The Film Director

The
Film Director

A PRACTICAL GUIDE TO

MOTION PICTURE

AND TELEVISION TECHNIQUES

Richard L. Bare

COLLIER BOOKS
A Division of Macmillan Publishing Co., Inc.
New York

To Gloria

ILLUSTRATIONS BY THE AUTHOR

Copyright © 1971 by Richard L. Bare

Macmillan Publishing Co., Inc.
866 Third Avenue, New York, N.Y. 10022
Collier Macmillan Canada, Inc.
ISBN 0-02-012130-X

Library of Congress Catalog Card Number: 76-130944

First Collier Books Edition 1973

11   10   9   8

Printed in the United States of America

CONTENTS

FOREWORD

No aspect of our society has escaped the flood of do-it-yourself books which have poured onto the market in recent years. Although many of them have served useful purposes, books on motion pictures—and most particularly motion picture directing—have left something to be desired. *The Film Director* is a welcome and needed exception.

Dick Bare is not only a professional and highly skilled director who is fully qualified to discuss his craft, he is an articulate spokesman for his fellow directors. As a result, *The Film Director* is both instructional and entertaining reading.

The point has often been made that film is an art form, and in order for it to develop to its fullest, directors should scrap existing rules and make free use of their own creative abilities. The obvious comparison is with painters who have broken with tradition, developing new techniques, even new schools of painting, to broaden the horizons of art appreciation. But while the comparison is valid, what should always be borne in mind is that only an artist who has mastered all of the rules can break them properly and make the fullest use of the medium he has chosen.

The value of *The Film Director* to the student or fledgling director is that it emphasizes the basic rules (not only of camera techniques and the use of film, but of helping actors create the needed emotion) and points the way to the free flight of creative imagination that breaks rules to provide exciting new uses of film and camera. In doing so, Dick Bare has made it clear that, like any other art form, film is constantly changing in both technique and content and the creative director must constantly strive to improve his skills, since yesterday's innovation may well be tomorrow's cliché.

This should not mean, however, that an idea once used must be discarded. When I was first handed the script for *The Sound of Music*, I questioned the opening because it was patterned after my concept for the opening of *West Side Story*, and I was reluctant to open my second musical with another high-angle helicopter sequence. But we were unable to come up with another opening that was as good—and I'm glad we couldn't. Nothing else could have set the mood of *Music* nearly as well and despite my preopening apprehension, even those critics who disliked the film did not contend that the opening was an attempt to copy a previous success.

These are the things, of course, that must be learned through experience. But the growing number of schools for aspiring filmmakers provides a solid groundwork which can hasten an understanding of the various factors on which experience is based. In past days, many of us started in the business as messengers and gradually worked our way through various crafts to reach the status of directors. Today's routine is different —the blueprint as spelled out in *The Film Director* indicates far less time consumed—but the novice comes to the medium now with far more understanding of the basics than we had. To paraphrase an old Hollywood joke, "to be interested in film is not enough—one must also have an understanding of it."

The Film Director goes a long way toward providing that understanding.

President
Directors Guild of America

ROBERT WISE

PREFACE

This is more than a textbook. It is a chronicle of one director's viewpoints and experiences set forth to illustrate the requirements of a fascinating but exacting job and to provide hope and inspiration to those who would like to crack the movie or television business.

Time and again film directors have maintained directing is an art, not a science, and have consistently taken the position that there are few rules or other criteria that can be successfully passed on to a newcomer. This is only true to the degree that Leonardo da Vinci was able to pass on his particular genius to his students, some of whom, I am sure, turned out to be reasonably proficient painters.

Veteran director William Keighley believed that certain basics of film-directing *could* be taught and, accordingly, conducted a class in this subject at the University of Southern California. I assisted him in this course, which spanned an eight-month period, and much of the material in this book is based on the approaches to teaching that were formulated at that time. Keighley made one point worth underscoring: he could show students how to make pictures, but he couldn't guarantee that they would be good pictures.

While this book covers the rudiments of film-directing, the mechanics and techniques of staging and handling the camera, as well as the dramatic and emotional processes involved in handling actors and telling a story, it also cites my own experiences in *getting to be a director*.

Admittedly one of the world's toughest professions to break into, film-directing can be one of the most rewarding, not only financially but in doing work that is fulfilling, exciting, sometimes important, but always *fun*.

Hollywood, California

Director John Sturges prepares to make a crane shot of James Garner, playing an American prisoner, and Richard Attenborough, an English one, in The Great Escape. *Sturges was a film editor before he broke into directing via an Air Force film he made with William Wyler.* (United Artists)

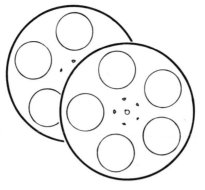

THE IMPORTANCE
OF THE DIRECTOR

His Eminence, the Director

Never before in the history of motion pictures has there been such a wave of genuine interest in the *making* of motion pictures. Over four hundred colleges in the United States offer courses in film education, and more than forty of these currently give degrees in the subject. Even some high schools provide classes for aspiring filmmakers. *Film* is fast becoming the art of the present generation.

To understand fully the subject of cinema is to delve deeply into the inner workings of the one who (today more than ever before) shoulders the greater responsibility for what reaches the screen. And this, most experts will agree, is the director.

There was a time, not so long ago, when most moviegoers first asked, "Who's in it?" Unless the answer contained the name of Cary Grant or Clark Gable or some other super-star of the day, there was not apt to be a long line outside the theater. The perpetrators of the star system had done their work well; the world had been mesmerized into believing that the biggest single ingredient of a picture's worth was the actor. There are still many who continue to identify a film with its stars, yet the trend is to find and separate the one person who can be held accountable for the result of the total product. *Film* has taken its place as the chief cultural topic on the campus; the "new director" substituted for the latest novelist at cocktail parties.

This new eminence given the director received its impetus in an article in the French magazine *Cahiers du Cinéma* in 1954. François Truffaut, a popular film critic who yearned to make his own films, wrote that movies were not group art, but rather the result of a singular authority over story, acting, and photography. The maker of a film brings to his work the same personal creativity as an artist in painting or sculpture, or the author in literature. Truffaut singled out the director as the true "author" of the finished film, hence the *auteur theory* of filmmaking.

Since then millions of serious film devotees have rallied to the support of their favorite director, seeing in his films the indelible and, to them, the unmistakable stamp of the *auteur*. Suddenly, film festivals sprang up on both sides of the Atlantic; films of Hitchcock, Huston, Ford, and Wilder were gathered together and studied like some newly discovered Dead Sea scrolls. Even Don Siegel a competent but never previously acclaimed director of such films as *Coogan's Bluff* and *Madigan*, had several of his films shown at a Siegel festival in Paris. His opening remarks, when asked to address the group, clearly expressed his surprise: "Where were you when I needed you?"

While the *auteur* theory has gained favor with many theatergoers in the United States and film companies find themselves giving directors complete autonomy, there remains one area in which the director is not the dominant figure. This is in series television, where week after week a program must perpetuate its original look and basic character. Some television shows have as many as a dozen directors during a season's programming. Each brings a different style of shooting, but the actors' characterizations must be constant from week to week. The man who molds all the elements of the show is the producer, usually a writer and often the creator of the format. He must supervise the writing, making certain that the various writers conform in style. He must be sure that the show is edited according to the form established in the pilot film. With the chores of story collaboration and much of the editing taken away from the director, there is only one place left for him to display his craftsmanship and that is on the shooting stage.

Whatever the arguments, pro and con, appear to be, the idea that a director "authors" a piece of film is true only to the degree that he conceived the original idea, shared in the writing, took over the producing chores, and then went on to overcome the infinite obstacles that lay ahead. All directors must master complex technicalities; the great director has something more—the talent to mold the complexities of human emotions into an inspired whole.

(RIGHT)
Director Paul Newman takes the Airiflex handheld camera to line up a shot of Joanne Woodward during filming of Rachel, Rachel. *Newman is one of the latest stars to turn director.* (Warner Bros.)

One of the qualified "auteurs" of his films, Richard Brooks writes, directs, and produces. His superb western The Professionals *has never been equaled in all-round craftsmanship. Here he chats with his wife, Jean Simmons, who stars in his* Happy Ending. (United Artists)

The Fortunate Four Hundred

It seems that practically everyone already connected with the motion picture or television business harbors either a secret or openly avowed desire to be a director. Sometime ago the word got around that this job is the most gratifying one in the motion picture business. For years the writers and the actors held obstinately that this wasn't so, but lately even they have come around.

Frank Capra once opened the annual banquet of the Directors Guild of America with these words: "Good evening. I wish to welcome all you directors. I especially wish to welcome you writer-directors, actor-directors, producer-directors, actor-writer-directors, writer-producer-directors, and just plain director-directors." Of course the crowd laughed and the business of the evening went on to hand out the coveted Directors' Award for the Best Director of the Year, which indidentally was won by William Wyler, a director-director.

According to the latest count, there are 2,472 senior-director members of the Directors Guild of America, an organization that embraces all theatrical and television directing in the United States, both film and live. The New York branch of the Guild claims 1,015 directors, the Midwest branch has 159, while the Hollywood branch boasts 1,298. These

On location in San Francisco for Guess Who's Coming to Dinner, *producer-director Stanley Kramer gets a high perch to watch the action. Kramer is one of the few producers who turned director, liked it, and stayed with it.* (Columbia)

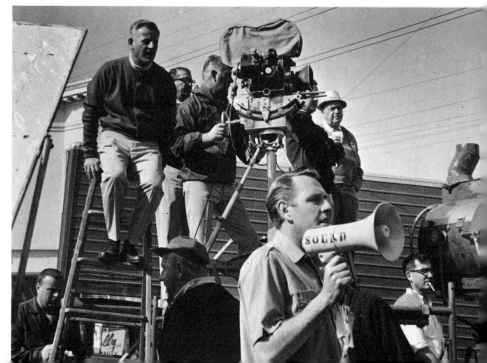

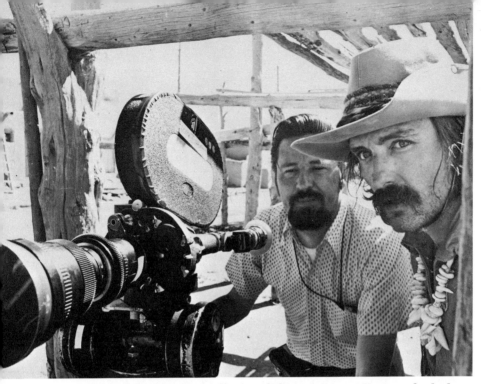

Cameraman Laszlo Kovacs (left) and director Dennis Hopper check the camera angle for a scene of Easy Rider, *starring Peter Fonda and Dennis Hopper. Hopper is an actor who made good as a director.* (Columbia)

figures tend to be somewhat misleading as the roster of both branches contains names of persons who have only directed one or two films and actors such as Frank Sinatra, John Wayne, Marlon Brando, and Mickey Rooney. Many directors on the list are retired or working in other fields, holding on to the coveted membership card on the chance that one day they will return. Of the entire Hollywood director membership, no more than 400 are regularly engaged in directing. Approximately 107 members make only theatrical films while the rest are divided between live and filmed television employment.

The above statistics are provided to illustrate the fact that the job of director is as highly competitive as it is coveted and many persons seek and obtain the opportunity to direct their first film on a commercial level, only to fall by the wayside in favor of the "fortunate four hundred."

But those who would seek entry into this exclusive group can take solace in the fact that its membership, by the nature of the demands of the business itself, is a rotating one. Nowhere in the world are there such opportunities for the young newcomer to reach the top in so short a time as in the film industry—especially if he has chosen directing as his life's work.

What Makes a Director?

Unlike some gifted artists, actors, and writers who were born with their talents, the director must learn his art, acquiring his knowledge and skill carefully through observation and practice. He can learn from watching films of other directors and he can learn from watching other directors at work. He can learn from reading cinema books and taking cinema courses but the best training ground for the would-be director still remains the motion picture business itself. At least this has been the avenue most used by the better than two thousand accredited film directors in New York and Hollywood today. One exception in this respect is my own experience, which will be related in a subsequent chapter and which points up the fact that a serious academic schooling in the fundamentals of filmmaking when combined with practical experience in *making films* can lead to a creative position in the movie or television industry.

Directors Arnold Laven and Don Weis used to be script clerks. So did Leslie L. Martinson, who directed many television and feature pictures for Warner Bros. These talented filmmakers took advantage of the close relationship a script clerk has with his director. If this director is a George Stevens, a Fred Zinnemann, or a John Huston, so much the better. The script clerk can keep the records of the shooting while quietly observing from a firsthand position just what goes on in the director's sometimes harried mind.

There are other jobs on the movie set which, because of their proximity to the director, are time-honored steppingstones to the director's chair. The film editor normally enjoys a close coalition with the man behind the megaphone, which incidentally, although a relic of the silent era, is sometimes still used on large sets today, and continues to be the most effective means of communication between the director and the actors at the far end of a large set. The editor, who prefers that title over the one most often used—cutter—learns how to be a director through years of handling the film turned in by a variety of directors, which range from excellent down to not-so-good. He vows that when he gets *his* chance he will never make *those* mistakes.

John Sturges, director of such films as *Bad Day at Black Rock* and *Ice Station Zebra*, started as an editor at the old RKO lot, and edited Air Force training films at Wright Field during World War II. Sturges became friendly with William Wyler and co-directed *Thunderbolt*, an outstanding war documentary made while the two were in the service. When the war was over, Wyler dropped a few words of praise in the right places, Columbia placed John under contract and he never cut another film except his own. He got his break and went on to direct some of the screen's top pictures.

William Fraker made the leap from cinema student, at the University of Southern California to still cameraman to head cinematographer on three top pictures in one year, *The Fox*, *Rosemary's Baby*, and *Bullitt*. When his ex-agents decided to turn producer, they hired Fraker as a director on the five-million-dollar *Monte Walsh* starring Lee Marvin. He, in turn, elevated his camera operator to first cinematographer.

James Wong Howe, Hollywood's only Chinese cameraman and a top man in his field for thirty years, has tried his hand at directing. George Stevens who piloted *Giant*, *Shane*, *The Diary of Anne Frank*, and a score of other blockbusters, started as a cameraman for Hal Roach comedies years ago. Somewhere down the line he watched how easy it was to direct the actors, since he knew what to do with the camera. Rudy Mate, the director of *Miracle in the Rain*, gave up his job as a cinematographer when he decided that directing wasn't all that hard. He had spent many years at the elbow of the industry's top directors.

Many cameramen have "directed" at times when a new and uncertain director has faltered, or become confused over the staging of a scene. Incidentally, it seems to be appropriate to mention here that cameramen, or "directors of photography" as they prefer to be known, will, almost to a man, come to the aid of the new director, offering solid counseling at a time when others may be waiting for him to fail.

There has been a recent assault on the directors' ranks by actors. Paul Newman, Gene Kelly, Ray Milland, and Edmond O'Brien are directors with at least one or two credits. Jerry Lewis is a clown in front of the camera but a dedicated and serious artist when he directs. Ben Gazzara, John Cassavetes, Don Taylor, Jackie Cooper, and Paul Henreid are all solidly established directors in television, while attractive Ida Lupino continues to grind out television shows as Hollywood's leading female director. Stephanie Rothman studied filmmaking in college and recently directed the feature film *The Student Nurses*. In New York, Elaine May has directed the Paramount film *A New Leaf* as her initial feature film effort, and Rita Gillespie has turned out such taped television shows as *Shindig* and *Kraft Music Hall*. Not only that, there is a Chinese woman director. Shu Shuen wrote, produced, and directed *The Arch*, a feature film made in Hong Kong and exhibited widely in the United States.

Otto Preminger was a fine actor and became a fine director with pictures such as *Anatomy of a Murder* and *Exodus*. Sheldon Leonard, one of the truly funny tough guys on the screen, gave it all up to direct the *Danny Thomas Show*, thus launching a new career behind the camera. The success Dennis Hopper had with his first directorial assignment on *Easy Rider* has made him a millionaire.

Logical, you might say, for actors to go into directing. They have had close contact with the best and worst of film directors over the years. They have watched, studied the director's technical problems, and waited. They were sure all the time they could do it better. Some have and some have not, as the degree of success among the actor-turned-director has not been, on the average, any more spectacular than any other group.

The screen writer has, perhaps, shouted loudest in his criticism of the director, and it has been understandable why so many have joined the ranks as directors. It is all too common to hear the expression, "I turned in a beautiful script but between the producer and the director it was hacked to pieces." The writer often dreams of the day when every word, every nuance, every bit of delicately written dialogue will find its way to the screen, unadulterated and tampered with by no one. He reasons that the only way this dream can become a reality is for him to direct.

One of Hollywood's most notable examples of the writer turned director is Richard Brooks who directed *The Professionals* and *In Cold Blood*. Names like Sam Peckinpah, Norman Panama, Mel Shavelson, and Tom Gries have gracefully made the transition from scenarist to megaphonist without taking a step back in the industry's esteem, while Blake Edwards has gone from actor to writer to director, and has turned out some first-rate comedies such as *Operation Petticoat* and *Breakfast at Tiffany's*.

David Swift, another director whose pictures for Walt Disney include *Pollyana* and *The Parent Trap*, became a director after he had risen to be a writer of delightfully funny scripts. His initial fame came in New York when he wrote and produced *Mr. Peepers* for television.

Hollywood has always been the end of the financial rainbow for people of the New York theater. Stage directors who have become outstanding in their field have little trouble in getting opportunities to direct film.

Mike Nichols, Josh Logan, and Morton Da Costa, to name only a few, have all sailed right into Hollywood and made their names bigger than ever. The producers must have known they could entrust their stars to these men; all they had to do was surround them with top cameramen, film editors, and script clerks who would insure that the picture would not suffer from the directors' inexperience in the medium.

Similarly, motion picture directors come from live television, and since the Directors Guild has taken over the live television director groups, this step is easier than ever. John Frankenheimer (*The Manchurian Candidate*, *Grand Prix*) started directing live television in New

Mike Nichols came to Hollywood after a successful series of Broadway hits and started out at the top directing Elizabeth Taylor and Richard Burton in Who's Afraid of Virginia Woolf? *Although his background was largely in comedy, he made the transition to dramatic director with flying colors.* (Warner Bros.)

York, then came to Hollywood and did such shows as *Playhouse 90*. George Roy Hill and Buzz Kulick used to direct from the control booth with no chance to do retakes. Now they shoot a scene on film until they get it right.

Stanley Kubrick (*2001, A Space Odyssey*), while still in high school, decided to take his still pictures to *Look* magazine. Mistaken for a messenger, he managed to see the editor, who promptly bought all his pictures and asked for more. At seventeen, Kubrick was a full-fledged staff photographer. And while still working for *Look*, he conceived an idea for a movie documentary about a prize fighter on the day of his big fight. That was in 1951 and once he had taken hold of the movie camera, Kubrick never relinquished his grip. It was a short road to Hollywood where he directed *Paths of Glory* at the age of twenty-eight.

Directors come from everywhere. Dick Moder was a wardrobe man just a few years ago, and worked on one of the pictures I directed at Warners'. The next time I saw him, he was an assistant director and doing well. Now he's a director—and probably giving the wardrobe man the same trouble he himself used to endure.

Directors evolve from dialogue directors usually with little effort or strain while making the transition. After all, there has been many a dialogue director who has put the polish on the performances while the director was concerned with the physical problems of staging and camera angles.

Irving Rapper and Frederick DeCordova both graduated in this fashion under the sponsorship of Warner Bros. Herschel Daugherty, who is now considered a top television director, served as dialogue director on several of my earlier television films. Observing the results he obtained from actors, I once asked him why he didn't make the break into the director's ranks.

Melvin Van Peebles (left) directs The Watermelon Man. *Although a native American, Van Peebles got his start in directing in France.* (Columbia)

"I don't know," he said, "I just couldn't handle all this cutting and camera stuff and get the picture done in three days."

I told him we should meet at nights; I would show him about cameras, lenses, movement, and production shortcuts, and he could tell me all he knew about actors. We never got together, but it wasn't two months after that day that he got his first chance to direct television, a film, incidentally he made in two days.

Until recently there were no black directors. Then Gordon Parks, a famous still cameraman, was given the opportunity by Warner Bros. to direct his own book, *The Learning Tree*. Ossie Davis was handed the directorial reins on *Cotton Comes to Harlem* for two reasons: Ossie knew Harlem and he had written for the screen and television. He was a fine actor and he settled into the director's chair like a veteran.

Melvin Van Peebles, although born in Chicago, had to go to France to get his break as a director. In Paris he wrote and directed a few short films. A writing award, a job as a French journalist, and four published novels led to his directing *The Story of a Three Day Pass*, which he had written as well. The picture was a hit and led to his being named the French delegate at the San Francisco Film Festival, where his picture was critically acclaimed. Then Columbia signed him to direct *The Watermelon Man*, which he attributes to his success in France. "It certainly didn't happen because I'm black and that I'm beautiful," he says half-kidding, half-serious.

Most people outside the picture business have the impression that the job of producer is the paragon of success in Hollywood. Too many top producers have moved over to become directors to give credence to this story. Stanley Kramer had many fine pictures to his credit before he tried his hand at directing. Joseph P. Mankiewicz (*All About Eve*, *Cleopatra*) was a top writer doing only the most important pictures when he became a producer. He apparently found a frustration behind the desk as well, for soon he was telling the actors and crew what to do on the set.

George Pal, one of the truly imaginative producers in Hollywood, became imbued with the spell of the megaphone and now directs most of his productions. Examples are *The Time Machine* and *The Brothers Grimm*.

Strangely enough, few assistant directors make the grade or even try to be a director. Since an assistant is more production manager than director and seldom concerns himself with the esthetics involved in making pictures, it is understandable that they do not move upward in this fashion. There have been a few exceptions, and former assistants like Robert Aldrich and Howard Koch have distinguished themselves as directors.

Actually, there are not many instances where a director has really coveted any other job. A few have moved upward and onward into that much maligned realm known as producing, but they usually hang on to the director's chores as well. For the director, with all his headaches, continues to have the most personally rewarding job of all.

What Is a Director?

A few years ago I was asked by the Academy of Motion Picture Arts and Sciences to write and direct a documentary short subject to be entitled *The Film Director*. This was only one in a series of public relations films they were producing in an endeavor to enlighten the public as to what went on behind the scenes in the making of a motion picture.

I tackled this assignment with proper dedication, knowing that here was the opportunity to make a visual statement concerning the importance of the director, one that might serve as a proper testimonial to a somewhat misunderstood profession. I was sure the audience as a whole still had the mental image of the typical Hollywood director as a rather noisy, flamboyant character who wore loud sport coats, a beret, and jumped around the set with his hands held before him in the time worn gesture of framing the shot. Here was the perfect chance to depict the movie director the way he really is; more often than not working in a conservative attire with no attendant hysterics or personal theatrics to awe the onlooker. Here the director could be shown as a hard working, responsible individual who was often first on the set in the morning and the last to leave the studio at the end of the day. At night, it would be explained, the director worked over the script and organized the next day's shooting, and many times his weekends were devoted to rewriting scenes with the producer or writer. Here was the opportunity to show the infinite problems that face a director during the shooting of a picture.

The film was made and was exhibited in theaters all over the country and answered to a great degree the question, "What is a director?"

The question of who does what in the making of a motion picture is one of perpetual mystery to those who view the finished work, and the reviewers seem to be more mystified than anyone when it comes to writing the notices after a preview.

For instance, a reviewer may comment, "Brilliant camera angles and dynamic camera movement by cinematographer Richard Roe." In most instances this should have been accredited to the director.

"George Spelvin's directorial touches far supass anything he has done in the past." Those touches, in this case, were written into the script

William Wyler is all attention as his actors enact a scene in an Italian studio outside Rome. The picture was Ben-Hur, MGM's all-time largest-grossing motion picture. (Metro-Goldwyn-Mayer)

by the author

"Producer John Henry has shown extreme taste and judgment in casting a Negro actor in a Caucasian role." Again, this was the director's idea, since he brought the whole package to the producer.

Invariably, the contributions to a motion picture are many and overlapping; sometimes even those who worked on the picture aren't quite sure who contributed what. That is why we so often hear the winner of an Academy Award say, upon accepting the Oscar, "Thank you, but this award would not have been possible without the help of everyone on the picture. It was a team effort."

The director's function is unique and all embracing. He preconceives

Although a native of England, John Schlesinger captured in Midnight Cowboy *a seamy side of American life with rare insight and won the Directors Guild of America Award for 1969. Here he lines up a shot for* Bloody Sunday *with the Mitchell Reflex.* (United Artists)

a motion picture as it will appear in its entirety and vitally participates in all phases of its preparation and execution. Since he is also in command of others, he must know something of their functions. He must know the rudiments of acting, writing, and photography. He should be able physically to edit his films. He should have a working knowledge of architecture, of costume design, of makeup, of music, else how can he communicate with those whose job it is to provide these ingredients? Above all, he must indelibly stamp his personality, his style, his *touch* on the film he creates, and the measure of his success is the extent to which he enlightens, uplifts, and gives pleasure to the audience.

Casting a Director

There has long existed in Hollywood a maxim that says a good director, with talented performers, can raise the level of an ordinary script to a
point where the public accepts the production as being extraordinary, at
least commercially. Seldom does this work in reverse; an incompetent
director cannot possibly manage to turn out superior screen entertainment even though he has an exceptional screenplay from which to work.

When Metro-Goldwyn-Mayer made the decision to produce the modern version of *Ben-Hur*, they sought the best man they could get for
the job, William Wyler. The studio was embarking on its most expensive
motion picture, and it should have the finest director obtainable, since
the financial risk they were about to take could bankrupt the company if
the picture failed to pay off. Wyler received a fabulous sum of money,
and *Ben-Hur* grossed over forty million dollars at the box office.

*Leslie L. Martinson started as a script clerk, swung into television direc-
tion, then made it in feature films. Here he is with the Mitchell BNC
on location in the Caribbean, directing PT 109. (Warner Bros.)*

Although the days of the studio-produced films seem to be past, occasionally a hit Broadway show or an about-to-be-published novel is acquired by a major film company. The first consideration once the property is acquired is, who will direct the picture. Invariably the studio will back its oftentimes astronomical investment in a new property with the insurance of a top director. When the Mirisch Company became interested in James A Michener's novel, *Hawaii*, it sent the galley proofs to Fred Zinnemann with the understanding that if he liked the material and would undertake to make the movie, they would acquire the novel for film production. Zinnemann agreed to direct and produce the picture, and the Mirisch Company put up $650,000 to secure the motion picture rights. But later Zinnemann bowed out over a disagreement and George Roy Hill took over.

Sometimes a director will motivate the purchase of a property, as did Billy Wilder with *Some Like It Hot*. He showed the producers, also the Mirisches, an ancient German silent film and told them how he would modernize it into a hilarious comedy. He was given free hand, and the rest is history.

Pictures were once scheduled for production as soon as the stars were set; today it is usually the director who is given the first consideration. The wise producer knows that a film's success, after the script has been written, lies in the hands of the man selected to mold the physical and emotional elements into a single tangible strip of film. A slow, indecisive director can run a picture hopelessly over budget, while an insensitive, mechanical director can turn out film listless and unalive.

But if the director is a man of taste and talent, the story is sound and the actors competent, and the producer provides the wherewithal to give the director the time and production values, a successful film should result.

Lloyd Shearer, the well-known motion picture critic, has this to say on the subject: "There is only one valid method of prejudging any motion picture: Find out who directed it."

Bette Davis, a temperamental star who has had more than one run-in with a director, admits frankly that "in films it's the director who's the supreme artist, who in the final analysis is responsible for the success or failure of the picture, who shapes his material, inspires the performers, controls, juggles and fits together all the pieces. We players are merely puppets a director dangles."

Charlton Heston wrote an article in the Directors Guild magazine *Action* and said the following about directors: "In a film, how the scene plays on the floor isn't necessarily all that important. One of the first significant things you discover acting for films is that your best performance of an entire scene may not be the one that is used. A scene doesn't even exist in the dailies. It doesn't exist until long after the actors are off salary. The vital fifteen percent is made in a Moviola with the director running the bits and pieces back and forth. Thus, who the director is is of vital importance to you."

Sometimes the star has the final approval of the director and it is always the actor who selects the director when the picture is being produced by the actor's own company. This usually results in a "cooperative" director being assigned to the production since the super-stars like to call their own shots and important directors will have no part of that. George Stevens has said, "It is most difficult to direct an actor who owns a piece of the picture. It is doubly difficult if that actor happens to be a millionaire. I am not about to direct any actor who insists on telling me how to direct."

The good directors of Hollywood insist on control and they never relinquish that control to the actors who play in their films.

Hollywood's Box Office Directors

Hollywood long existed on the star system, and pictures were sold to the exhibitors mainly through their stars. Cary Grant, Clark Gable, and Joan Crawford had their fans at the box office and even the success of todays less pretentious films are making newer stars, such as Elliott Gould and Donald Sutherland. But through it all, we find some directors with as much "box office" as many stars. For over thirty years the name Cecil B. De Mille on a marquee insured success for the pictures he directed. Alfred Hitchcock is perhaps the best-known film director in the world, largely due to his television appearances and the fact that he plays a small bit in each of his movies. Telling the public that Hitchcock directed means added money at the box office.

Among the art theater circuits, the names of De Sica, Antonioni, and Ingmar Bergman are featured prominently in the advertising, for exhibitors know the drawing power of these directors.

Mike Nichols made an auspicious film debut with *Who's Afraid of Virginia Woolf?* As a result, Nichols was besieged with offers. That he chose *The Graduate* for his second screen venture was a fortunate thing for both himself and the picture. It has since become the highest grossing non-hard ticket attraction in history, and won for Nichols the Directors Guild Award.

Norman Jewison is one of today's foremost new directors. His films, combining entertainment with statement, have the knack of intriguing

John Frankenheimer started his career as an actor, but soon he was working as an associate director in live television. In 1954 he got his chance to direct and turned out such shows as You Are There *and* Danger. *Now firmly established in feature filmmaking, Frankenheimer has turned out such stylized pictures as* Manchurian Candidate *and* Seconds. (United Artists)

the masses as well as the hard-core movie buffs. *The Russians Are Coming, The Russians Are Coming*, spoke for peaceful coexistence; *In the Heat of the Night*, against racial bigotry; while *The Thomas Crown Affair* spoofed the establishment as represented by banks and big business.

Although an Englishman, John Schlesinger made a tremendous impact on American audiences with *Midnight Cowboy*. As a result, he can pick and choose almost any project he wishes on two continents.

Sydney Pollack graduated from filmed television shows to feature pictures with *The Slender Thread* with Sidney Poitier and Anne Bancroft. Since then he has directed such films as *The Scalphunters* with Burt Lancaster and *They Shoot Horses, Don't They?*, a grim story of marathon dancing in the 1930's. Producers know that they will make a safe investment with Pollack at the helm despite his few years in the business.

William Castle, just a few years ago an obscure quickie director, made himself somewhat of a name director by specializing in horror pictures, each one with a novelty gimmick, such as a skeleton that slid on a wire over the heads of the audience, or electrified seats that sent a tingling though harmless bolt of electricity into each patron. Castle demonstrated the importance of the director in each venture he undertook.

Directors can become "typed" just as players, and certain ones are almost never given assignments foreign to their reputations. John Ford is invariably identified with the large epic western, while George Cukor is known for his expert handling of women in pictures. Jane Fonda, who was directed by Cukor in *The Chapman Report*, had these significant remarks to make about him: "He creates a character; he hypnotizes himself and becomes the woman he wants you to be. He has impeccable taste and a sense of subtlety, and he knows if anything is too much. He shoots everything fifteen or sixteen times, and you know he will protect you because he forces himself to love and believe in you."

Many directors, through their individuality and characteristic viewpoint, bring a distinct trademark to the screen recognizable from picture to picture. Pioneers like Ernst Lubitsch and King Vidor brought an unmistakable stamp to their pictures, as did Orson Welles (*Citizen Kane*) on his initial visit to Hollywood. Stanley Kubrick, in the unusual film *2001, A Space Odyssey*, reaffirmed a style first seen in *Dr. Strangelove*.

King Vidor, whose earlier films were infused with serious themes, maintains the movie director has a strong and articulate voice, and he

Mark Rydell, on location for The Reivers, *directs a scene by long distance. He looks through the Panavision 250 mm lens at the action, then shouts instruction through an electric megaphone.* (Cinema Center-National General)

should use it well: "In my opinion, the motion picture is the greatest medium of expression ever invented. The films that have expressed the greatest unity, and given the most satisfaction to the viewer, have been those in which the guiding hand has been imposed on every section of the film's many divisions. Story, casting, settings, photography, acting should all bespeak *one* mind."

It is obvious that Mr. Vidor is referring to the fact that in his opinion, the director is the most important single person in the creation of film entertainment—a doctrine formulated over thirty years before Truffaut conceived his *auteur* theory.

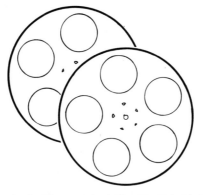

2

THE DIRECTOR
AS PSYCHOLOGIST

Temperament and Tricks

William Keighley, one of the first important directors to conduct classes
in film directing at the University of Southern California, placed a high
degree of importance on the psychological factors involved in directing.

Keighley had been under contract to Warner Bros. since the early
days of sound and had risen to the position of director via the route of
dialogue director, having originally come from the theater. In his early
days as a full director he had the occasion to direct many temperamental
stars and was forced to devise unusual if not devious techniques in
directing.

On one such occasion, Keighley was attempting to get a performance
out of a particularly high-strung and nervous leading lady, an important
star of the day. After several takes it was apparent that the actress was
not doing the scene correctly and tension was mounting. Each time he
would ask for the scene to be done over, she wanted to know why; *she*
thought it was good. It took all the diplomacy and expertise that
Keighley could muster to persuade the lady to make another take. Finally
on the ninth take, as the scene was nearing the end, Keighley knew he
would have to shoot it again. But how would he tell her? Spotting a
bucket lying near the camera, he slowly moved alongside it and with a
furtive movement kicked it against the camera dolly.

"Cut! CUT!" he cried, turning around to face the crew. "Who did
that? You spoiled a perfect take!"

The astonished crew looked from one to the other, while Keighley
walked up to the actress, put his arms around her, and expressed a profound apology for the clumsy idiot who ruined the scene just when it

was going so well. Now they would have to do it again. In this way, the director got what he wanted out of a star who, because of a feeling of insecurity in her own work, was not giving a performance equal to her reputation.

Often a director is handed a leading lady who has passed her prime and is faced with the dilemma of how to make her look the age of the role she is playing. The cameraman, of course, can do much to bring a flattering and youthful look to the actress by the manner in which he positions his lights. The addition of diffusion filters on the lens, the purpose of which is to wash out wrinkles and sagging chin lines, can also work miracles. But, the director can add the finishing touch to this metamorphosis, and a good way is to keep her laughing. There is nothing like a touch of humor initiated while the camera is starting to roll to bring the lady's face up to her former levels. By the time you say "action" and the scene starts, she is relaxed and smiling; and this youthful expression will many times hold for the entire scene.

In Norman Lear's first try at directing, the writer-producer turned director handled a difficult crowd scene like a veteran. The location was a small town in Iowa; the picture *Cold Turkey*, starring Dick Van Dyke. The scene Lear was shooting called for Van Dyke to exhort a large crowd of townspeople into signing a no-smoking pledge. But the crowd's lack of professional acting ability marred the scene; the proper reactions to Van Dyke's appeal were not forthcoming. Finally, in desperation, Lear started screaming at the top of his lungs at Van Dyke, calling him stupid and incompetent for the way he was playing the scene. Van Dyke, in on the ruse, hurled insults back at the director. The crowd buzzed and reacted with proper realism while the cameras slowly panned over their astonished faces. After the scene the director explained to the townspeople that he had wanted a shocked reaction from them and that fooling them with the temper tantrum was just a director's device.

The Overzealous Actor

The art of directing is an extension of the actor's development. A good director does not run a school of acting, but rather guides the performers along in their own interpretations. He must be sure that these interpretations fit correctly into the overall interpretation of the script, which should be his alone. I have seen actors so charged up with their own delineation of a character that they completely failed to coordinate it with the other characters in the story. This usually happens when an actor, who has been used to more important things, accepts a small part intending to make it "memorable." The director, whose job it is to de-emphasize the overzealous actor, sometimes finds he has a handful. Various psychological techniques can be used, but the one I find most helpful is to explain to the actor that the performance is so outstanding that it is sure to be cut out of the picture after the star complains to the producer. Desiring to stay in the picture rather than to end up in the "out takes," the actor usually conforms.

Once when I was directing a young lady of some prominence in Rod Serling's *Twilight Zone*, I experienced, not too happily, I might add, a situation that almost developed into a full-fledged imbroglio. The actress apparently had been persuaded to do a rather bland role and accepted knowing she would bring an interpretation to the character far and away beyond anything that was on mere paper. The character, as written by Serling, was a drab, unsophisticated waitress working in a remote roadside café in Nevada. She was not supposed to be anything but that, else why would she stay year in and year out in such dull and unexciting surroundings? But the young actress who had a considerable amount of ability thought she could make her part stand out in the minds of the audience. She proceeded to interpolate, to improvise sophisticated mannerisms of speech and action, and generally to "brighten" the character she was playing. She apparently had no conception of the relationship of her part to that of the others in the story. All she was concerned with was doing an attention-getting job of acting, which would boost her stock in the industry. Actually, all she succeeded in doing was to inject a false note in what otherwise would have been a much better film.

With no rehearsal time available prior to shooting, it was all one could do to maintain the shooting schedule and still cope with the situation. As the shooting progressed, the actress's hatred for me mounted with every take. I was holding her down, she claimed, making her give a listless and dull performance. Trying to explain my reasoning to her was of no avail.

The scene that brought the shooting to a standstill was one in which she was simply and mechanically, if you will, to walk to the window and look out.

"What motivates me to go to the window?" she challenged.

"The same motivation that's clearly indicated in the script," I retorted. "Now let's see you do it."

The by-now surly leading lady sat down in a chair. "What am I thinking? How do I feel?"

"You're thinking it would be nice to walk to the window and look out. That's what you're thinking!"

She stood up, in a mild snit. "You're a *result director!*" she snapped.

(ABOVE, TOP)

William Keighley, who directed many important pictures for Warner Bros., believed in preserving an actor's ego and used many psychological tricks to obtain the correct performance. Here he sits on a couch with Rosalind Russell and James Stewart who starred in No Time for Comedy. The cameraman crouched below the camera is Ernest Haller, himself an Academy Award winner. (Warner Bros.)

(ABOVE, BOTTOM)

Director Don Siegel explains a set-up to the camera crew during filming of Two Mules for Sister Sarah. Siegel is one Hollywood director who has been "discovered" by the auteur groups in France, although his pictures all had different producers and writers. (Universal)

(ABOVE, RIGHT)

Director Norman Lear gives orders through an electric megaphone to his actors who, judging by the length of the lens on the Mitchell NC camera, are some distance away. The lens, incidentally, is a 500 mm. The picture is Cold Turkey. (United Artists)

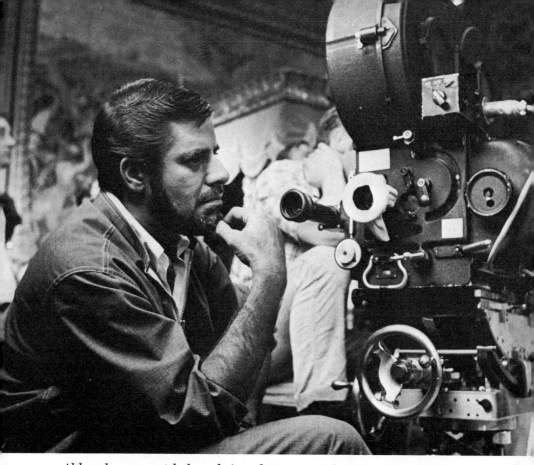

Although a congenial clown before the camera, when Jerry Lewis takes on the responsibility of direction, he becomes a thoughtful and crafts-manlike filmmaker. Lewis was one of the first directors to rig a closed-circuit television camera to his motion picture camera, enabling him to see an instant playback on tape of his scenes. (United Artists)

"Right. And that's what I want out of you—results!"

Needless to say, the results obtained were something short of per-fect, since nothing I could say regarding her interpretation would change this girl's mind. If she was going to do a minor role, she was going to make something out of it. The unfortunate part was that the director and actress didn't have the time to iron out their differences before going into production—a condition that continually exists in most television filming today.

The Value of Patience

Although the foregoing incident perhaps represents an extreme in my relationship with actors, I have always firmly believed in the moder-

Women have been among the ranks of directors since the early silent days, but none has been more feminine than Ida Lupino. After starring in dozens of pictures and quietly observing the style and technique of some of the industry's best directors, she decided to explore the world behind the camera and turned out Never Fear, Outrage, *and* Beware My Lovely. (RKO-Radio)

Michael Sarne, one of the leading exponents of the now *generation, came to* films from "pop" singing and making a prize-winning short subject. His first two features were Joanna *and* Myra Breckinridge, *both for 20th Century-Fox. Sarne is shown here with the French Eclair camera.*

ate approach, calmly and quietly working with the players, suggesting rather than giving orders. The director who screams in anger and impatience does a great disservice to both himself and his cast. It is difficult for anyone to react emotionally one way when those same emotions are stirred up in another way. How much better it is to quietly communicate with one's actors, giving guidance where necessary and encouragement where deserved. Patience and understanding are two virtues that are not to be underestimated in dealing with people, whether they be actors or other members of the crew.

One director I know is one of the most charming people I have ever met—off the set. But when he has a stage full of people at his beck and call, he becomes an entirely different man. He will harp and pick at an actor until the poor fellow's nerves are frayed. He will embarrass a bit player by shouting his dissatisfaction so all can hear, then will lapse into melancholic periods of self-persecution wailing, "Why are you all against me?" Yet, despite all his agonizing, he manages to turn out first-rate films along with his ulcers.

I was directing *House Across the Street* for Warner Bros. some years ago and the studio had flown a Broadway actor out especially to play an important part. As it turned out he had page upon page of dialogue to learn but not enough time in which to learn it. Together with this, it was the first time he had ever faced a motion picture camera. He was literally frightened to death, and his face perspired profusely, keeping the makeup man busy with tissues. The assistant director hovered close by, annoyingly looking at his watch, as we were behind schedule.

After sixteen or seventeen takes, it looked like we weren't going to get anything on film worth using. Then, I introduced an approach that I have had occasion to use many times since. I told him two things: we had lots of time and plenty of film. It was only after I *took the pressure off* him that we began to print usable takes.

Of all the attributes a director should have in dealing with actors, patience is near the top of the list in importance. The word finally found its true meaning one day when I was directing a leading man in a feature film.

While a highly skilled player, this man is also an excitable and restless individual whose boundless energy has a wearing effect on all who work with him.

We had spent six weeks on the picture and were trying to finish on schedule. Every suggestion I made to the actor caused a discussion. Not an argument—a discussion. If it were simple mechanics, like "Come in the door, light up a cigarette, then think about the call you want to make and pick up the phone." He would nod agreement. Halfway through the rehearsal he would stop and say, "How about this? I come in the door and pick up the phone first, then light up the cigarette."

Knowing that if I disagreed a thirty-minute discussion would ensue, I shrugged my shoulders and said fine, it didn't make that much difference.

But instead of going on with the change of business, this man would explain at great lengths *why* he thought it was better, as if he felt that his viewpoints needed some intensive selling before they were completely acceptable to me.

"Okay," I said. "Let's do it your way. I think it's a good way."

And so it would go all the rest of the shooting. He never understood when to quit while he was ahead but continued to take up valuable time in discussions that couldn't have been less important. It is during such times, when the director is fighting the clock to finish, that he needs all the patience and understanding he can muster.

Needless to say, this actor and I never had any important disagreements. Otherwise, the whole picture would have stopped dead still. But it is typical of a wearing experience the director can always do without.

One of the most important of the director's psychological tools is the ability to show that he has confidence in himself. One of the traps that new directors sometimes fall into is allowing the impression to get around that he isn't quite sure of what he wants, whether it be an interpretation from an actor or a camera setup.

Some actors are like little children. They respect authority, but will behave outrageously when they think they can get away with it. They most certainly will take advantage of the director who frankly asks them what to do in a scene. It is well enough to lead the players into a situation in which you are in a position to extract their ideas, but never let them suspect that you are depending on them. Similarly, to maintain the proper relationship between director and crew, one should never ask his assistant or the camerman what to do next. If you don't know, you somehow reached the position of director without being ready for it.

The director can be compared with the captain of a ship. He has been commissioned to guide the vessel safely over rough waters, and the voyage is in his hands. Any incompetence can lead to mutiny.

Directing Stars Is Different

Just as George Stevens would rather direct actors than stars (particularly those stars who are "bosses"), most directors feel they can contribute most creatively when they control all elements that go into

One of the great directors of all time, John Ford (Long Voyage Home, Stagecoach) *developed a style of shooting all his own. During a period which discovered the camera's mobility, Ford, instead of dollying in on the actors, had them move to the camera for a closer look. Here he is shown in a typical pose, comfortably seated next to a rigidly anchored camera.* (Republic)

making a motion picture. And the large studios seem to agree with them since many companies are bypassing the producer in favor of the producer-director. This new modus operandi has come about since the studios abandoned the mass production methods that were in vogue before television became a national institution. In the old days each studio had dozens of stars under contract. They were *assigned* to pictures, not coddled into them. And they were told who was to direct them, more than likely a director from the studio's own contract list. Today the big star picks his stories, his studio, and his director, more than likely a director who he feels will allow him some say in the direction.

In this connection, it is the wise director who refrains from trying to change an actor's personality or, in other words, to make him *act*. The greatest stars Hollywood has ever known were never really considered *actors* as one would consider a star of the theater. Gary Cooper, Clark Gable, and Errol Flynn were *personalities*. John Wayne and Jimmy Stewart are much the same in every role they play and woe be the director who would try and change that. It has been the great star-personalities who helped make the motion picture business the giant that it is, not the handful of actors who, as competent as they were, portrayed different characters from picture to picture.

Once I had the occasion to direct Gary Cooper. It was a patriotic short subject, and Cooper was donating his time and talents. We discussed the brief scene he was to do, and I was impressed by his forthright manner and articulate speech. Even his rehearsals were direct, precise, and not at all the Gary Cooper I had seen on the screen. But when I said "action" and Cooper stepped onto the set, there he was in all his characteristic shyness and faltering speech. I learned then that his screen personality was all an act, and that he had obviously learned years ago that this was what was expected of him. Changing it could only lead to destroying the image he had built up. In this respect, Cooper has been totally underestimated by those who maintained he couldn't really act.

In the opinion of those of us who remember with unabashed fondness the "Golden Years" of Hollywood, today's new crop of stars lack the magic of those of the thirties and the forties. Perhaps it is because the major studios no longer make five hundred or so pictures a year and accordingly do not develop and guide new stars along the road to prominence. Or perhaps it is due to the changing tastes of today's audiences that support the glorification of the antihero and reject the gloss and artificiality of the majority of yesterday's films. Dustin Hoffman, Jon Voight, or Mia Farrow, as splendid as they are at what they do, would never have made it to the top were they born into the world of Gable, Grant, and Garbo.

At any rate, there are few opportunities today to direct the superstar with the one-dimensional approach to characterization, and more pictures are being turned out today with unknown actors than at any time in screen history. This should make many young directors (as well as Mr. Stevens) happy as the absence of status-conscious stars can only ease the strain of filming.

Many times it is difficult for a director to find the right words to tell an actor that a performance was not good, especially if that actor is a star. William Keighley had a method that worked well and illustrates the effectiveness of psychology. When a particular take was flat or slowly paced, or dramatically uneven, Keighley would let the scene play out, then walk to the actor and in a confidential tone suggest that they do it again, this time the way it had been done in rehearsal. The actor's ego was not damaged, since the implication was that he *had* given the correct performance in rehearsal and all that was expected of him was to repeat this achievement.

J. Lee Thompson, who directed *Doctor Dolittle*, says in this respect: "I like to listen to actors attentively and with sympathy, making them think they can do no wrong. The actor may be right; if he is, I'm delighted. But he is often wrong, so you employ tact and diplomacy and avoid saying let's do it your way or let's do it my way. I never make one version for the actor and another for me. If I know he's absolutely wrong, I stick it out; but first I talk it over and by the time he walks away he thinks he has really won his point, that my way was really his way."

And yet surprisingly, one of Hollywood's biggest stars, Charlton Heston, has this to say on the subject: "One thing I don't think a director has to do—and there are a lot of actors who get a lot of money who don't agree with me on this—is create an atmosphere or a mood particularly comfortable for me. I get a lot of money for acting and I think part of what they pay me for is to be able to work any way the director wants. If he wants to work in a kind of drum-tight atmosphere of watch-building tension like William Wyler, scratching and niggling at one little point and then another—that's fine. All I care about is the work. Many actors, and that includes most of the women in this business, want to be babied and coddled.

"I think all the hand holding and the making happy with the work is a bloody waste of time . . . the director doesn't have to hold my hand; he doesn't have to make me happy; he doesn't have to begin by saying: 'Chuck, that was marvelous, that was simply great, but look, baby, let's do just one more good old take, huh, and if you could just give us a little teensy bit of this . . . ' I don't need any of that. And I think that an actor who does need that is a child."

While we're on the subject of reshooting scenes, there is one rule of paramount importance: never ask an actor to do a second take unless you can make constructive criticism of his performance. Nor should the director show the actor what he wants by acting the part out himself, particularly if the actor is a competent one. Discuss with the actor the concept of the character, what motivates him, and the overall result that should be accomplished. Then let the actor bring his own interpretation to the part. Chances are it will be at least as effective as your own anyway.

The established director invariably "suggests" to an actor, never commands. Some wise philosopher once said, "Men must be taught as if you taught them not; and things unknown proposed as things forgot." No one likes to be ordered about, and a director can go far toward winning the instant respect of all his co-workers if he adopts a confident but casual manner in the way he gives cast and crew instructions. If an actor knows anything about psychology, it will be apparent to him that the director's "suggestions" are really orders to be followed faithfully.

Occasionally a director is faced with what seems to be an insurmountable problem in his relationship with a star, and a breach develops so wide it would seem that reparations of damage are all but impossible.

I was signed to direct a Technicolor feature for Columbia. The day

before the picture was to start I had yet to meet my leading lady, who was confined to her bed with a touch of virus. The producer suggested I drive out to the lady's house in Santa Monica and discuss the part she was going to play. She was a fast-rising actress of the day and had just won an Academy Award for her work in an important picture.

As I stood on her doorstep waiting to be admitted, I didn't realize the trap I was about to walk into. Sitting by her bedside, with her mother not once leaving the room, the actress and I went over the entire script, scene by scene, almost line by line. She would ask me from time to time how I would interpret the various scenes, and I confidently expressed my opinions since I had also worked on the story for many weeks. I knew it cold, or so I thought.

When the discussion was over and I stood up to leave, she made the announcement that was to almost bowl me over. "I'm glad we had this meeting because I have no intention of playing the role the way you described it."

I was dumbfounded. I muttered something about working things out and found my way out the door. I thought of all the things I could have said on the way back to Hollywood. I could have been resolute, telling her that she'd play it my way or else she could quit the picture before it even started. I could have double-talked, saying that perhaps I had explained the interpretation badly and that I was sure that we would see eye to eye once we started shooting. But, of course, I said none of these things in rebuttal to the leading lady who had just declared war on her director.

The next morning, when the first call for rehearsal was made, the actress made the first move. "Mr. Bare, I've been thinking over what you said yesterday. I think I see what you mean—and I want to apologize for saying what I did."

I was almost as dumbfounded as I had been the day before, but I shook her hand and inwardly sighed with relief. I knew then what had happened. Her mother, not one to see her daughter's career go down the drain, had set her straight on the obvious pitfalls of starting a picture by declaring war on the director.

(LEFT)
Gene Kelly, who directed Hello, Dolly!, *brought the multimillion-dollar film in one day below its ninety-day schedule. Many directors leave the direction of extras to their assistants, but Kelly personally handled the details of the crowd scenes something in the style of a college cheerleader. The 70 mm camera is shooting the Todd-A-O process.* (20th Century-Fox)

The lesson in this, to me at least, was that sometimes things have a way of ironing themselves out. Had I taken any tack except the one that I did, I am positive that the picture would have been a complete disaster for the lady as well as myself.

Winning Friends and Influencing Actors

Since directing deals with the emotions as well as the mechanics of staging and photography, the director must have a thorough knowledge of human nature and the psychology of dealing with others. He must be a born diplomat and a father as well. There is only one good way to get people to do what you want them to. And that is by making the other person *want* to do it. One of the best ways to accomplish this is to follow the advice of William James who said, "Everybody likes a compliment. The deepest principle in human nature is the craving to be appreciated." And, since actors are no different in this respect they respond amazingly well to the director who shows when he is pleased, and directors have many ways to express their pleasure. One contemporary of mine carried a bag full of small pieces of chocolate wrapped in foil to give the appearance of gold coins. Whenever an actor did a scene well he was handed a chocolate coin, the value of which equaled the director's estimation of how well the scene was played. Of small importance one might say, yet this director gained the reputation of being an "actor's director"—one way of saying that they enjoyed working with him. What is of greater importance is that his pictures are noted for the high level of performances they contain.

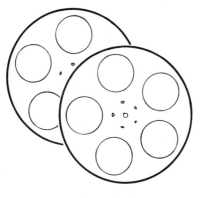

THE DIRECTOR
PREPARES FOR SHOOTING

Working with the Writer

The director's first duty upon being assigned to a feature motion picture is to spend some time with the writer who developed the script in conjunction with the producer. It is here that the director's interpretation first becomes a force, and usually certain portions of the script are rewritten or polished according to the director's viewpoints. This, of course, varies directly with the stature of the director and the importance of the picture.

There was a time during the old contract days of the major studios when a producer would assign a story to a writer, then turn it over to another for "polishing." It might go through five or six writers, each adding his touch, then it was assigned to the director for whatever directorial changes he thought was necessary. The picture could be written, photographed, and edited without the director and the writer ever making contact. Today's feature films are made with the writer and the director working in close concert. Most of the multimillion dollar pictures are made by directors who have almost complete autonomy, and in many instances these films carry no producer credit.

Billy Wilder (*The Apartment* and *The Fortune Cookie*) says, "It isn't necessarily helpful for a director to know how to write, but what is vitally important is that he know how to read. It isn't easy to ask the writer 'What did you mean by this, I don't get it?'"

Through close contacts with one another, the director and the writer become one another's collaborators; the director becomes a co-writer while the writer takes a hand in the direction.

Because more writers are becoming directors, the distinction between the two functions is tending to disappear. John Huston, one of the first writers to take up the megaphone, has made a fine art out of combining his talents. So has Richard Brooks, who not only wrote and directed, but produced as well, the taut and exciting *The Professionals*, one of the best all-round examples of cinematic story telling ever made.

Clive Bell, the English critic, calls true film art "that which has significant form, i.e., a deliberate design in which all parts contribute to a harmonious, unified whole." The fusion of director and writer makes for such unity of form and does much to dissuade the detractors of the *auteur* theory.

Director Robert Mulligan has a different approach to the writer-director subject. "Not every director should write, any more than every writer should direct. I don't write in the sense of putting words on paper, but I collaborate with the writer effectively every step of the way. When the film is shot I show it to him. If he has objections or suggestions, I listen very seriously. But the writer knows that the decision will be mine."

Since the director may be spending days, weeks, or even months with the writer on the final phases of the script, it becomes essential that he know something of the evolution of the screen story from its origin to the form from which the picture will be shot. If the story was a novel or a play, the beginning is obvious. If it was an original for the screen, it first became an *outline*, or synopsis, which delineated the characters and generally explained the plot. When a story is in this form there follows what is known as the "cut off" point; either the idea is abandoned or further development proceeds. The original writer may or may not be assigned to continue on the project. In any event, the next phase of story development is usually the *treatment*. This is an amplification of the outline that details the action and characterization and divides the story into scenes and sequences. Some writers even furnish at this stage relevant bits of dialogue, but generally dialogue and camera directions are absent from the treatment. If the story now satisfies all concerned, the writer goes into *screenplay*, which brings the story into a *continuity* that the actors and director use to interpret the author's words. The screenplay is what a blueprint is to a builder; the architect's aesthetic ideas set forth in technical terms.

There have been some pictures that have been marred by poor direction. On the other hand, I know of no case where a picture was a hit unless it had a basically good story, even though it had been brilliantly directed. No one who aspires to direct will deny Shakespeare's words, "The play's the thing."

When the director's contribution to the script has been accomplished, it is mimeographed as a *"final script,"* and sent out to all the various craft departments in the studio. William Keighley always did one thing before the script was mimeographed, however. He removed *all reference to the camera.* This may seem strange when the camera is such a vital part of telling a motion picture story, but Keighley had his reasons. He would go through the script and completely eliminate all camera angles, such as close shots, long shots, pan shots, dolly shots, leaving only the dialogue and those directions that pertained to the locale of the scene and the actor's business. He maintained that a screen writer (who did not intend to direct the film) could not properly visualize in advance how and where a pan shot or a dolly shot would be effective. Keighley freely admitted he usually didn't know himself until he started to stage the action on the set that had been built for the scene. Dramatic action can be much different on the sound stage from the way it had been imagined by the writer as he faced his typewriter. By delaying the camera treatment until the action, dialogue, and business is worked out, the director is able to photograph the action as he sees fit, according to the situation at hand, rather than follow what had been set down in the script. This does not imply that a director does not have preconceived ideas how he will shoot his scenes, only that he will not be bound by the writer's conception. Fortunately, there is a growing tendency among writers to turn out scripts that avoid camera directions since they, too, have come to recognize that a director will in most cases disregard them.

Stanley Kubrick, who directed *Dr. Strangelove* and *2001, A Space Odyssey*, in his advice to would-be screen writers, has this to say about the subject: "All it takes to write a movie script is to record what people say and do. Don't bother with all the camera information. The director will change it all anyway."

Where most writers and directors are in agreement is in the division of units of a screenplay. These units are *the shot, the scene,* and *the sequence.* Although Keighley always believed that the shot should not be indicated in the script, it sometimes appears, so it is only proper that we give it a definition.

A shot indicates a separate component of a scene, while a scene is a succession of shots, although sometimes a scene can be composed of only a single shot.

A sequence is a unit of action in which there is no lapse of time and can be made up of several scenes. For instance, a ten-page sequence in an apartment, with continuous action, may be composed of individual scenes. Let's presume that our script *sequence* has to do with the preparations for a dinner party, the arrival of the guests, and the comic events connected with preparing the food.

The first *scene* takes place in the kitchen with the newlywed wife

Cameramen will do almost anything to get the shot the director wants, and if that director happens to be Billy Wilder, and the camera is an Airiflex, he will even lie down in a grave. Wilder, shown behind the camera, has been nominated twenty times and has won six Oscars.

fixing a shrimp soufflé, the husband arriving at the last moment with the news that his boss is unexpectedly coming to dinner. Conflict ensues when it is brought out that the boss is allergic to seafood. The second *scene* begins when the husband greets the arriving guests and shows them to the living room. He shakes up some cocktails, and makes excuses for the wife who has gone out the back way to buy a cooked turkey for the dinner. The husband behind the bar is covered in a *medium shot,* while the boss moves about the room looking at the husband's old football trophies in a *panning shot.* The third *scene* has the wife telling the husband that the delicatessen is closed and the husband concocting a meal out of canned goods. The fourth and final *scene* covers the social disaster at the dinner table resulting in the boss and his wife storming out. The complete *sequence,* including its *scenes* and *shots,* has come to a close, either with a *fade out*, a *lap-dissolve*, or as in most pictures today, the *quick cut*, which is no more than an abrupt transition to the next sequence.

Most scripts indicate *parallel action* at least someplace in the story, and this means interplaying two scenes through the use of *cut-backs*. The grand daddy of them all had Little Nell tied to the railroad tracks with cut-backs between the approaching train and Harold Trueheart riding to the rescue. Parallel action can take many forms, and can be slow and suspenseful as well as frantic.

Another term that had its origin in early film scenarios is the *flash-back*. This often used device labels scenes that portray events backward in time.

It is not the purpose of this book to dwell on all aspects of screen writing or the techniques, past and present, of good film stories. There are many definitive books on the market for the interested student.

The Warner Bros. studio art department outdid itself on the lavishness of sets for Camelot. *Notice the size of the man on the lower level of the great hall as compared with the production crew in the foreground. Directed by Josh Logan.* (Warner Bros.)

How the Cast Is Assembled

If the director has been assigned well in advance of the shooting date, he will be concerned with casting; and in all cases where a star is not involved, he will usually have a complete veto over casting. He may not get every actor he desires for his picture, but seldom does a producer saddle him with a performer he does not want.

The studio casting department, while its usefulness is not to be questioned, merely acts as a procurement agency, and the casting director a suggestor and collaborator with the producer and director in the matter of casting the various roles.

If the director is not familiar with a performer he will ask him to read, just as actors audition for parts in the legitimate theater. Many actors protest this method of selection; in fact, some refuse under any condition to read for a part—yet it remains the best way (short of making a screen test) for a director to become acquainted with an actor's talent and personality before arbitrarily casting him for the role. The most often-used expression connected with a reading is when an actor maintains, "I'm a terrible cold reader." Still, the director will make allowances; and many times after such an audition, I've commented most enthusiastically: "That's the hottest cold reading I've ever heard."

When the reading is not feasible, the director can either believe the superlatives of the actor's agent, or he can avail himself of some recent film showing the actor in question in a role that may have similar qualities. While not cooperating completely with one another, the major studios have always allowed pictures to be screened for the purposes of casting, especially when the producer makes the request.

The Academy of Motion Picture Arts and Sciences publishes a voluminous work known as the *Player's Directory* that contains the pictures of several thousand thespians. An obvious aid to the director in casting, it has always been a "must" for an actor, yet some actors in Hollywood foolishly refuse to pay the low yearly fee to be included.

The first television film that Warner Bros. produced was the initial episode of *Cheyenne*, which I had been assigned to direct. After having spent some time with the writer, my attentions were turned toward finding not only the cast for the episode, but a star as well.

I tested half a dozen potential western leading men and among them was Norman Walker, a 6' 5½" giant of a man, with a velvetlike voice, who had been a bouncer at one of the clubs in Las Vegas. His discovery was due to a Hollywood agent spotting him in the gaming room, and then asking him the time worn question, "Do you want to be in pictures?"

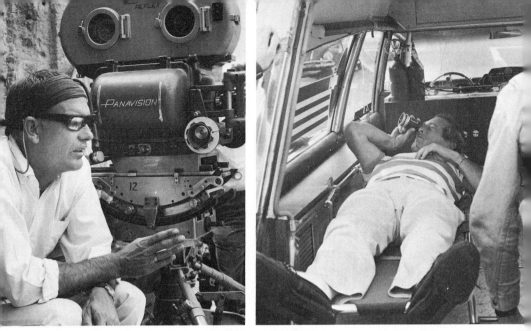

(ABOVE, LEFT)
Director Sam Peckinpah (Ride the High Country, The Wild Bunch) *specializes in violent stories of the old west. Here, reflected in his eye, is the scene that holds his attention. The huge Panavision camera, another rival for Mitchell's supremacy, awaits the order to "Roll 'em."* (Warner Bros.)

(ABOVE, RIGHT)
Paul Newman in his first feature-directing stint is not lying down on the job. He is lining up a shot through his director's finder for Rachel, Rachel. *The picture was nominated for an Academy Award as best picture.* (Warner Bros.)

"Nope," said Walker.

"Well, if you ever change your mind, here's my card. Come and see me," said the agent as he walked over to the crap table.

Six months later, Walker lost his job and remembered the agent and the movie proposition. He jumped into his battered car and drove to Los Angeles. The agent took him to William T. Orr, a studio executive who was overseeing the brand new television activities. That's how Walker came to be tested that day.

Later when we sat in the projection room with Jack Warner, I noticed that he viewed the various tests with little enthusiasm until Walker's test came on. Although the neophyte actor was rough in technique and a little nervous, there was something—some vague quality, call it personality—that Warner recognized.

"Put the big fellow's test on again," he ordered through the speaker to the projectionist.

When Walker's test was again shown, he was sure of it.

"That's the boy. What's his name?"

"Norman Walker," I said.

J. L. cast an upward glance to the ceiling.

"Can't call him Norman. Too mild. We'll call him Clint. That's it— Clint Walker."

Conferring with the Staff

While the director is interviewing actors for the many parts in a feature picture, he must determine with the art director the style, size, and arrangement of the sets that will shortly be constructed. Again the budget on the picture, whether it be for theaters or television, will determine the degree to which the director may influence the design and construction of sets. Most art directors will, if the opportunity presents itself, confer with the director on the design of important sets where the placement of doors, windows, or other physical elements will have a bearing on the staging of the action.

The director who has the ability to draw—even the most elementary sketches—has a decided advantage when it comes to discussions involving sets. This method of communication between director and art director not only provides a positive short cut to understanding, but saves many disappointments on the stage later when it is too late and too costly to make set changes.

Sets are designed today with careful attention given to the aspect ratio with which they are to be photographed. This will be discussed in a later chapter, but in general the wider the screen the wider the sets must be.

Sets sometimes are designed especially for the stars who are to work in them. Once all the sets in an Alan Ladd western film were scaled down to create the illusion that Ladd was larger than he really was. As soon as the feature was finished I inherited these sets for an episode of *Cheyenne*. Six foot-five Clint Walker looked slightly ridiculous having to stoop as he came through every door in the film.

During the preparation period of a motion picture, the director confers with the property man, the wardrobe people, and exchanges concepts of photography with the cameraman. The production department is kept advised of any unusual effect the director plans to use in the picture, and matters such as the number of shooting days, the scheduling of sequences, and the like, are all discussed in detail. It is at this time, and this time only, that the director will have the opportunity to influence the production department to shoot the picture in a sequence as near to the correct order as possible. Unless he speaks up now, he may find he is shooting the tender and dramatic denouement on the very first day. While we're on this subject, production managers don't deliberately try to shoot pictures backward, but sometimes due to the exigencies of budget, the availabilities of stage space or actors, a director is required to make many concessions to his aesthetic nature. But an experienced director understands the need for a proper balance between the pragmatic and the artistic.

The Shooting Schedule

When the assistant director first lays out a shooting schedule, one of the things he takes into consideration is the number of script pages the director will be able to shoot in a day and whether or not his schedule is realistic. The schedule might be one way for a Don Siegel and another way for a George Stevens. The director whose background was in film editing might be expected to turn in his picture faster than the man who came from the theater or had been a screen writer.

When the budget is complete, the director may be asked to make certain concessions, especially if the picture is a modest feature or made for television. These concessions may range from eliminating a costly location jaunt to the obtaining of less expensive actors. The experienced director knows in what areas he can afford to be cooperative and conversely when budget slashing is apt to hurt the quality of his picture.

Selecting Locations

The director will next want to scout his locations—that is, his exterior locales away from the studio. In a major studio this is done in collaboration with the location department. On a smaller picture, it may become the director's sole responsibility to cruise around the countryside more often than not in his own automobile, using his own gasoline. Few directors complain about this, however, when they have genuine enthusiasm for the script they are about to direct.

The modern feature film utilizes natural backgrounds to an extent never realized by the studios when they were in assembly line production. Today's more critically aware audiences demand realism in sets and locations as much as in story content and performances. Director Richard Brooks shot the entire production of *Happy Ending* in and around Denver, Colorado, using both exterior and interior locations. Not a single set was constructed nor was a single scene shot in a studio. The money saved on set construction went for transportation costs, and this sometimes evens out. Only the sound recording budget goes up disproportionately as most of the sound must be done over, or *dubbed,* back at the studio.

If the locations selected by the director are within a municipality, police protection must be obtained to control traffic and interested on-lookers. If they are in the open countryside, other factors should be analyzed; weather conditions, isolation from highways and airways, which will contribute to maximum quality in sound recording, and accessibility of the trucks and equipment to the camera site. Many a director has enthusiastically walked to the highest ridge only to find that the spot he has selected is almost completely inaccessible to camera and sound equipment.

But with the advent of the new wave director, particularly the commercial maker, a demand has been made for new lightweight cameras and recorders. With this new equipment there is virtually no place an energetic director can't shoot his scene.

The Director Plots His Action

Preparing can be an extremely important phase of the director's contribution to the picture, for it is only with careful planning that a smooth production will result.

There is a wide divergence of opinion among directors in Hollywood regarding the working out in advance of camera angles, *coverage* (the amount of angles from which a scene is shot), and the positioning and movement of actors. They range from the man who works out on paper each movement of the actor and each corresponding movement and angle of the camera to the man who gives this no advance thought whatsoever. Frankly, I have had occasion to use both methods, and each can be a perfectly valid system of working. There is little sense in intricately mapping out in advance each movement of camera and actors in a short scene involving a small set and only two performers. But when a director is under the pressure of a tight schedule and has many and varied sets to shoot in one day, each with a large number of actors, it will behoove him to give some considered attention to how he will stage each setup to gain maximum advantage. For instance, let's consider a grand ballroom scene that covers twenty script pages. There is an archway at the far end of the set. During the course of the action nine different actors make their entrance, and there is need for a close shot of each as they come through the arch. The experienced director will take advantage of the camera and lights being set up for the first actor's entrance, and will then bring all the actors through one after another, thus saving many hours of repositioning the camera and sound equipment and relighting the shot. Of course, Wyler, Stevens, and Hitchcock might find this an annoyance, but then with the budget they are accustomed to they can afford many luxuries.

There is much to be said for the director who, otherwise proficient and knowledgeable of his craft, prefers to work out all the mechanics of the scene just before he shoots it, providing this method does not add to the production schedule. Moving his people around the set like chessmen enables the director to obtain many values which are not apparent on paper. Seeing people in three dimension, in the depth and breadth of the set, and being able to watch the action through the camera will provide many opportunities for a freshness and vitality not otherwise obtainable. I have seen directors who, because they had worked the action out on paper the night before, failed to take advantage of sudden inspirations and proceeded to stage the scene in a static and unimaginative way. And actors sometimes have excellent ideas for staging. It is prudent to have a guide, and perhaps most of the time the guide will work, but it is the wise director who will deviate from his own preconceptions when either an actor or the cameraman has an obviously better idea. Incidentally, the taking of ideas from others will not in itself lower a director's prestige, and the director who announces to his crew that he is not in the market for suggestions shuts himself off from many valuable sources for touches in direction. It is much better to encourage these suggestions from people, taking what one likes and discarding the rest.

Robert Aldrich, director of such films as *What Ever Happened to Baby Jane?* and *The Killing of Sister George*, is one of the most throughly prepared directors in Hollywood. He rehearses for two to three weeks on the sets and with the props and in some instances the wardrobe the actors will wear. He claims that actors respect a director who is well prepared and once they feel that a director is in charge and knows exactly what he wants they become secure and give better performances.

As a last word on preparation, a director can find himself in a situation where there is practically no preparation whatsoever. Such a thing happened to me once as I was driving out of the studio for the day. I had been under contract to Warners for some time and had done several features since being elevated to that status from the short subject department. But right at this time I was unassigned.

As I reached the gate, the gateman hailed me down and told me that a certain producer wanted to see me right away. I turned the car around and headed back to the main administration building.

When I reached the producer's office he told me that I had been assigned to direct the picture that was to start the next day and that he hoped I would like the script. Naturally, I was confused, having known for weeks another director had been assigned to do the picture and that he had worked hard in all phases of preparation.

This producer, never one to mince words, quickly set me straight.

"We had a slight difference of opinion," he ventured, "one that centered around the way a certain scene was to be shot."

Intrigued, but still confused, I told him that since I was going to start shooting the next morning a script I had never seen before, he had better fill me in.

He went on to explain that the other director had refused to stage a scene in which the leading man was to extricate himself from a thirty-foot well the way the producer wanted him to, and had even taken his case to Mr. Warner. He parenthetically indicated to me that if I, too, wanted to be removed from the picture all I need do was similarly bother Warner.

When I asked what the producer's method of having the actor gain his freedom from the well, and how this differed from the previous director's intentions, I found out what the difficulty was. The producer thought the actor would climb out of the well by extending both arms and both legs and working his way up inch by inch over the cobble stones in a horizontal position. The director differed, maintaining steadfastly that a superhuman achievement such as this could only have believability if the actor remained in an upright position, pulling himself up inch by inch with his hands.

When I had been properly indoctrinated with all the facts and who said what to whom, the producer, who incidentally doesn't produce pictures any more, sat back in his big leather chair and said rather testily, "Now, how do you see it?"

"Well," I said, "It doesn't make much difference to me, because with a stunt like this I'm going to have to use a double and pull him out with a wire."

With that, I took the script, went home, boned all night, and started shooting *This Side of the Law* the next morning.

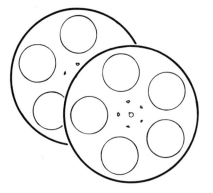

4

THE ART OF REHEARSAL

And a Fine Art It Is

A perfect rehearsal is a wasted take.

Insufficient rehearsal causes imperfect takes.

Unused takes cause a waste of valuable time and money.

Knowing at what point a cast and camera crew are sufficiently rehearsed is something that cannot be learned by reading a book. Only experience teaches a director the fine art of rehearsing his players up to the point where they are ready for filming. If they are overrehearsed, chances are that take one will not be printed; something is apt to go wrong, or the scene will lack spark or vitality. If the players are not well enough rehearsed, some error in movement or a fluff in dialogue will surely occur. The knack is to run through the scene so that everyone knows his mechanics and his dialogue, but is not emotionally exhausted to the point that he has "given his all" before the camera even starts grinding.

Personally, I strive to rehearse and shoot a scene so that take one will be a print. I may go on to make a second take for protection, but usually count on the first one for the spontaneity and energy that the scene demands. Too many run throughs and eight or nine takes can only have an enervating effect on actors and a resultant letdown in their performances.

A famous director at Metro-Goldwyn-Mayer, after shooting a long and important scene, said: "Print Takes 36, 27, 25, and 2." The producer on the picture, in an attempt to discourage the director from wasting so much film and time, had the cutter rearrange the slate numbers on the head of each take. When the director ran the dailies in the projection room with the producer, he defended his position by insisting that "Take 27 is the best—anybody can see that." No one in the room dared tell him that he had actually selected take 2, except the producer who did so with considerable relish.

The Cast Is Assembled

When the cast for a picture has been assembled it is important for the director to meet them in an informal reading, at which time the story, dialogue, and characters may be discussed by each player both individually and in relationship to the other characters of the story.

This get-together is important in other ways as well. It serves to "break the ice," to become acquainted and stay acquainted. It allows the director to become familiar with the players with whom he must work. It allows the actors to become acquainted with the personality of the man who will guide them through the picture, and who will be responsible for exposing their own personalities to the audience through his staging and use of the camera. At this first meeting, it is well for the director to let it be known that he knows exactly what he wants and that he intends to get it. It is in this first meeting that the director's leadership must be firmly established. Respect must be won, and all misunderstandings or disagreements should be settled now, for it will be disastrous to carry any divergence of opinion regarding characterization to the shooting stage.

A well-known television player once stomped off in high dudgeon as a result of a director refusing to make changes in the dialogue of a script in one of these early readings. To say the least, the player was summarily replaced by another actor, and shooting started as scheduled. For the director to have acquiesced in favor of the actor would have had a cancerous effect when shooting since this particular actor has a reputation for undermining directors, and took every advantage that occurred to him. In this case, he and the director had it out before the shooting started, and in that way each knew exactly where one another stood. The fact that he chose to give up the assignment rather than acquiesce to the director only points up his own immaturity and unprofessional behavior; but these are the kinds of temperments directors often come in contact with, and one should prepare for the eventuality.

When the first reading is finished, if practicable, a run-through of some of the more important scenes should be given on the actual set if it is available. Even though the entire picture or television film cannot be completely rehearsed, just singling out one or two important scenes can do much to establish a rapport between director and actors, and will

Morton Da Costa presents the script of Auntie Mame *to Rosalind Russell, who starred in the picture. Da Costa is a director who firmly believes that "the play's the thing" and that actors should use any approach to acting that is comfortable to them. (Warner Bros.)*

On location for What Ever Happened to Baby Jane?, *director Robert Aldrich (dark glasses) shares camera platform with the Airiflex. Aldrich is one of the few successful directors who came from the assistant director ranks. (Associates & Aldrich–Warner Bros.)*

serve to illustrate the tone and shape of the direction that will follow during the course of filming. The reading is the place for a mutual meeting of the minds about the way each character is to be portrayed. Every misunderstanding that can be cleared up before cameras start to turn is money in the bank for the director, and the production company as well, as many hours and even days can be added to the schedule of a picture by directors attempting to communicate with actors regarding the interpretation of a scene.

The Importance of Being Articulate

It is appropriate, at this point, to dwell on the value of the director's ability to communicate. Nothing will serve the director more than a well-organized, articulate approach in his communication with others, and the man who has the ability to speak clearly with the proper vocabulary will find himself hours ahead each day and held much higher in esteem than the inarticulate director who, while knowing exactly what he wants, finds it difficult to express himself.

Originality, leadership, persistence, patience, and a true sense of the drama are all requisites of the successful director, but unless he has mastered the power of communication, his road will be rough.

While it is not the best way to direct, there are certain times when it becomes expedient to "show" an actor the way to play a scene. Perhaps you have an hour to go on a three-day television schedule, and you have run into an incompetent or miscast actor. That training you had in the little theater, or as the lead in your high school play, will hold you in good stead at this point. Sometimes the finest vocabulary in the world fails (after all an actor must have the same vocabulary to comprehend what you're talking about), and other methods of indicating what the director wants must be resorted to. I once lost my voice, because of a severe attack of laryngitis, while directing *Maverick*. I never realized how much I depended on the transmission of ideas without using my full vocabulary, until I was forced to whisper certain instructions to the script girl, who in turn relayed the information to the cast. Without being able personally to speak to the actors, I had to convey the mechanics and business, as well as indicate the way more humor could be derived from the scene—and all this through another person.

Correcting Actors' Mistakes Early

One of the most serious errors a director can make is to allow misreadings or other false interpretations to go uncorrected in early rehearsals. Things have a way of becoming implanted on an actor's subconscious through repetition, and if the director would have it eliminated or changed by the time he is ready for a take, then the mistake should be corrected the first time he hears it. Actors sometimes criticize this method as being picayune, especially if they have not yet learned their lines; but I find that it is better than wasting takes to correct some slight but important part of a performance.

Robert Aldrich has his own methods of correcting early mistakes: "One thing I've discovered about actors is that they don't like surprises. A sudden change in the way a scene should be filmed or a role altered throws them off balance. My own formula for working with actors is to have at least a two-week rehearsal on a sound stage without interruptions. Sitting around a long table, I impart to them my idea of the story, the characters, and the problems we face. They, in turn contribute their ideas. We discuss costume, character backgrounds, and motivations and relationships to each of the other characters in the story. When the scenes are actually shot, the actors will know what is expected of them so that none can say, just as we are set to roll the camera, he doesn't understand the scene or that the dialogue doesn't fit. They will have had plenty of time to have ironed that out during the rehearsals."

Aldrich believes that actors respect a director when they know he is firmly in charge. When an actor has complete confidence in his director, he can go about his own preparations and performance with confidence in himself.

Good Rehearsing Is Good Directing

The late George Bernard Shaw had many thoughts on the art of rehearsing and although he was a man of the theater, many of his ideas are applicable to motion pictures. He believed strongly in the kind and character of criticism. If a thing is wrong and the director doesn't know exactly how to set it right, it is much better to remain silent until he or the actor comes up with an idea. It discourages and angers the actor to hear you tell him you are dissatisfied without being able to criticize constructively.

Shaw had thoughts on the director's disposition, too. He deplored directors who lost their tempers or displayed bad manners in any way. This, he felt, destroyed the dignity of the director—and in his words, "make a scene which is not in the play."

During the rehearsal of *Pygmalion* in London, Shaw saw to it that his actors did not stop the forward movement of the play at any time. They were told to sit on a line and rise on a line, and that the last word of an exit speech must get the actor off the stage. If he were to cross on the stage, he must move as he spoke and not before or after.

Morton Da Costa, who directed *Auntie Mame* and *The Music Man*, made a speech to his cast on the opening day of rehearsal for a Broadway show a few years ago. The following excerpts are set down as they are appropriate in the motion picture field; "Welcome to the cast. You have all been selected with great care. You use different methods of approach to acting. You have studied at different dramatic schools with different teachers. Please continue to use whatever method is comfortable—I endorse any method that makes you a better actor. However, it would be impossible for me to accommodate myself to your various terminologies and systems, so I suggest it would be much easier for you to accommodate yourselves to mine.

"I will welcome suggestions for authenticity, but will not be a slave to realism. The stage is fundamentally a place for selective realism. The phrase 'The character wouldn't do so-and-so' is most often suspect to me, just as is 'The character would positively *do* so-and-so.' Many things can be justified depending on the completeness of the understanding of the character, and the will or the desire to justify them.

"I beg of you to impress the idea 'The play's the thing.' If you serve this play well, I promise you, you will serve yourselves well. Let us set aside the usual preoccupation with our so-called position-protocol and other inhibiting factors in favor of being a group of dedicated craftsmen, to try to put aside the insecurities common to most sensitive, creative people and become a family, a happy one, I hope."

Leslie Stevens, who directed the interesting feature *Private Property*, rehearsed his cast in natural locations for two weeks—then, went on to shoot the entire picture in six days. Each move made by an actor, and the corresponding camera position, was carefully charted in advance with the result that when actual production commenced no lost motion occurred.

One of the inequities in modern television filming is the lack of rehearsal time extended the director. Certain shows like Rod Serling's *Twilight Zone* always included several days' rehearsal just prior to shooting; but too often a director must not only start filming on the first morning of his schedule, but meet his actors for the first time as well. If he is lucky, unimportant scenes will be scheduled the first day, and the dramatic moments of the film will be saved until he and his cast have properly become acquainted.

5

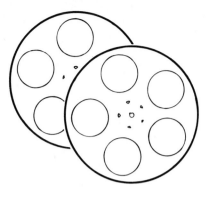

STAGING AND PLOTTING ACTION

Left to Right and Vice Versa

Every director leans to a certain extent on his script clerk whose job it is to keep the records of the shooting as well as remind the director of the first rule in the book, "Keep 'em going left to right."

Or right to left—but keep the direction of actors, trains, stage coaches, Indians, and almost everything else that moves across the screen and progresses from shot to shot going only one way.

Directors who observe this rule provide an even flow to the action easier to comprehend by an audience, whose point of view shouldn't unnecessarily change any more than if they were seated in a legitimate theater watching a play.

Motion pictures, capable of sustaining the continuous action of its actors over a multitude of backgrounds, early set up standards of consistent movement as a less confusing arrangement than having the audience, in effect, change positions from shot to shot.

This technique, in addition, has always been used to denote actors who were going as against actors who were coming. Planes that flew from San Francisco to New York invariably were seen in flight going left to right, as one would view a map. East to west flights were always depicted going right to left.

An actor moves across the screen from *right* to *left*, walks up the steps to a house and knocks on the door. The door is opened and the actor enters the house—cut. Now the crew moves inside the house and prepares to continue the scene. If the director insists on reversing his position (that is, crossing the proscenium—discussed later), the actor will now be seen entering the door from *left* to *right*. When the two shots

SHOWING AN ACTOR
AT A WINDOW

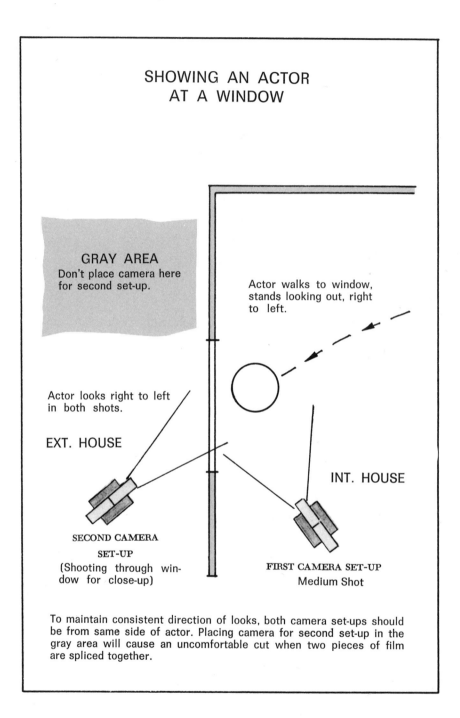

GRAY AREA
Don't place camera here for second set-up.

Actor walks to window, stands looking out, right to left.

Actor looks right to left in both shots.

EXT. HOUSE

INT. HOUSE

SECOND CAMERA SET-UP
(Shooting through window for close-up)

FIRST CAMERA SET-UP
Medium Shot

To maintain consistent direction of looks, both camera set-ups should be from same side of actor. Placing camera for second set-up in the gray area will cause an uncomfortable cut when two pieces of film are spliced together.

BRINGING AN ACTOR
THROUGH A DOOR

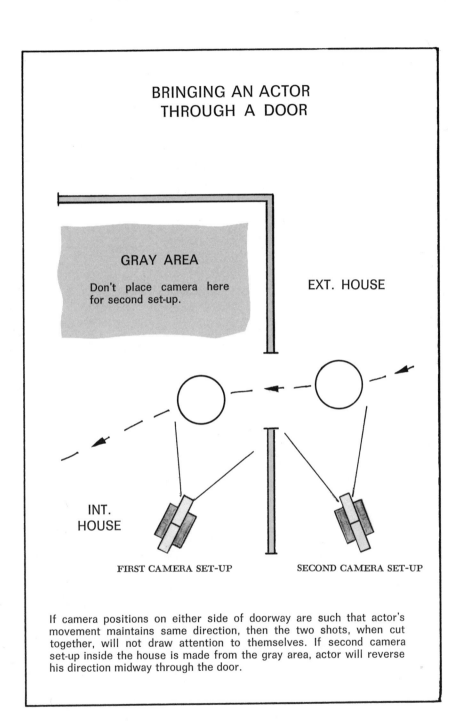

GRAY AREA

Don't place camera here for second set-up.

EXT. HOUSE

INT. HOUSE

FIRST CAMERA SET-UP   SECOND CAMERA SET-UP

If camera positions on either side of doorway are such that actor's movement maintains same direction, then the two shots, when cut together, will not draw attention to themselves. If second camera set-up inside the house is made from the gray area, actor will reverse his direction midway through the door.

When Alfred Hitchcock made Rope, *starring James Stewart, he did something no other director had ever done. Every "take" ran a full one thousand feet, with actors and camera moving about the multiroomed set in complicated patterns. Here one can see how the walls were constructed to swing aside, making room for the large Technicolor camera, then close again as the camera passed through the doorways.* (Warner Bros.)

are cut together there will be (to most viewers) a disturbing element introduced. The technique of cutting will not call attention to itself if the progress of movement is consistent on both sides of the door.

Now, as I have pointed out, this is a rule—and rules are sometimes effectively broken. John Ford was perhaps the first of the directors to ignore the rule of maintaining a constant direction. The new directors break rules to provide shock effect, to purposely make an audience uneasy, even restless. When the first director threw away the tripod in favor of the handheld camera he was breaking an iron-clad rule.

John Sturges (*Magnificent Seven, Marooned*) makes an appropriate comment: "For a long time, starting back in the thirties, I guess, the motion picture industry became very stylized. The product itself was stylized, and so was the way it was made. Now it's a whole new ball game and we're moving ahead, exploring to see just what you really can do with film. It's more exciting now and it's more creative. Will we keep anything of the old? Sure. There's something rewarding in familiarity. And in quality. You don't hear Beethoven's Fifth Symphony and say 'I don't like that because I've heard it before.' "

However, Sturges, a modern filmmaker, usually does not break the rule of maintaining consistent directions.

The Consistent Direction of Looks

There is one rule that has been rigid as long as film editing has existed and that is the rule of *opposite looks*. Even the most rebellious of the young directors seem to obey this technical mandate, holding it sacrosanct while breaking all other cinematic rules willy-nilly.

Actors who stand facing one another are established in their opening shot each looking in a certain direction. When the individual close-ups are made of these actors it is mandatory to keep consistent the direction in which they are looking with reference to the position of the audience. If two actors are speaking to one another, one has to look left-to-right, the other right-to-left. Yet strangely enough this fundamental rule acknowledged by all professionals in all countries of the world is still one of the hardest to grasp by most of the people who work in this business. I have witnessed near knock-down and drag-out arguments between directors and their script clerks, or their cameramen, over the simplest matter of which way an actor looks—camera left or camera right. The corresponding scene may have been made days previously, with the script clerk making notes exactly the way it was shot. The cameraman speaks up, and confuses the issue by saying that he looked through the lens and remembered vividly that it was not a left look but a right look. All I can say, when these disagreements occur, is that the director had better be sure he either calls the shot correctly or shoots the scene both ways to save embarrassment in the projection room later.

Transgressions by directors in this respect are referred to as *crossing the proscenium*, or *crossing the imaginary line*, and it is the director's ultimate responsibility to see that the directions of looks and movements by his actors are consistent.

The imaginary line can be visualized by plotting on paper the positions of actors and camera. Draw two circles to indicate the actors and a small square for the camera. Project two lines of a "V" from the camera to encompass the actors, representing the camera's view or angle. (See

A BASIC RULE
IN DIRECTING

Don't let camera cross
imaginary line

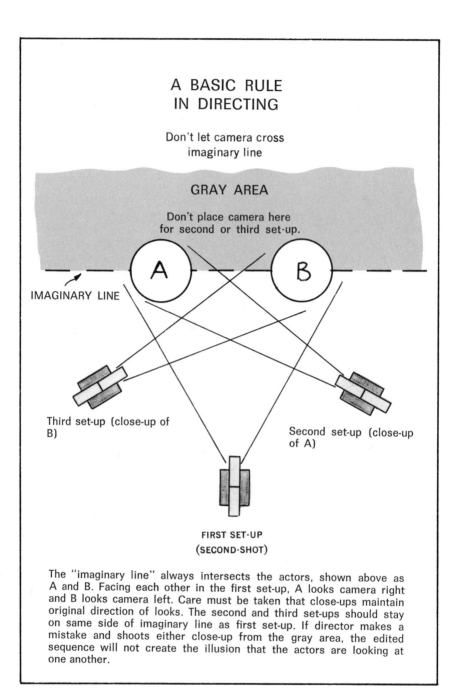

GRAY AREA

Don't place camera here
for second or third set-up.

IMAGINARY LINE

Third set-up (close-up of
B)

Second set-up (close-up
of A)

FIRST SET-UP
(SECOND-SHOT)

The "imaginary line" always intersects the actors, shown above as A and B. Facing each other in the first set-up, A looks camera right and B looks camera left. Care must be taken that close-ups maintain original direction of looks. The second and third set-ups should stay on same side of imaginary line as first set-up. If director makes a mistake and shoots either close-up from the gray area, the edited sequence will not create the illusion that the actors are looking at one another.

diagram.) Now, draw a dotted line right through the circles, which indicate the actors, and you have the imaginary line. At no time during filming of a scene, which is to be broken up with one or more shots, should
the camera cross this line. For to do so, takes the audience across the
line too, just as sure as if during a play the audience walked up on the
stage and viewed the action from the other side of the actors.

This does not mean that in a scene staged with multiple actor and
camera movement the camera cannot cross the imaginary line; it only
means that for purposes of cutting the various component shots of the
scene together, the audience's viewpoint should remain consistent. A
scene that begins with a given set of left and right looks can reverse itself
midway, then return again to the original audience viewpoint, since the
consistency of looks need only be respected in relation to the cutting in
of other shots. What will work at one point in a moving camera scene will
not work at another point.

Imagine an apartment living room with a window on the left, a door
on the right, a small bar upstage center and a couch downstage center
facing camera. The director decides he wants to make a master shot of a
five-page scene, the subject matter of which is one in which a girl rejects
her boy friend.

The boy enters the room through the door, walks to the girl who is
seated on the couch talking on the telephone. The girl looks up at him,
camera right. The boy looks down at her, camera left. She tells him to
fix himself a drink. He walks to the deep end of the set and goes behind
the bar, with the camera moving *beyond* the imaginary line that has been
drawn through the first positions of boy and girl, i.e., at the couch. (See
diagram.) Now, intercutting between the two becomes mandatory, since
the master shot includes only the boy, with the girl being off camera. The
complimentary shots at this point have the boy looking camera right and
the girl looking camera left, over her shoulder while still talking on the
phone. When the phone conversation is finished (filmed separately) the
girl enters the master shot while the boy is still at the bar. Surmising by
the tone of the telephone conversation that he is being brushed off, the
boy moves to the window, camera following him alone. At this point,
close-ups would be cut in and the direction of looks must again be consistent—the boy looks right, the girl left. She again steps in to the shot,
and then the two walk downstage to the couch, she sitting on the right,
he on the left. Close-ups are made here, too, and her look will be left and
his right. The camera has moved all over the set, crossing the imaginary
line, and then returning to its original viewpoint, but it did this deliberately, causing no bewilderment on the part of the audience. All that is
necessary to make the scene editorially perfect is to have the looks of the
close-ups correspond to the looks in the master shot. And this is where

THE IMPORTANCE OF LOOKS

RIGHT

After the direction of looks has been established in the first set-up, a two-shot, both actors in their close-ups look in opposite directions and appear to be looking at one another.

WRONG

This is what happens when the camera is placed over the imaginary line for one of the close-ups. Although in the two-shot, Eva Gabor is carrying on a conversation with Eddie Albert, she appears to be looking away from him in her close-up.

VERTICAL LOOKS ARE IMPORTANT, TOO

To keep the close-up looks consistent with the master two-shot, Eva Gabor looks below the lens in her close-up and Eddie Albert looks above the lens in his—regardless of the height of the camera. This simple rule can plague the director who doesn't concern himself with camera height.

COVERING A THREE-SHOT

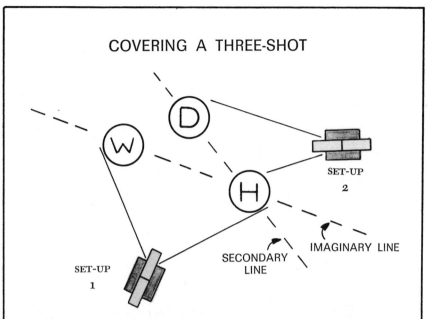

Husband discusses fees with doctor as wife stands by. Master three-shot has been photographed from set-up 1, and normally all close-ups or two-shots should be made with camera respecting the imaginary line. However, when wife has considerable dialogue with both men, first speaking to one, then the other, it is permissible to move the camera across the line and shoot the wife, framing the shot with the doctor on one side and the husband on the other. Shifting angle this way establishes a secondary line, and all succeeding close-ups should, in turn, respect the new line.

SHOOTING TROUBLESOME TABLE SCENES

SOMETIMES THE CAMERA MUST MOVE BEYOND THE IMAGINARY LINE.

The direction of actors' looks in close-ups made around a table can be confusing as well as annoying to the director. Actor E has several lines to B. E looks left in his close-up and B looks right. But then E turns to A and looks right. A's close-up must have him looking left, which when related to the master group shot would seem to be all wrong. Match each exchange between actors with opposing looks rather than matching with the master.

the danger lurks, where the confusion occurs. The girl receives three separate close-ups while she is seated on the couch. One was when the boy stood alongside her after making his entrance. The second was when she spoke to him while she was still on the phone and he was at the bar. The third was after she had brought him back to the couch. No doubt the close-ups will be made all at the same time, and the script girl must note that two of these shots require a camera-left look and one a camera-right. It is relatively a simple matter to match looks when the camera remains stationary; it is quite another when it roams freely about the set.

When shooting telephone conversations, care should be taken that the two corresponding shots of the persons talking are made with opposite looks. While this is not as fixed a rule as if the actors were standing facing one another, it does help to create the illusion that they are talking to one another.

Another common pitfall for the director has to do with the vertical matching of looks from one shot to the next. The establishing two shot, let us suppose, was made with a man standing and a woman sitting. He was looking down at her; she, up at him. But, when the camera is moved in for a close-up position of the woman, the director and cameraman must be extremely diligent lest a mishap occur. Since women are more flatteringly photographed with the camera looking slightly down on them, our subject must still look higher than the lens to give the illusion that she is looking at the man. Actually, she may be looking too high in relationship to the actor, who will stand beside the camera to play the scene with her, and a box may even have to be provided for him to stand on so that he can properly meet her correct look. Care must be taken with the man's close-up look also; for unless the camera is just below the imaginary line of sight between the two actors, as established in the master two shot, the scene when cut will result in both actors looking up.

Certain latitude may be taken with the height of the camera to accomplish a better composition or perspective as long as the fundamental rule is observed: the high actor looks below the lens; the low actor looks above the lens.

What It Means to Cheat Backgrounds

William Keighley, who was as efficient a director as he was a teacher, always at the end of a shooting day would walk through the sets to be used in the next day's filming. He and Bill Kuehl, his prop man for many years, would move a chair grouping or place the couch downstage center in place of the spot the set decorator had put it. He would mentally move his actors about the set, and in general line up the first shot for the next morning for the camera and electrical crew.

THE MOVING CAMERA AND
THE IMAGINARY LINE

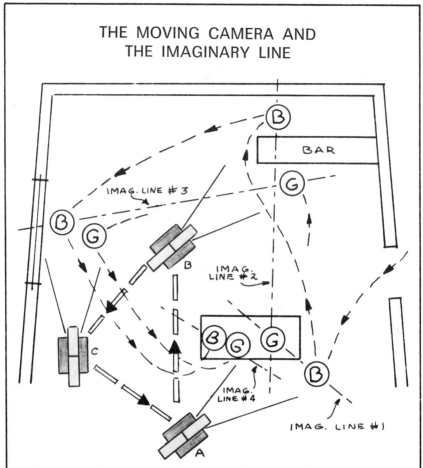

The Action: The boy enters the room, walks to the girl seated on the couch talking on telephone. She tells him to fix himself a drink at the bar. When phone call is over, girl goes to bar, but boy walks away from her to look out window. Girl then follows him to the window and takes him downstage to sit on couch.

Camera Movement: Camera (on crab dolly) starts at A with two-shot of girl on couch and boy coming through door. Camera follows boy to bar, to position B. Girl then walks into this shot, but boy goes to window, camera following and moving to C. Again girl enters the shot, and takes boy to couch, camera moving back to A.

Pitfalls: The moving camera has established four separate and distinct imaginary lines. The first is at the couch following the boy's entrance. The second is when camera has moved to B and the line intersects boy behind bar and girl on couch. The third is when camera is at C with the boy at the window and the girl at the bar. The fourth is at A again with the boy and girl seated on the couch. One danger lurks in the fact that while seated on the couch the girl gets three separate close-ups, one at the beginning when the boy stood beside her at the couch, the second when she speaks over her shoulder to the boy while he is at the bar, and the third when she is seated next to the boy on the couch for the finish of the scene. Each close-up is from a different angle, and each will have a different look to match the master shot.

Rule: Camera may cross the imaginary line in a dolly shot, but in so doing a new line is established for subsequent close-ups.

A SIMPLE RULE FOR MAINTAINING THE CONSISTENT DIRECTION OF LOOKS
IN SCENES INVOLVING MORE THAN TWO ACTORS

MATCH TO THE MASTER

Stage the master scene, or group shot, in the most natural or appropriate manner, then film coverage shots to match the original looks.

CLOSE-UP HUSBAND

Husband looks at all others, one direction only—left to right.

TWO-SHOT WIFE AND

MOTHER

Mother looks left to husband—right to soldiers. Wife looks right and *up* to soldiers.

TWO-SHOT SOLDIERS

Soldiers look at all others, one direction only—right to left.

Keighley never photographed anybody sitting on a settee with it shoved deep into the set or up against a wall. It was always moved downstage so that the entire set was shown in the background, much to the pleasure of the cameraman. He also, wherever possible, had his actors make entrances through doors that were downstage or nearest the camera. He kept his action down front, taking advantage of the depth of the set for showing full production values.

Michael Curtiz once shot for a week in a living room set that contained a large grand piano. When it came time to make a reverse shot and show the other wall which had been behind the camera, the problem of what to do with the piano came up.

"Take it out!" ordered Mike to his bewildered set decorator.

It was forthwith removed, and I am sure no one ever missed it in the theater except the set decorator.

The camera with its two-dimensional characteristics allows great latitude in "cheating" items of furniture, backgrounds, and the like completely out, and when one knows where to draw the line much time and money can be saved in ignoring so-called matching from one shot to the other.

One of the most glaring mistakes an inexperienced director can make is to insist on moving in a wild wall as background just to make an individual shot of an actor who, in the master shot, was standing with his back to camera. To be technically correct, if the director moves his camera around to get what amounts to a *reverse shot*, the unseen wall, which actually is the open side of the set, would be behind the actor in question. But, the audience has never seen this wall, so will accept anything the director provides, as long as it isn't just like something they have become used to in the scene. To save time (which is money), the director, who knows his way around, will "cheat," shooting his close-ups against another background instead of waiting for the grips to move in the wild wall. Anyone of the existing three walls will do, and usually all that is needed is to rearrange furniture and pictures on the wall to create the proper background.

Cheating is an accepted part of movie making, but sometimes even the experts can go too far, as Alfred Hitchcock did once in *North by Northwest*. Several times we saw the dignified columns adorning the facade of the stately manor house, but once, when Cary Grant drove up to what was supposed to be the same housefront, the columns had disappeared. This, I am sure, was because of the fact that certain sequences had been filmed on location in the East, and that later a Hollywood home had to be doubled. In this case, I am not so sure that the audience overlooked it.

Speaking of Hitchcock, this talented man only serves to prove the point that the rules of picture-making are only there to be broken by those who dare, and who can get away with it by virtue of their standing in the profession. In this same film, Hitchcock builds an exciting and sus- penseful sequence in which Cary Grant and Eva Marie Saint are hanging by their fingertips to the cliffs of Mount Rushmore, with the villains beat- ing and stamping at their hands. Just when it looks as if there is no chance of rescue or of avoiding a crashing fall to the valley below, Hitch- cock confidently dissolves to the two people safe and sound in the com- partment of a speeding train, with nary a word of explanation as to how they got there. I am sure that Mr. Hitchcock looked upon this incident with the same casualness as the time when a concerned co-worker ques- tioned a sequence earlier in the picture when Cary Grant, being chased by the heavies, decided to get onto a certain train, which he barely caught in the nick of time, only to find one of the accomplices, in this case Miss Saint, already calmly seated waiting for him.

The co-worker wanted to know how the heavies knew precisely what train Grant was going to jump aboard so that they could plant Miss Saint there. Hitchcock turned to him, and in his characteristic manner known so well to TV fans, said: "Don't be droll, dear boy."

A director who has the studio's production department at heart will plan his day's shooting so that the large, physical problems come either the first thing in the morning or the first thing after lunch. This will give the electrical crew more time to light a large area, and the grips time to move out wild walls to better position the camera for shooting. Since the crew usually takes a shorter lunch period than do the actors and director, all this comes under the heading of an efficient operation.

The Illusion of Reality

To maintain the illusion of reality is one of the director's prime responsibilities, and he has limitless tools and techniques at his command to rise to this responsibility.

He has the vast, almost limitless, potential of the camera with its bag of tricks. He has the modern techniques of *optical superimposition, matt shots, glass shots,* and *process.* And, he has the scores of studio technicians: prop men, special effects men, miniature men, powder men, and many other artisans who can construct almost anything the director or writer calls for. All these cost is money.

There is an infinite number of short cuts to creating the illusion of reality; and the director who, by virtue of his own ingenuity and imagi- nation, manages to effect these short cuts will be of great value to the production company, particularly if the picture he is working on has a limited budget.

CREATING THE ILLUSION OF REALITY

USING A POINT OF REFERENCE TO
COMBINE TWO DISTANT LOCATIONS INTO ONE

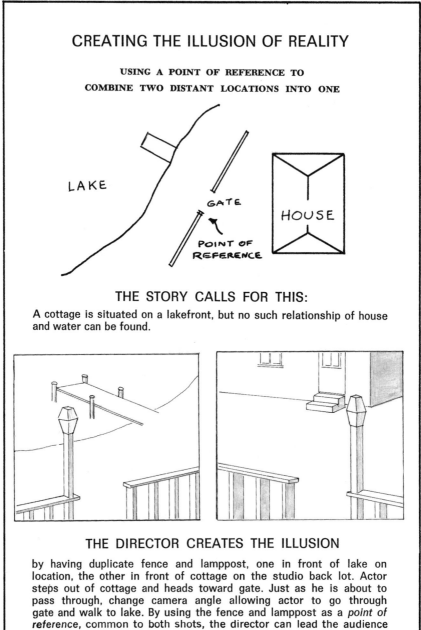

THE STORY CALLS FOR THIS:

A cottage is situated on a lakefront, but no such relationship of house and water can be found.

THE DIRECTOR CREATES THE ILLUSION

by having duplicate fence and lamppost, one in front of lake on location, the other in front of cottage on the studio back lot. Actor steps out of cottage and heads toward gate. Just as he is about to pass through, change camera angle allowing actor to go through gate and walk to lake. By using the fence and lamppost as a *point of reference*, common to both shots, the director can lead the audience to believe the cottage and lake are contiguous.

HOW TO TURN A LOCOMOTIVE AROUND

The Situation: The sun is setting, the movie company is working without lights. One more scene has to be shot, but on the *other* (shady) side of the locomotive.

The Solution: Shoot the scene on the sunny side of the engine, then turn the film over in the laboratory on the optical printer. Don't forget to change the part in the leading man's hair, or the brooch on the leading lady's dress. Also be sure to avoid the lettering on the engine's tender.

SHOOTING IMMOVABLE TRAINS

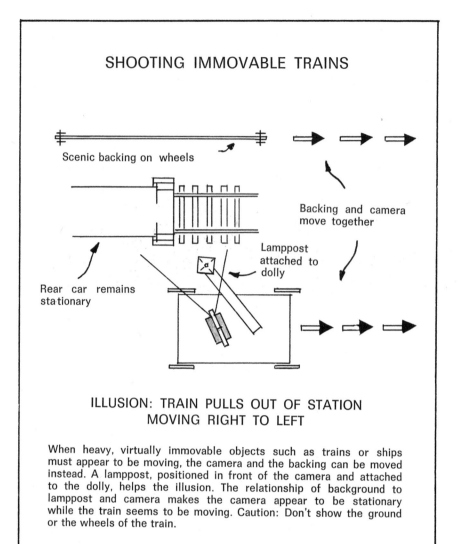

Scenic backing on wheels

Backing and camera move together

Lamppost attached to dolly

Rear car remains stationary

ILLUSION: TRAIN PULLS OUT OF STATION
MOVING RIGHT TO LEFT

When heavy, virtually immovable objects such as trains or ships must appear to be moving, the camera and the backing can be moved instead. A lamppost, positioned in front of the camera and attached to the dolly, helps the illusion. The relationship of background to lamppost and camera makes the camera appear to be stationary while the train seems to be moving. Caution: Don't show the ground or the wheels of the train.

Suppose the script calls for a certain kind of house to be situated on the shore of a picturesque mountain lake. The director finds the right lake and the right house, but not situated in the proper relationship to each other. How to create the illusion that one can step out of the house, walk a few feet and touch his toes to the water could be troublesome and expensive, unless the director has learned an elementary rule involving a *point of reference*. In this case, he will order a small section of fence with a distinctive gate or lamp post, and he will have it erected in front of the house. He will film his exits and entrances, in and out of the house, with his actors going through the gate, apparently heading toward the lake.

Then, he will move the company to the lake-front location and will have the same section of fence and gate erected a few feet from the water's edge. The actors who went through the gate previously, will do so again, this time continuing on to the lake. When the two pieces are spliced together the illusion of reality is perfect. No one in the audience will believe for a moment that the fence and gate don't divide the house from the lake.

The utilization of a point of reference to bring two diverse landscapes or backgrounds together can be used in a wide number of ways. A horseman can gallop down a hill toward the camera, pause to survey the landscape near a wooden shrine, then proceed on away from camera toward the village in the valley below; only, in this case, the shrine is moved three miles to create the illusion that hill and village are contiguous.

Almost any object that can be transported can be used as a point of reference; the only requirement being that the actor comes into some relationship with the object.

Recently, I was faced with a problem that occurred late in the day; one which, had I not come up with a short cut to creating the illusion of reality, would have burdened the studio with considerable expense by having to shoot an extra day.

I was filming on the back lot of M-G-M and had been working with a railroad locomotive of ancient vintage. All day we had shot scenes on the near side of the engine; now came one scene that called for the actors to be on the far side. Our sunlight was failing, and we were within twenty minutes of completing the sequence. It was impossible to get the cameras on the other side and to turn the locomotive around would take a crew of technicians the better part of the night, and the company would have to return the following day to complete the scenes instead of doing interiors at the studio as scheduled.

My assistant director and I were pondering the situation rather hopelessly when the solution struck me. We would turn the film over! We would shoot the scene with action on the near side but, when viewed in the projection room, it would appear that the action was on the far side and without moving the heavy locomotive as much as an inch.

Quickly, the set decorators reversed the positions of the dressing on the station platform while I set about supervising the re-parting of an actor's hair to the other side. A female star (fortunately with no part in her hair) cooperated by switching a large brooch from one side of her

A TYPICAL FLUID-CAMERA SHOT

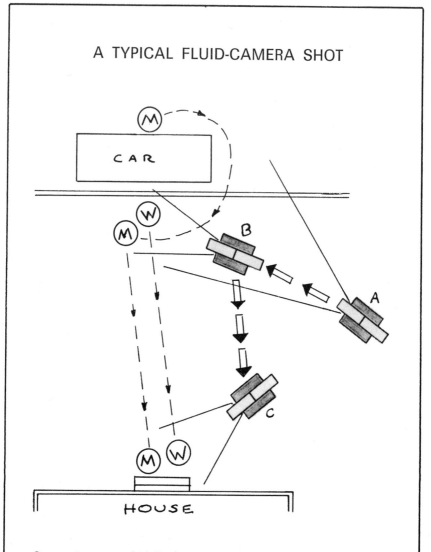

Camera is on a crab dolly or a small crane with a 40 mm lens. Car pulls up to curb as camera shoots full shot from position A. As man gets out of car and moves to help woman out, camera dollies in to position B. As man and woman start toward house, camera dollies slightly ahead to end of track at C, where camera then pans around taking actors into house.

dress to the other. I placed the camera so that no signs or other printing were in view, and started shooting. The script clerk made a notation to have the print optically reversed, or flopped over, before being screened by the producer. No one who viewed the scenes made that day ever questioned that the scenes were not made on the other side of the locomotive.

A director can be called upon to cooperate with the budget department, particularly if he is engaged in television filming. He may be denied the use of a stunt double, and be expected to use his own imagination in filming a hazardous piece of business. One such occasion occurred while I was directing a television film starring Alan Young. The script called for Young's wife to walk down the street, slip on a banana peel, and come crashing down while her preoccupied husband was trying to snap candid camera pictures.

As was to be expected, there was no stunt woman, so again my ingenuity was taxed, and I was faced with maintaining the illusion of reality at all costs. My solution in this instance was to rely on the proper piecing together of the shots I was to make. The first had the woman walking toward the reposing banana peel. Just as she was about to step on the peel, I made a close-up of her right foot as it came to rest on the peel, and started to slip forward. Then, I made a medium close-up of the woman's startled face as she lost her balance and fell over backward onto a prop man's mattress (just out of view). Following this, I made a shot of the husband looking up from his camera to see his wife's predicament; then a shot of the wife sprawled out on the sidewalk rubbing her hip painfully.

When edited properly, the illusion was perfect; and I am sure the audience actually believed it saw a woman slip on a banana peel.

Coverage

When the director plots his action, whether on the spur of the moment or at home on paper the night before, he ponders the question: How will I shoot it; how will I break it up? What scenes can be made in only one shot, and which ones must be *covered*; in other words photographed from a variety of angles? These and other problems, including movement, business, and the emotion of his actors are prime concerns of the motion picture director.

The *long shot* has its special dramatic use. It can serve to orient the audience with the scene's locale, or to keep the audience detached from the character shown; or it can represent another character's point-of-view. In script parlance, this latter shot is referred to as a *P.O.V.* When long shots are used to introduce the locale, they are known as *establishing shots*. A full shot usually denotes a full figure, and the term is more apt to be affixed to an interior scene. A *medium shot* generally is one that takes in the subject or subjects from the waist up. a *close-up* is a character's face only. A *medium close-up* is a halfway between a medium shot and a close-up, while the word *extreme* can be applied to both ends of the scale to denote an increase in size either way. A script may call for an extreme long shot or extreme close-up to underscore a dramatic effect.

The *over-the-shoulder* shot is about the size of a medium close-up, except that the head and shoulders of one actor are included as he stands facing the principal subject.

Sometimes a screenplay will be sprinkled with such shot designations as *dolly shot* (or *truck shot*), *pan shot, up shot, two shot, down shot, moving shot*, and *insert*—each with its special meaning to the director. An insert is usually a close-up of some inanimate object such as a letter, watch, or gun.

How the director combines the above mentioned shots is called his *coverage*. Alfred Hitchcock has this to say about it: "If I have to shoot a long scene continuously I always feel I am losing grip on it, from a cinematic point of view. The camera is simply standing there, hoping to catch something with a visual point to it. What I like to do is photograph just the little bits of a scene that I really need for building up a visual sequence. I want to put my film together on the screen, not simply record something that has been put together already in the form of a piece of stage action. This is what gives an effect of life in a picture—the feeling that when you see it on the screen you are watching something that has been conceived and brought to birth directly in visual terms."

Feeling as strongly as he does about the above, it is only a tribute to Hitchcock's pioneering spirit that he directed *Rope*, a picture in which there were no cuts, save for a few that hooked the thousand-foot rolls of film together. Each ten-minute take was rehearsed over and over on a trick set composed of walls that were raised up to the cat-walks as the camera glided through the multiroomed sets, never once losing contact with the performers. Of course, this technique can only be utilized where the action of the script covers a short continuous period of time.

Normally, scenes are shot first in a *master shot*, which usually covers the entire scene (if not too long) in a continuous take. Some directors will even make more than one master shot, each having a different camera approach. Then the over the shoulders and the close-ups are made. However, the prudent director will consider another method, particularly if his leading lady is getting along in years. That is to shoot her close-ups first when she is fresh. Many times people look fine in medium shots and tired and wan in their close-ups, especially when the close-ups are made late in the day.

Close-ups have another important function, one that serves to facilitate editing, especially in the television field. Films for television differ from films for theaters in that they must be edited to a precise length irrespective of the dictates of the story or the director's ideas on pace. Therefore, on a half-hour film that is first edited in *rough cut* form to, say twenty-nine minutes, must be pared down to twenty-four minutes, leaving the balance for the insertion of commercials. Something has to come out, and if the director has covered his scenes with plenty of close-ups, the job will be easier and the film will not suffer because an entire sequence had to be eliminated, thus making the story disjointed and confusing. The editor, by *line cutting*, that is by deftly removing parts of actors' speeches, can create the illusion that nothing is missing. This can only be done if there is more than one camera angle made, preferably the close-up, with the complimentary reaction close-up.

Even in feature-length films, where there is not a mandatory length limitation, cutting out lines has its merits. Rarely will a director, not under the pressure of time, shoot a sequence from only one point of view. Rather, he will give it as much coverage as the budget and schedule will allow, for he well knows what a skillful editor can do if he is provided with enough film. He can even make bad actors sometimes look good, and in many cases patch up some mistake of the director as well.

Many directors insist on perfect master scenes; in other words, if there is a *fluff* of a line, or if an actor misses a mark on the floor or the microphone boom fails to get a clear pick-up on a line of dialogue, the director will insist on starting all the way back at the beginning of the scene. Some scenes are intricately laid out with complicated actor movement and a corresponding amount of camera positions. Now, what these directors don't put into proper perspective is that this almost perfect master scene is going to be hacked to pieces by the cutter when he inserts the close-ups and other angles. What the director who fully understands the complexities of editing will do is to order a print on the master take that took so long to film. If a line had been fluffed he will correct it in the actor's close-up. If the sound mixer claims that a word or two weren't clear, due to the inability of the boom man to swing the mike through a part of the shot, the director will make a *wild track* by having the actor record the line without the camera turning. Almost any variety of inadequacies can be eliminated if the director will think in terms of his combined coverage. Of course, if there is to be only one angle of the scene, and it plays well in this angle, then the master shot must be perfect in all respects.

All shots, whether the master or the coverage shots, need not be done completely over from the beginning each time something goes wrong. The director can call for a *pick-up*, which means making another take from the point of the difficulty, knowing that by *cutting around* the mistake, that is, cutting to another character's close-up, the error will never have to be in the final assembly (See Chapter 9.).

There can be one extenuating circumstance that might cause a director to disregard the pick-up shot—the performance of the actor. A highly charged dramatic scene more than likely needs to be constructed in proper context, starting from the beginning each time it is taken. Certain actors, completely in control of their performances, know where they are at any point in the scene and these actors can survive the technique of "picking-up." Other actors can only find their level of effectiveness if each time they start back at the beginning.

William Keighley, who came from the New York stage, was a dialogue director at Warner Bros. before he became a full director. He was also the first important director to conduct a class in film directing at the University of Southern California. (Warner Bros.)

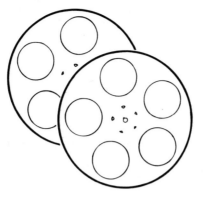

6

MOVEMENT AND PACE

Movement, the Primary Must

The motion picture as an institution reached lofty heights because of *movement*; one only has to view the early silent slapsticks and serials to realize that this was the foundation of the movie business. The pioneer filmmakers knew the value of keeping an audience alert; yes, even awake, by creating a tempo of action across the screen that stirred and excited. Not that all pictures of the silent era raced; there were those that were ponderously slow despite the way some old classics are seen on television today. While we are on this subject, it might be well to explain that the modern projector runs film at twenty-four frames per second, while the standard speed of silent pictures was sixteen frames per second. This accounts for the jerkiness and comical pace that seems to characterize all silent films. One only has to see them projected at the speed that they were photographed to realize that many silent films are truly immortal.

When the motion picture found its voice it was so aware, almost self-conscious, of this newly acquired talent that it almost completely forgot to *move*. Early talking picture cameras were completely immobile, stuck away in soundproof "bungalows," and actors and writers became more obsessed by the spoken word than by pantomine or movement. Several years went by before technical advancements produced cameras with *blimps* that could once again be mounted on dollies and booms.

Today, the element of movement still remains as a primary "must" in the making of entertaining films, and the foremost directors accomplish this in many different ways.

The four basic methods are subject movement, background movement, camera movement, and editorial movement.

In the case of subject movement, the actors move about the set, roaming freely from chairs to couches to windows, each character making his moves under the director's supervision and in strict accordance with his part in the story. An actor may move upstage or downstage, from a full shot in the background to a large close-up in the foreground. Or he may move laterally in front of the camera, his image in the lens maintaining the same relative size.

The second way to get movement in a scene is to move the background, for instance, playing scenes in moving automobiles or trains. The very fact that the actors, though sitting, are going someplace gives the scene a forward movement and thereby becomes more interesting than if the same dialogue were played in a living room or on a doorstep.

Sometimes in television the economics of the industry forces the director to pull some ancient tricks out of the bag and on the show *Green Acres*, which I directed for six years, I had many occasions to use my ingenuity. If you ever saw the train pull out of the station on that series it was always done by dollying the camera and the scenic backing behind the train in a synchronized movement. In other words, the train stayed still but with both camera and backing moving parallel to the tracks the train seemed to pull out of the station. Sometimes, I would add a lamp post affixed to the camera dolly and placed in front of the lens to add to the illusion.

I have solved the problem of how to bring the train into the station in another way. Again I have moved the camera instead of the train, which is virtually immovable. I have the grips take a short four-foot-wide window section of the train's interior and mount it on outriggers on the camera dolly. By moving the dolly along the tracks and shooting through the window we bring the train to a gradual stop in front of our leading characters who are waiting on the platform. This not only accomplishes what the script demands but gives the scene more style than an otherwise normal set-up would provide were the shot made at a real railroad station. And at only a fraction of the cost.

The exceptional film *Spectre of the Rose*, written and directed by Ben Hecht a number of years ago, made excellent use of background movement to enlighten the foreground action, which by its nature, was static. Two young lovers sat on a settee in a crowded hotel lobby and made subtle love with their eyes, while the place swarmed with people all about them. The audience shared with the actors a decided emotional experience, feeling the young people's frustration in not being able to express more freely their love for one another in the crowded room. Had Hecht isolated them in a secluded corner, the scene would not have been nearly so effective.

The director has at his command two other methods to introduce movement into his scene. One is camera movement. A dramatic scene in which two people in love have what they believe is their last meeting can be given movement by the handling of the camera. It can slowly, almost imperceptively move from a full shot to a medium shot, then move swiftly in to an extreme close-up as the lovers kiss, then pull back for a medium shot as they walk away.

Most scenes combine both subject movement with camera movement. For instance, the actor who walks laterally across our set must be followed in a *pan shot*, unless the camera is shooting from a stationary full shot. If he moves longitudinally toward camera, chances are the director will order a dolly shot, to maintain the same size figure during the actor's movement.

A typical shot that combines camera as well as subject movement might be one in which a woman pleads desperately with a man, attempting to persuade him to change his mind about something or other. In a two-shot, the woman approaches the man pleadingly. The man, troubled, moves away with the camera following him in a medium close-up. Then the woman moves into this shot, which widens to a two shot, and she continues her arguments; but the man evasively moves out of the shot, leaving the woman alone in a close-up. As she moves after the man, now at the window, the camera dollies back, widening the angle to a medium shot. When the climax of the scene comes, the man moves to the door, camera panning but widening its angle to a full shot. The woman enters this angle, and follows the man to the door, where the scene ends. A complex series of actor and camera moves, requiring perfect timing on the part of the performers, camera operator and the *grips* who operate the dolly.

In the pioneering days of pictures, cameras never moved, only actors. The camera was placed on a tripod, and every scene was introduced by a long shot. Actors scurried in and out of doors in camera angles that took in all of the set. Medium shots and close-ups were made, but always after the actors reached center stage, never while they were in movement. By the time the silent picture reached its highest form, near the end of the twenties, cameras had begun to free themselves from tripods. Perambulators, as they were called, began to move with the actors, and gear heads allowed the camera operator to pan and tilt with the actors wherever they went. The old-fashioned hand crank was replaced with the motor drive, and the operator's right hand was freed, which enabled him to give his camera mobility.

Today, the fluid camera is as much an accepted part of filmmaking as a standard close-up, which was originated by D. W. Griffith, the first really imaginative director. While the use of the fluid camera is almost mandatory in modern filmmaking, there can be no rules set down as to its use. Camera movement is dictated by the dramatic content of the scene, and nothing more.

Modern *zoom lenses* are becoming more popular with the newer directors and these provide a form of apparent camera movement. Apparent because while the size of the picture changes the camera itself remains stationary.

The final method of providing movement to otherwise static scenes is in the use of a variety of camera angles and the editing thereof. A slow and tearful scene played in an empty cathedral can be heightened in interest by a constantly changing point of view. First, the camera is on the girl who kneels silently in prayer. Then, her point of view: the altar and the Virgin Mary. Next, a long shot taken from a point high in the rear of the church. Then, a medium shot, shooting over the girl as she prays, with the altar in the background. Now, an extreme close-up as a tear falls from her cheek. And so on.

The about-to-be director should study the dynamically directed *La Dolce Vita*, made by Federico Fellini, which more than any other contemporary motion picture demonstrates the full powers of movement on the screen. From the opening scene in which a statue of Christ is, perhaps irreverently, flown over Rome dangling from a helicopter until the last ironic shot of a gay crowd examining the carcass of a whale, the picture is one splash of movement and cacophony. One may not agree with what *La Dolce Vita* has to say, but the picture is a director's triumph, and Fellini has made an indelible impression on his audience notwithstanding.

William Keighley placed strong emphasis on getting a story, any story, started with a punch, and always approached every script he directed with this in mind. He felt that if exposition or character delineation could be postponed until the audience was properly hooked, he had money in the bank. One such picture he directed opened up with a train speeding down the main line and a car on the highway alongside, obviously racing the train. By introducing his main characters, one on the train and the other in the car, he got the immediate attention of the audience; and when the train narrowly missed hitting the car at the crossing, the sequence had already paid off.

John Sturges has his own opposing views to this: "For some reason in America they think you can't begin a picture slow. They want to hook the audience before they get bored. Charlie Brackett summed it up beautifully when he said that in Europe you could open a picture with clouds, dissolve slowly to clouds, and dissolve again to more clouds. In America, he said, you open with clouds, then a plane comes out of the clouds and in the next shot the plane has got to explode."

The director who stands his actors against a wall, then ties his camera down and proceeds to shoot a lengthy scene, is denying himself (and his audience) of one of the motion picture's most cherished endowments. Nothing gains and holds attention like a well-designed flow of movement across the screen.

The Director Sets the Pace

Bryan Foy, who has produced many action pictures on modest budgets, once told me: "Keep it moving. You can't see the teeth on a buzz-saw." What he was really referring to was that if a show is well paced, the flaws in writing or directing will not be apparent. Not that he condoned flaws, but discrepancies have been known to creep into the best of well-regulated movies. A fast-moving picture was insurance according to Foy.

No one is more responsible for the pace of a picture than the director. His pace as a director is somewhat akin to his personal pace as a human being. The director who thinks, speaks, and moves around slowly can hardly be expected to bring great tempo and vitality to the picture he directs. Not that bustling around the set like a jumping jack is the key to directing well-paced movies; there are many screenplays, the mood of which calls for a slow overall tempo. But since the majority of screen entertainment benefits by a crisp forward progression of dramatic action, I will confine the discussion of pace to mean the opposite of lagging action.

What is pace? It can be defined as the tempo with which all things at the command of the director move in telling the story. This can mean the tempo with which the actors move about and speak their lines. It can mean the tempo of the cutting from one camera angle to another and the variety of those angles. The script itself, although not always under the control of the director, can contribute immeasurably to the overall pace of a picture by utilizing short, action-filled scenes as against long-winded and talky ones.

George Stevens displays less pace in his directing today than he did years ago when he made *Gunga Din*, which moved like Bryan Foy's mythical buzz-saw. Stevens, a careful and thoughtful filmmaker, has de-emphasized pace in his later films such as *Giant* and *The Diary of Anne Frank* in favor of mood and characterization.

King Vidor, always a director who appreciated the value of pace, devised a technique that he called "silent music." This involved the creating and putting together of action and shots in time to a metronome, the result of which would be a perfectly rhythmical series of movements on the screen.

He had first used this technique in the silent days during the filming of *The Big Parade*, and with musicians doubling as assistant directors, he created a visual symphony of moving trucks, marching soldiers, and flying airplanes.

When he made one of his first sound films, *Our Daily Bread*, he planned an eight-hundred-foot sequence about the digging of a ditch for a community irrigation project. He dispensed with the sound equipment and used a metronome and a bass drum. The workers drove their picks into the ground on the counts of one and three, while the shovels scooped dirt on the counts of two and four. Each shot was enacted in strict four-four time, with the metronome gradually increasing its speed on each succeeding cut.

The finished sequence is one of the most memorable scenes ever devised, and Alfred Newman's musical score complimented the visual action in a most adroit manner.

D. W. Griffith, pioneer director (right), also pioneered in other areas. Here he is shown with (left to right) Douglas Fairbanks, Mary Pickford, and Charles Chaplin, who combined to form their own company, United Artists. Griffith conceived the close-up and cutting as we know them today.

Nothing can kill a comedy quicker than a director who lacks pace, or doesn't understand the mainstay of all comedy, *timing*, or fails to appreciate the value of reaction.

There's an often-repeated axiom in Hollywood: "Screen actors don't act—they react." While this is perhaps not an accurate appraisal of the movie actor's functions, it does serve to illustrate the importance of reaction, and the director who fails to make his reaction shots only exacts part of the value of his scenes.

George Bernard Shaw maintained the secret of pace was found in the actors' deftness in picking up their cues and cautioned never to have a single moment's silence on the stage except as an intentional effect.

An interesting sidelight to Shaw's theory is that in some cases actors have to be conditioned to *avoid* picking up cues. The first six months of directing Eddie Albert and Eva Gabor on *Green Acres* found me continually retaking scenes because these two talented performers instinctively picked up their cues when they should have paused, waiting for the laughs that they could not hear. As long as canned laughter is added to the sound tracks of television comedies, actors in those shows must *imagine* an audience's reaction and stall, yes, literally stall, until the unheard laughter subsides.

Pace is an instinctive thing, as varied with each director as are his other tastes and desires. It is perhaps the most difficult thing to teach, and little was said about it in the cinema courses at the University of Southern California. I can only add that the interjection of pace into a motion picture is more often than not directly related to the director's own enthusiasm and personal energy. One of the true pitfalls in directing motion pictures is the tendency to be lulled into a state of lethargy due to a long and tiresome shooting schedule. A director who lets down, becomes bored, will not only lack pace but will end up with a dull and listless product. Never has a great film been made without the enthusiasm of all who contributed, and this is especially important in the case of the director who, of course, sets the pace for all.

One important device that the director has at his command, and one that is sometimes overlooked in modern filmmaking, is the advantage of *manufacturing* pace by varying the speed of the film as it receives its exposure in the camera. The silent directors, especially of the Keystone Comedy variety, often slowed down the cranking of their cameras, or *under-cranked*, which made screen movement appear faster. While 16 frames per second was their norm, a comedy scene would be shot anywhere from 8 to 12 frames per second, while certain dramatic scenes would be slowed down to 18 or 20. Today, varying the frames-per-second is almost a lost art, but in a western it is most helpful in speeding up your

Veteran director King Vidor, whose career spans back to the silent days, is shown here, megaphone in hand, shooting Duel in the Sun *from a high camera platform. Vidor was the first director to use a metronome to establish rhythm for the movement within his scenes. He is one of nine directors who have received the D. W. Griffith Award of the Directors Guild of America.*
(Selznick International)

leading lady (who can't ride) as she gallops down the road, or to inject more danger or excitement in any situation that involves threatening moving objects. Conversely, slowing down the speed of screen movement (by increasing the speed from the sound norm of 24 frames per second) can have interesting results. I once directed a comedy in which there was a scene that called for an actor to receive a dose of ether by mistake. By slowing down the screen action, his every mannerism and movement as he incongruously floated through the halls of the hospital, became extremely funny. His movements, seen in direct contrast to the normal actions of the other actors in the same scene, were photographed at 48 frames per second; and consequently, all the other actors were required to speed their own actions up exactly double, so that when the film was projected they would appear to be moving normally. This is the most difficult part of this kind of filming, having your leading character act normally, while all the others walk and move twice as fast, with your only problem being the proper visualization of the end result!

Samuel Fuller, who has directed such interesting films as *Steel Helmet* and *Naked Kiss*, has said: "Enthusiasm is the heartbeat of movies. It breeds ideas, breaks down barriers, encourages imagination, and gives pride in the making of a movie. Enthusiasm has been the key word in the arts since man scratched an animal on a cave wall. It is the magic that triggers the making of a successful movie."

No one who fully contributes to the success of a complex entertainment motion picture can do so without using his maximum energy. Energy is the mother of enthusiasm; enthusiasm fosters pace. One seldom appears without the other.

The Rigors of Directing

The one requirement of all directors I have failed to mention is physical stamina. If ever a want ad were placed for a film director, it would surely carry the line, "Only the strong need apply." It has been mentioned that the director is usually one of the first on the set, and the last to leave. He stands on his feet practically the whole ten-hour day and then goes to the projection room to see his daily rushes before leaving at night. His nerves are unduly strained after hours of concentration to detail, and the burden and responsibility of his position cause tensions to build up inside his body.

Since the early days, the public has heard of the derring-do of the cameraman, up in planes, down in mines, perched precariously on the bowsprit of a ship, operating dangerously close to explosives, grinding the camera atop a speeding train—all these and more. But what has received less publicity is the fact that the director is usually right along side him—taking all manner of chances, even risking his life sometimes, all for the sake of the picture. When someone in the theater said, "The show must go on," little did he know what a doctrine he had created. Hardly a day goes by in Hollywood, or anyplace films are made for that matter, that someone doesn't place his life in peril for the sake of the show.

Once during a serial film, director J. P. McGowan donned the actor's wardrobe and took a leap from the top of a fast moving boxcar and ended up in the hospital with a broken back. There have been other instances where directors have fallen from high camera parallels and speeding camera cars, each case within the call of duty.

Metro-Goldwyn-Mayer once dispatched me to the Caribbean to film scenes for *The Islanders*, a television series for which I had just produced and directed the pilot film. The completed first episode had been in New York for seven days, and it was still too early to know whether or not it had been bought for sponsorship.

Now I was in Miami, doing the job of producer, director, production manager, and assistant director. In fact, I was all alone, another illustration of the amount of endurance and stamina a director sometimes is called upon to show. I had to hire the camera crew from the Chicago local, make arrangements for camera equipment out of Miami, interview and hire photographic doubles for certain players unable to come from Hollywood, and charter a seaplane.

The next day, I took off ahead of the crew who would fly to Jamaica in the seaplane, a somewhat antiquated Grumman Goose that had been recently purchased from the government of Honduras. Upon my arrival in Kingston, I rented a small car and toured the perimeter of the island, searching for and spotting bays and lagoons in which the Goose could made safe and picturesque landings.

The stars of *The Islanders*, Bill Reynolds and Jim Philbrook, flew in direct from Hollywood, and we all made a rendezvous at Montego Bay, a popular resort on Jamaica's north shore.

For five days we toured up and down the coast, photographing landings and takeoffs against the lush tropical backgrounds. The weather was, as to be expected, hot. Reynolds and Philbrook ran over half the island while I filmed a chase sequence against natural backgrounds. On the sixth day, I had shot over ten thousand feet of negative, and started making arrangements to proceed homeward. We were at Port Antonio, staying in the hotel Errol Flynn once owned, the Jamaica Reef. Howard Smith, the pilot, had rowed out to the plane, which was anchored in the bay opposite the hotel, only to find the bilge half full of water. When George Schmidt, the first cameraman, and his assistant, Glen Kirkpatrick, came out in the second boat, they helped bail the water out, which apparently was leaking in through the metal seams in the plane's hull. Jim Philbrook and the doubles had already started back to Montego Bay in the limousine we had rented, and now the question of how the precious negative would be transported came up. I wanted Bill Reynolds to take it in the other car we had, since I didn't want it to be the sole responsibility of the Jamaican driver. But, Bill didn't want to make the hot ride in the car along the narrow winding road, and begged to go in the plane with the cameramen and myself, who were going to make a few more aerial shots enroute. Bill Reynolds later wished I had been more adamant, but as it happened, I agreed that he could come along with us. That settled the question about the negative; it, too, would go along in the plane.

With the plane's bilge dry once again, Howard Smith revved up the engines, and with Schmidt, Reynolds, Kirkpatrick, and myself aboard, the seaplane took off with the usual roar. Smith, without any previous movie flying experience, had demonstrated a daredevil style of piloting, and the ten cans at my feet were filled with some exciting footage of his landings and takeoffs. But, now we were on our way home, and George Schmidt occupied himself with making aerial shots from the plane's windows. Suddenly, and without warning, both engines quit. I was standing at the moment directly behind the pilot, with my hands on the bulkhead. Instantly, Smith put the plane into a dive to avoid stalling. The three hundred feet of altitude we had at the moment of losing power was fast diminishing, and Smith frantically hit switches, turned knobs, and activated the wobble pump in an attempt to find the trouble and restart the engines. For approximately six seconds I stood frozen in the aisle, then when it was apparent that we were going to crash, I hurried to my seat and started to fasten the seat belt. It never got fastened. My next recollection was a return to consciousness, a cooling plunge in the darkness of the water and the knowledge that I was floating free and not entangled in seat belts or other wreckage. But, where was I? In the plane, or out of it? Instinctively, I swam to the surface, and then saw what was left of the Grumman Goose. The left wing and engine nacelle were completely ripped away from the main section and were sinking. My first exclamation was "Save the film!" I heard a voice from the other side of the wreckage, "To hell with the film!", and that is when I discovered I had been injured. The first thing I did when I rose above the surface of the water was to feel my head and upper portion of my body. Although there were a few abrasions, I was not bleeding too much and my mind was clear. I quickly stripped down, getting my shirt off preparatory to swimming, if necessary, to shore. I reached down to pull off my shoes, when I discovered a frightening fact considering we had crashed more than four miles off shore. I had two broken legs.

The pilot, Howard Smith, was floating thirty feet from the main section of the plane, which was sinking fast. He was in a state of semiconsciousness, and when I first saw him he had his face under water. I managed to get him to raise his head by calling his name, and presently he caught hold of the plane's nose section that had completely broken off and was floating in the water like a giant eggshell.

On the other side of the plane, I saw Kirkpatrick treading water, his head a mass of blood. Bill Reynolds and George Schmidt were floundering near the fuselage, which had a gaping wound in one side, obviously where we made our escape at the moment of impact. In a matter of seconds, the wreckage had sunk, all except Smith's nose section, a piece of pontoon that was for the moment holding up Kirkpatrick, and the four cabin seats, which had broken away and were floating. I had always carried the impression that the reason passengers in planes fastened seat belts was to stay with the frame in case of a crash. In this vintage Goose, the seats broke away like so much papier-mâché. But, they did float, having been packed with kapok by some thoughtful Hondurian aide-de-camp, since this had once been the private plane of the Latin country's president.

George Schmidt reported in as having something wrong with his legs, but minimized the trouble as he climbed aboard one of the chairs. Reynolds had pushed one to Kirkpatrick, and as I pulled myself onto another, began giving orders. I had for five days been in charge of the troupe, so no one questioned my commands at this decisive moment. Reynolds, who had one broken leg, and I, with two, were still in the best shape, so we would head for shore together to get help. By lying on our backs, with the chairs supporting us, we were able to do a backstroke and to maintain our injured legs in a neutral and, fortunately, painless position. Reynolds, a former collegiate swimming champ, took his strokes rhythmically and efficiently. I, perhaps, splashed the water too fast, but all I could think about was, where were the sharks? Weren't all Caribbean waters shark infested?

Soon the swells obstructed our vision, and Reynolds and I could see no one but each other as we headed for the Jamaican shore. I had estimated that at our rate of speed, and with no sharks, we could make shore by nightfall. But, what then? How do two fellows with only one good leg between them get off the beach of a lonely stretch of coast line and get to a doctor? These, and other thoughts plagued me; I couldn't help thinking of my wife, my children, and what would happen to *The Islanders*, on which we had all worked so hard. There is one scene I now feel eminently qualified to direct, and that is the one where a character, anticipating sure death in a plane crash, reacts to his impending fate. In the case of Schmidt, Reynolds, and Kirkpatrick, there wasn't a sound. Pilot Smith was only cursing as he frantically worked to avert disaster. Myself? I was feeling but one emotion, anger. I was just damned mad to have to die in such a stupid fashion. My whole life did not flash in front of my eyes, I only briefly thought of wife and family, but I *was* mad.

Two and one-half hours later, Reynolds and I heard the putt-putt of an outboard motor, and two young native fishermen hauled us, broken legs and all, into the thing they called their boat—a carved-out cottonwood tree with a free board of no more than an inch and a half.

We were taken ashore at Annotto Bay, transferred into a jeep, and then to a country hospital. The fishermen put to sea again in their crude dugout in search of the others.

Later, awaiting the Jamaican doctor's return from a Friday afternoon cricket match in Kingston, I counted the survivors as they came into the hospital one by one. I heard planes roaring overhead, searching the area of the crash, but hours passed and George Schmidt did not arrive. Three days later they found his body, washed ashore, apparently dead from loss of blood.

Eight days after that, I said goodbye to Reynolds and Kirkpatrick, as they prepared to take a plane back to the States. A few days later, I was transferred to a hotel at Ocho Rios, leaving only Howard Smith in the Annotto Bay hospital still speculating the cause of engine failure—a thing that to this day remains a mystery.

This move to the hotel was, of course, arranged by M-G-M, never an organization to miss an exploitable opportunity. They had invited Ollie Treyz, president of the American Broadcasting Company and Terry Clyne, account executive for Chesterfield Cigarettes at McCann-Erickson advertising agency in New York, to join George Shupert, Metro's head of television, on a trip to Jamaica. The point, of course, was to meet the creator of *The Islanders*, who had so spectacularly crashed in the Caribbean.

So, while basking in the tropical warmth of Jamaica's infectious climate, Treyz and Clyne considered the purchase of the series. Before they left, Clyne had promised to sponsor, Treyz had cleared the air time. And I had sold my first television show—the hard way.

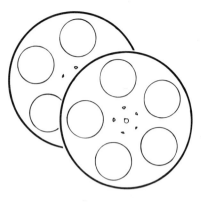

7

THE CAMERA AS
THE DIRECTOR'S TOOL

Why a Director Should Know Camera

When I was sixteen years old I graduated from the New York Institute of Photography, and was well on my way to becoming a Hollywood cameraman, or so I thought.

This feat is not quite so amazing when you understand I was still in high school and all the lessons were through correspondence. Still, it did give me a basic education in photography, which has been invaluable in my work as a film director. Later, I taught Cinematography at the University of Southern California, and helped train Combat Cameramen with the 164th Signal Photographic Company during World War II.

One of my first jobs in Hollywood was as assistant cameraman, and later I was on George Pal's photographic staff making his series of Puppetoon shorts for Paramount. As I said in an earlier chapter, everybody wants to be a director—even the cameraman—but in my case I wanted to be a cinematographer, a Gregg Toland or a George Barnes. And, I feel I could have been, except for one thing. The cameraman's union, Local 659, I.A.T.S.E., was closed to newcomers unless the applicant happened to have a father or a friend who was a cinematographer. They allowed me to work around in the independent field, or for Pal's Puppetoons, but as far as being invited into the inner circle of major studio cameramen, it was out of the question.

So, I decided to be a director—since the opportunities for succeeding were not dampened by a union that invaded the sacred domain of the right to work. The Directors Guild has from its inception held that any man who could get himself a job and who could pay the initiation fee was duly qualified for membership, an encouraging thing for any young person attempting to get a start as a director.

Second only to the ability to communicate with and inspire actors into giving creditable performances is the ability to use the camera in telling a story. From the earliest silent films, the camera played a predominent part in the director's interpretation of the author's words, and today the man who fully understands the camera's powers is a step ahead of his fellow directors who do not have that understanding.

Occasionally, the director will work with a cameraman, who for one reason or another, either fails to comprehend what the director wants or is not inclined to try for it anyway; and it is here that the knowledge of the camera's limitations is important. The director who freely admits that the camera is a mystery to him is at a decided disadvantage, but the director who can communicate with the cameraman *on his own terms* will usually end up by getting almost any known or experimental effect he desires.

Lenses and What They Do

The standard lens on a motion picture camera, one that photographs a scene as near to the way the eye sees it, is the 50 mm, or two-inch lens. The lens that has come to be used as a standard lens under most conditions is the 40 mm lens. Lenses that have smaller numerical designations than either the 40 mm or 50 mm are known as short focal-length lenses, while lenses that have larger numerical designations are called long focal-length lenses. The short focal-length lenses, also known as wide-angle lenses, are the commonly used 35 mm, 30 mm, 25 mm, and the occasionally used 17.5 mm lens, which has an extremely wide angle of view.

The usual long focal-length lenses are the 75 mm, 100 mm, and a 300 mm, or six-inch, sometimes called a telephoto lens.

The long lenses tend to bring objects closer, while the short lenses make objects appear farther away and sometimes tend to distort their shape and size. The shorter the lens the more distortion, especially when photographing objects close up.

When the director understands what these lenses can do, he can properly stage his action and camera movement to compliment the camera's point of view and thus obtain a pleasing screen effect.

Since the 40 mm and 50 mm are the normal lenses with little or no distortion, we'll consider what the lenses that are longer than the 50 mm do for the director.

LENSES AND WHAT THEY DO

30 MM

This lens takes in virtually the whole set, reproducing it sharply in focus. Establishes where the actors are in relationship to one another and to the room itself. The 30 mm tends to make the set look larger than it really is.

40 MM

The normal lens, used under most circumstances. The scene as now photographed makes the room look its normal size and there is an absence of floor and ceiling; in other words, the center of attention is directed toward the people, with a minimum of accent on the set.

50 MM

Now we have eliminated three of the actors on the right. This lens is used when it is impractical to move the camera closer or when camera shadows from the keylight show up.

75 MM

All other actors have been eliminated. The use of this lens, which is the standard close-up lens, directs viewer's attention to the subject, and tends to "fuzz up" or hold background in soft focus.

In the first place, since there is an absence of distortion in these lenses, they are ideal for close-ups of beautiful women. In this respect, the 75 mm and 100 mm are most often used. These long lenses will tend to blur the background, and will be called upon by the director when he wishes to place all attention with the foreground action.

Obviously, when a universal focus effect is desired, one in which all things in the scene are crisp and sharp, the director does not ask for a long focal-length lens, but rather, requests that a wide angle lens be used by the cameraman.

Another thing about long and short lenses: the size of the picture is determined by the selection of the lens. With the camera placed well back, a long lens will only photograph a portion of a given set, while a short (or wide-angle) lens will take in practically the whole room.

When the director wishes to photograph his action from a particular point of view, but in order to do so would have to remove a wall to accommodate the camera with a 40, he merely calls for a 30 or a 35, and ends up with the same size picture without wasting the valuable time it would take to remove the wall from the set. Conversely, when the camera and the subject are separated by objects nontransversible, such as a river, a canyon, or a city street, he calls upon the long focal-length lenses to bring his action closer, therefore making the image the desired size.

Remember the shot you've seen of an actor walking directly toward the camera—he walks and walks and *walks*, but he never seems to get any closer. That shot was made with an extremely long lens.

You've seen those shots where one actor's face looms large in the foreground, slightly three-quarter angled, while another stands squarely facing the camera, slightly farther away? Chances are the shot was made with a lens at least as wide as a 30 mm, with the overall intensity of lighting built up to accommodate a small lens f. stop.

The f. stop indicates the amount of light reaching the film, the wider the opening in the lens, the more exposure. "Stopping down" or narrowing this lens opening increases the sharpness of the image. Shots made with a wide-angle lens have a way of looking around the curve of the face, so to speak, and are dramatically quite effective. Both faces will be in sharp focus, and the distortion seems to add to the mood created, especially if the face that is closest to the camera is not the one of your glamorous leading lady.

Then there are the shots of your leading man as he walks in close-up along the sidewalk on the far side of a busy city street. When you see fuzzy objects such as automobiles or street signs blur by in the foreground between you and the actor you will recognize this shot to no doubt have been made with a 250 mm lens. And when the close-up zooms

Elaborate preparations are made to film a close-up of the driver of a moving automobile. Most of the time the cameraman merely rides in the passenger's seat and makes the close-up of the driver against the moving scenery outside. But in The Rain People *director Francis Ford Coppola insisted that the view of the driver be outside the car, hence the specially designed camera mount.* (Warner Bros.)

back into a 25 mm wide-angle view, you will realize that the lens used is a French made Angineux, a popular one with the commerical and new wave directors.

Orson Welles, together with Gregg Toland, revolutionized the technique of universal focus in their exceptional film *Citizen Kane.* Extreme depth of field was obtained by using short lenses and building up the key light so that an exposure could be made at a small f. stop. The result was dramatic and astounding; an actor standing in the foreground in a huge close shot, while another actor stood full figure in the background. Both were in critically sharp focus.

There are times when extreme motion, or jiggling, of the camera is unavoidable, as when it is tied down on the rear end of a speeding camera car. In this instance, the wider lens will do much to eliminate the effects on film of the jiggling of the camera.

The zoom lens places another tool at the director's hands by allowing the camera to, in effect, dolly without ever leaving its stationary position. The camera can zoom from a long shot into a huge close-up in a much faster time than two grips could push the dolly forward. Knowing the characteristics of lenses is a valuable and time-saving talent on the part of the director, and he who understands the capabilities and limitations of the "glass," as the cameramen call them, is far ahead of the game.

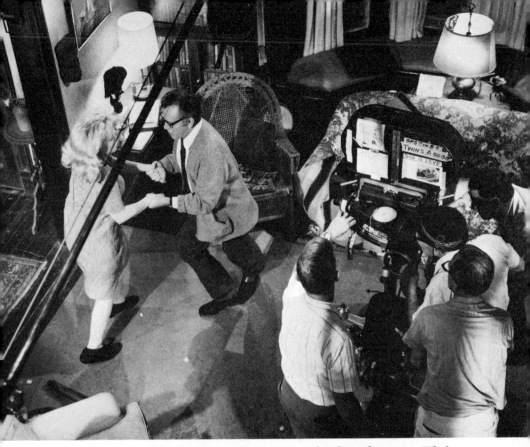

Richard Burton leads Sandy Dennis in a drunken dance in Who's Afraid of Virginia Woolf? *while the Mitchell Camera records. Judging by the distance from camera to subject, the scene was probably filmed with a 30 mm lens, which, when cropped top and bottom by theater projectionists to become so-called "wide screen," resulted in a waist figure of the actors. Directed by Mike Nichols. (Warner Bros.)*

Camera Movement

The proper use of the motion picture camera, of course, takes into account its ability to move about the set, in almost any position, vertically or horizontally. All it takes to achieve this maximum mobility is time, for the more the camera changes its basic point of view the more lights and intensity changes are required.

To illustrate that there are actually *no* limitations to this camera movement, consider a shot I once made for Rod Serling's *Twilight Zone*. The scene called for a bridge game, and since the results of the game had no story value, and the scene itself was only one to denote a passing of time, I pondered how to make it interesting. The first angle I set up was from below the glass-topped table, showing the cards and faces of the players as the cat might view them. The second, and the one that demonstrates the complete scope of the camera, was made by placing the camera in the center of the table and panning it from the face of the leading man, across the faces of the other players, as they made their bids, and right on around through 360° until the leading man came into a close-up again. While this took a little doing, it was accomplished by first enclosing the open side of the set with wild walls to make a four-wall room, and then removing all lights and grip equipments, from around the camera. All crew members were obliged to leave the set, and the scene was lighted by lamps suspended from above. As the camera was panned from face to face, only the operator and myself walked around behind it, keeping out of its view.

On this same picture, I had occasion to use the camera in other ways for an effective overall result. The idea of the story was to depict a group of persons who were planning to leave for another planet in the face of the threat of a terrible and destructive war. Only at the end, when they were safely aboard a space ship did one character ask another the vital question.

"What is the name of this planet we're heading for?"

The pilot of the ship thoughtfully perused his radar scope and replied, "It's the third from the sun—it's a place called Earth."

The sudden twist at the end is what made the film, and the problem in the scenes that led up to the climax was not to betray Serling's secret that we were actually watching members of another planet preparing to come to ours. It was decided to use conventional-looking, acting, and sounding players, living in conventional Earth-like surroundings; but they would be treated differently with the camera.

I ordered the widest angle lens that Metro-Goldwyn-Mayer Studios had, a 17.5 mm bug eye. I mentioned to the cameraman that I wanted this lens used exclusively, even on close-ups and even on close-ups of women. I explained I wanted the distortion that this lens gave everything, and suggested that the cameraman work out unorthodox sources for his lighting that would bring an unusual aura to the film. In addition to this, every camera set-up was cocked to one side or the other, which further served to take away the feeling of normalcy. What I was striving to do was protect Serling's surprise ending, and yet give the feeling of oddness so that when the picture was over the audience would understand why the "kooky" camera treatment was used. In this respect, I would say, never make an unusual or self-conscious angle unless there is a reason for it. The director who abuses the privilege of a mobile and versatile camera calls attention to himself as if to say, "Look, ma, I'm directing."

The Standard NC Mitchell Camera, with "sticks," forerunner of the blimped BNC, is still used in exterior scenes for which sound recording is not critical, and can even be used close to the microphone when wrapped in a "barney," a blanketlike covering that absorbs the camera noise. Shown alongside is Richard L. Bare directing Twilight Zone. (Columbia Broadcasting System)

In the sixties filmgoers were bombarded by every conceivable camera trick, old and new, ever thought of by a director or cameraman. Zooms have been used to distraction, selective focus shots to point of no return (a selective focus shot is one in which only one plane in the scene is actually sharp). And such effects as shooting the sun, wildly aiming the camera at the tops of buildings so that they swirl dizzily, and duplicating shots in a pattern of multiple images not only call attention to the fact that the picture is being "directed," but distract from the pure involvement of the audience in the story.

Billy Wilder, director of numerous artistic and successful pictures (*Lost Weekend, The Apartment*) says: "In film making, I like the normal setup, like Wyler uses, like John Ford, like Chaplin. I'm against this fancy stuff. It reminds an audience that artisans have intruded. I don't want them to grab their partner and say, 'My God, look at *that!*' Besides, we tried all those things in the old UFA days," he added, referring to the famous German studio.

Arthur Penn used a variety of camera tricks, including the first of the slow-motion death scenes, in making *Bonnie and Clyde*. When he got around to making *Little Big Man*, he had changed his directional approach. "It has no slow motion and no camera tricks. It is an effort in orthodoxy. The fascination with camera techniques is getting a bit ripe. If it contributes to the whole experience, then it is valid. When it becomes something independent of the film, then it's of no use."

The three basic types of conventional movement are: (1) movement of the camera head on the tripod or dolly, called *panning* and *tilting*, and which is used to follow actors about the set when they move on the same lateral plane; (2) movement of the camera on a dolly, which causes the camera's viewpoint to change laterally or longitudinally; and (3) movement of the camera on a crane, which combines the above with a vertical dimension, as well as allowing the shifting of viewpoint from any one point in the set to almost any other—in other words, complete mobility.

The use of the panning and tilting feature of the camera is so basic that anyone who has held an 8 mm movie camera understands its uses and limitations. The same rule that all the camera stores warn of: namely, don't pan too fast, applies in professional production. This is because the background will blur if scanned too quickly. Of course, if the camera is centered on a moving object and stays with it, there is no limit to the speed of a pan shot. *Whipping*, that is, the fast panning off of one subject and on to another, can be used effectively as a technique to bridge two scenes together when a quick cut or a dissolve is not to be desired.

It is when the director becomes involved with the movement of the camera on the dolly that he had better know his lenses, and the other virtues and limitations of the camera.

However, the director who gets the reputation of being a "dolly rider" needlessly slows down the cameraman's work, viewing each rehearsal through the viewfinder as the camera makes its moves about the set. I have found that, after lining up the shot with a *wild finder*, it is best

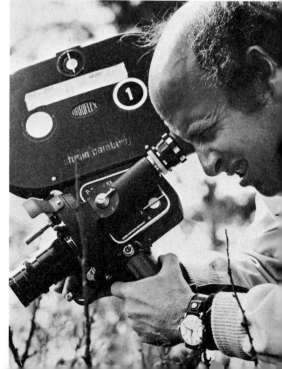

Today the modern director picks up the camera and starts shooting —too bad if the sun is not in the right place. With realism the key word, the photographic results have accidentally started a new vogue—erratic photography. Here Richard Lester, native Philadelphian who does most of his work in London, grinds the Airiflex with determination. (Columbia Broadcasting System)

It sometimes takes hours to construct a dolly track such as the one shown here. The director normally will lay out such a shot in advance so that the grips won't delay the shooting. Here Guy Green, director of A Walk in the Spring Rain, *inspects the track before making the shot.* (Columbia)

to work with the actors away from the camera. Then, when the cameraman notifies you that he has lighted the set, and is ready for a camera rehearsal, all that is necessary for a director is one "ride," watching the action through the camera. This is merely to confirm that the cameraman interpreted the shot as the director lined it up originally.

There was a day when the director was known by his megaphone, but today he is more apt to be recognized by the small object hanging by a chain around his neck. This is his *director's finder*, a device that approximates all the lenses on the camera. There are two types of finders, one with a small inexpensive viewing lens on one end and a slot on the other end into which various matts are slipped, each one corresponding to the scope of the lens it matches. The other is an optical type that works like a zoom lens allowing the director to rotate the barrel of the finder and select any image size he desires. By referring to a scale on the barrel he can determine which lens corresponds to the image size he has selected.

Most experienced directors avoid as much as possible what is known as *unmotivated camera movement*, that is, when the camera pans from one subject to another without anything to carry it across. The most widely used device—in fact, it has become a cliché—is, when shooting restaurant or night club scenes, to use the waiter to cross from one table to the next, thus giving the camera something to concentrate on as it moves its view from one point to another. There are many interesting ways a director can move his subject action about to give proper motivation to the movement of the camera.

The newly arrived director, if given the chance, usually becomes obsessed with the crane, and stays up nights thinking of ways to confound the cameraman whose job it is to light the shot. One such fellow photographed a long scene on a huge set at Paramount one day, taking all day to get one take. The scene started with the camera angling through a brandy snifter, then followed the drinker over to a piano that was being played at the edge of the dance floor. The camera dipped under the archway, one-half of which was swiftly pulled to one side by the grips, then proceeded to shoot the piano player from a point of view under the drinker's arms. Then, when the music was finished, the camera wandered over (motivated by a crossing waiter) to disclose the full figure of the leading lady as she entered the café. After twelve takes, the scene was pronounced a masterpiece of rhythm and motion by the director, who thought he had accomplished enough that day and wanted to go home. When the cameraman asked him what set they were going to shoot the next morning, the director told him that he wasn't through in this set yet—that he still had to make close-ups.

"You mean you're going to cut close-ups into that scene we took all day to get?" asked the tired but incredulous cameraman.

"Of course," replied the director.

"Then why did we have to get the whole damn scene in one take?" the cameraman demanded.

"It's for the front office—they love to see this kind of stuff."

The next day, the company spent all morning doing several close-ups, which would be cut into the involved master shot, the complexity of which would never be appreciated by the audience.

The longest and most involved moving camera scene to my knowledge was done by Robert Siodmak in *The Killers*, which had the camera alternately moving from interior scenes to exterior scenes involving hundreds of people, and at least that many individual camera moves. The effect was spectacular to those of us in the business; but I doubt if the layman recognized the feat.

Stanley Donen in the Cary Grant picture, *Indiscreet*, once made a moving camera shot that defied previous limitations. The camera followed Grant into a building, moved inside the elevator with him, rode up several flights with him, then followed him out into the corridor and moved down several doors with him until he disappeared through a doorway. Battery operated cameras and battery powered lights facilitated the making of intricate shots as never before and now these shots are becoming commonplace.

Movement of the camera is not merely confined to broad sweeps from a close-up of a champagne bottle to the waiter's dash to a table in a busy party scene to a long shot of the floor show. More subtle movements have a definite dramatic value, and their use can give positive illusions. One of these illusions created by camera movement is that which creates the feeling of flight in an airplane, or headway in a boat when you are using mock-ups of the real thing. The gentle but slight tilting and panning while a scene is in progress provides the unsteadiness an audience always associates with movement of planes, ships, and even Conestoga wagons. Many a trek close-up has been filmed with the wagon dead still, the camera tilted toward the sky so as to avoid the horizon, and both the camera and the wagon rocked a little to create the conditions of travel movement.

The pilots in the cockpit of a four-engined transport are usually photographed on the ground, a painted cloud background visible through the window, with both the camera and the keylight moved up and down to simulate the slight rock of the airplane.

These rules are for studio made shots; shooting the real thing poses another problem of camera movement—how to minimize it.

I once made a film in its entirety in and around the Hawaiian Islands, most of it aboard a fifty-five-foot sailboat at sea in the Molokai Channel, admittedly one of the roughest bodies of water in the world.

The problem here was how to keep camera movement to an absolute minimum, lest the actors bounce all over the screen. This was the first feature picture I had ever made in which there was not one dolly shot. During the land sequences, actors were moved to and from the camera to give impact to their scenes in the best John Ford style. But on board the *Samarang* on the high seas, not only was dollying out of the question but how to keep the subjects in camera range and the camera steady became the paramount question.

It had been decided that we would take aboard only one camera, an Airiflex with a lens compliment of a 75 mm, a 50 mm, a 40 mm, and a 25 mm. The camera was, of course, battery operated and tied in with a sync-pulse system to a Nagra portable recorder. A tripod was taken aboard and a few shots were attempted with this, but a strange illusion resulted when the first dailies were projected back in Hollywood. The camera being tied down to the deck photographed the actors in a relatively vertical attitude producing no illusion of the boat's rolling movement. However, the horizon rolled back and forth annoyingly. When the

Sometimes as many as three cameras are used on the "insert car" to get different angles on action shots. Here William Holden prepares to gallop behind the car while long shot, medium shot, and close-up are filmed simultaneously. From Boots Malone. (Columbia)

The Airiflex camera proves its worth in the filming of I Sailed to Tahiti by obtaining shots the Mitchell could never get. The sound man holds an overhead microphone to record dialogue for a "cue track" only. All sound had to be "looped" back in Hollywood with actors adding new voices to the picture. Wind, waves, and camera noise are thus eliminated, with the wind and the waves added again in proper perspective. (United National)

Here is an example of selective focus, although not as extreme as would be accomplished by a six- or ten-inch lens. All the gaiety of a drinking party is depicted, but the eye goes to Dyan Cannon who is fulfilling a story point. This Rebel Breed, directed by Richard L. Bare. (Warner Bros.)

A few scenes were shot with a Mitchell NC and tripod, tied down to the deck. When the boat heeled over, so did the camera with the result that the boat seemed to stay still but the horizon pitched wildly. I Sailed to Tahiti, directed by Richard L. Bare. (United National)

Acceptance of the handheld camera as the prime photographic instrument has brought a new mobility to feature production. Under such adverse conditions as shooting on the deck of a 55-foot sloop, the cameraman is able to counter the roll of the boat and keep the horizon level. I Sailed to Tahiti, directed by Richard L. Bare. (United National)

tripod was abandoned and the Airiflex was handheld by the operator, the proper illusion of a boat at sea was given. Audiences can be subject to an inner ear imbalance when the horizon does not remain relatively constant and one only has to remember the first Cinerama pictures to be convinced. So, the balance of sea shots were made with the handheld camera and with the operator attempting to hold the horizon level with his viewfinder, no little chore in light of the heavy seas encountered. I recall that at least three of us steadied him with our bodies, forming a kind of human tripod to keep him from losing his balance and falling overboard. One last word about shooting under these conditions: only wide-angle lenses can reduce the unsteadiness of shots made on a rocking boat, and in this case almost all were made with a 25 mm lens.

Of all the directors who understood the camera, Josef von Sternberg, perhaps, made the best use of it. It would be nothing for von Sternberg actually to operate the camera himself on a long and intricate crane shot rather than to stand to one side and depend on the camera operator's interpretation of what he wanted.

Von Sternberg knew the value of the mobile camera and its ability to convey an abstract thought, or merely to suggest what was not possible to photograph. In his early talking picture, *The Scarlet Empress*, which starred Marlene Dietrich, his camera traveled down a torture chamber disclosing, one by one, several executioners placing their victims' heads on the chopping blocks. At the end of the chamber, the camera came to a stop on a chief executioner who gave a signal to proceed with the grisly event. Von Sternberg's camera then started to move back, retracing its course, but this time as it passed, only the executioners were shown—the blocks and the kneeling victims being below the frame line. As each man came into view, he sent the axes into the blocks with a thud. There was no doubt in the observer's mind as to what had happened, yet he actually saw little of the gruesome sight. The continuous scene, done without cutting and with but slight change of angle, can do much to create the illusion of reality.

Once while shooting a Warner Bros. western, *Shootout at Medicine Bend*, I had occasion to combine what I had learned about the psychology of handling actors with von Sternberg's technique of the continuous camera treatment.

We were halfway through the feature, and the script called for James Garner, Randolph Scott, and Gordon Jones to be swimming in a river while their clothing was being stolen. Randy had never mentioned to me, or anyone else as far as I knew, that he wouldn't go in the water. When we got around to setting up for the wet work, the assistant director came up to me and told me what Randy had just told him, that he wasn't going in the river. I knew that talking to Scott would do little good, so I proceeded to task my imagination. I first asked the assistant if Scott minded stripping down to his underwear. No, that was all right; he didn't mind that. It was just that he had a cold and wasn't going to get in that dirty river. With this hurdle accomplished, I proceeded to stage the scene. I put Randy's double out in the middle of the stream with Garner and Jones, and placed the camera behind a fallen log that was lying on the water's edge. I put Scott behind the log and told him to crouch down out of sight. Just as the camera rolled the prop man dumped a gallon of warm water over him, and the boys in the river started to swim a dash to the shore. As they approached the shore and disappeared momentarily behind the log, the double stayed hidden, and Randy popped up alongside Garner and Jones, breathing heavily and looking for all as if he had been swimming right along with them. I was happy; we stayed on schedule; and Randolph Scott, no doubt, picked up a few more fans.

Component Parts of the Camera

The standard sound camera of the Hollywood professional motion picture industry is the Mitchell BNC, an expensive and complicated piece of equipment that has come through years of evolution. It is self-contained in its own soundproof *blimp*, for it could never be used close to a microphone in its basic state. It evolved from the Mitchell NC, which is still used on exterior production where sound is not necessary, and when used with the microphone it is enclosed in a horse-blanket affair called a *barney*.

In silent days, Bell & Howell had a corner on the camera market in Hollywood; but the Mitchell, with its exclusive *rack-over* device, soon became the most popular camera. The rack-over, as it is called, allows the body of the camera to be slid to one side, leaving the photographing lens exposed to the eye, and the scene which is to be recorded may be viewed through the lens exactly the way it will appear on the film. This device is so important and the patent so encompassing, that no other camera maker has been able to rival Mitchell since the decline of Bell & Howell.

In 1967 Mitchell developed and put on the market the BNCR, a reflex-type camera that eliminated the rack-over viewing and substituted a direct system of viewing through the lens while shooting. But back to the BNC, the camera most used in production.

The *finder*, attached to the side of the camera parallel with the lens, is used to watch the scene while the camera is operating. The camera operator does not see the scene exactly the way it is being recorded on film due to a condition known as *parallax*. (The reflex type cameras eliminate this parallax altogether and for critical shooting they are better.)

The other primary parts of the camera are the *magazine* (which holds the film), the *matt box* (which acts as a sun shade), the *drive motor* (which turns the camera in synchronization with the sound recorder), the *lens mount* (which serves as a fastening base for the lens), and the *intermittent movement* (which pulls the film through the *gate*, exposing one frame at a time, while the *shutter* is briefly open).

The Mitchell BNC, worth somewhere near $25,000, is so heavy it must be handled by at least two grips, who place it on the *crab dolly*, an innovation that allows a camera to be perambulated around corners rather than on straight metal tracks as previously.

Once it is lined up on its dolly, and *threaded* by the assistant cameraman, with either black and white or color *negative*, the lens *focused* for distance by the assistant, and the proper *stop* determined by the first cameraman, the camera is turned over to the whim of the director.

Of course, the director has already rehearsed the action of his actors, and has lined up the course that the dolly will travel. He has instructed the camera operator to avoid the palm tree across the street, since the locale of the story is in Philadelphia. He has probably ridden in the operator's seat and watched the scene through the camera during the first rehearsal, giving the grips instructions to move the dolly with the action of the scene. When the leading man drives up to the curb in a full shot, the dolly must be on No. 1 mark. When he walks around to open the car door for the leading lady, the dolly must be on No. 2 mark—no sooner and certainly no later. He has called the makeup man to remove the perspiration from the leading lady's face since the time of the year is supposed to be December, not August, which it really is. He gives a last word of advice to the actors, and turns to his assistant and says, "Let's make it!" When the camera crew, the sound crew, the electricians, and the grips have all indicated their readiness, the assistant calls, "Quiet, and roll it!", and the camera and recorder start to turn. The assistant cameraman slaps the *clap sticks* in front of the lens simultaneously with getting a *slate*, and the camera operator calls out "Speed." The director calls, "Ready—Action!", and the scene as rehearsed proceeds. The car drives up, the actors get out with the grips pushing the camera to the proper mark. The actors walk toward the house, the camera panning with them so as to avoid the palm tree, and then dollying with them to the porch, where the camera then swings around and takes them into the house in a full shot. The director calls "Cut!" and everybody takes a breath and starts talking again. The director asks the camera operator and the sound man if they're happy, and if so, prints the action and moves on to the next shot. That's the way it goes, set-up after set-up, all day long. The director, with little time to sit down, is either rehearsing the actors or lining up the shot with the cameraman, working out the camera movement smoothly so that it will not call attention to itself. On the other hand, the movement of the camera sometimes is designed to shock and startle—the content of each scene dictating the style of such movement.

Composition

Since the *framing* of a shot by the cameraman is subject to the director's approval, the art of composition should be part of the director's basic training.

The fact that a landscape is pleasing to the eye is not necessarily a reason for it being pleasing in a picture. While the eye takes in a wandering, all-encompassing angle of view, the camera has an outside boundary, a sharp edge on all four sides; and a picture even though real in its illusion can represent only a portion of nature. With the landscape captured or framed, the eye can only see what the director wants it to. If the eye

An example of foreground objects which "frame" or set off the main action. It is kept darker or, in this case, silhouetted to throw the center of attention deeper into the shot. The Wild Bunch, *directed by Sam Peckinpah.* (Warner Bros.)

Some cameramen go to great lengths to control the harsh rays of the sun and to give their scenes photographic "balance." Here is a movie troupe on location at Lake Arrowhead working under the protective cover of a huge scrim. However, today's style is to shoot it "as it is." (Universal Pictures)

There is no spot where the camera can't go, say some of Hollywood's more cooperative cameramen. "Give the director what he wants" is the mode of the day. Here Lucien Ballard (top) prepares the huge Mitchell BNC to shoot a somewhat thorny scene. (Warner Bros.)

COMPOSING INDIVIDUAL SHOTS

RIGHT

This medium close-up is properly composed—proper head room, sides and bottom.

WRONG

Here there is much too much head room and bottom of shot gives no base for judge's arms.

RIGHT

With camera moved slightly back, picture is still pleasing to the eye.

WRONG

Here there is not enough head room and too much bench for good composition.

RIGHT

This close-up crops the top of the head in a "Warner Bros. close-up" as it is known in Hollywood.

WRONG

This close-up is too close and disturbingly cuts off part of actress's chin.

COMPOSING A
TWO-SHOT

RIGHT

This medium shot properly depicts the subjects in their relationship to one another, the man impudently lying on the bench making notes on the judge's calendar.

WRONG

The composition of this shot fully shows where the man lies on the bench but has placed the judge too far to the left sideline, diminishing his importance.

RIGHT

This close two-shot gives both subjects equal prominence, and when followed by the longer shot above, leaves no doubt as to the man's continuing impudence.

WRONG

This two-shot is too close. Not only are both heads too close to sidelines, but the shot doesn't include the man writing on the calendar.

COMPOSING SHOTS FOR
BOTH WIDE-SCREEN AND TV

Most films for theaters are shot in so-called wide-screen (aspect ratio: 1.85 to 1). It is incumbent on the director and the cameraman to protect the composition of these films when they are shown on television, which uses the aspect ratio of 1.33 to 1.

This scene, composed for standard wide-screen (1.85 to 1), will not compose satisfactorily when shown on television. Both the girl on the left and the man on the right will be cut off.

This scene, although composed for 1.85 to 1, will not suffer in its television showing because ample room was left on sides, top, and bottom.

This shot has too much head room and is not pleasing to the eye, despite the subject. Proper head room is a matter of individual choice, but most directors and cameramen would agree that the above head room could be reduced by 50 percent.

Although this shot has the same head room as the picture on the left, the scenic background gives the top part of the picture additional interest that warrants the breaking of the head room rule.

strives to go beyond the limits of the picture, the result will be a restlessness on the part of the observer. This is why objects that are important, which attract the eye, should be placed near the margins of the picture.

A photograph has two functions: to represent nature in a realistic manner and still to be decorative and artistic. The lines and masses contained in the picture must have a balance or rhythm in order to please —hence the importance of composition.

The director has several ways at his command to achieve a pleasing, well-composed picture. He can move his subjects, the actors, to positions either pleasing or displeasing to the eye. He can pan or tilt the camera, thus changing its angle of view to include another background against which his actors play their scene. He can shift the height of the camera, either up or down, backward or forward, or move it to a completely different spot to obtain a better overall composition. It is necessary that all parts of the picture contribute to its general effect, and extraneous objects that cause a division of interest detract from the force of the picture.

When Alfred Hitchcock directed Rope, *he made no "cuts," but, rather, shot the film in twelve ten-minute takes. The huge Technicolor camera roamed about an elaborate set with moving walls. All lighting had to be done from above, since many of Hitchcock's shots involved 360-degree pans.* (Warner Bros.)

The subject of a picture is its most important part, and is generally placed near the center of the frame with the subordinate components leading to or balancing it. Unless one portion of the picture is more attractive and interesting than the other, the eye will shift from one side to the other, creating a restless or monotonous effect. This condition exists many times in the two shot, wherein two actors stand facing one another, showing their profiles to the camera. Each actor is equally important, and the eye has no choice but to flick from one side of the frame to the other. This fact, I'm sure, contributes directly to the tendency of film editors to use a preponderance of over-the-shoulder shots in putting together a lengthy dialogue sequence. Here, there is only one point of interest, the person speaking, with the other person becoming subordinate in the composition.

While good composition is something that should come naturally to a director, there are a few basic rules that can serve as a guide in setting up a shot for the motion picture camera.

The idea that the picture should be divided into thirds is one of these rules. Let's take a sea view, for instance. You might position the camera so that the waves lapping the shoreline occupy a position one third of the frame up from the bottom, while the horizon in the distance coincides with the imaginary line one third down from the top. On the right side of the frame is a steep cliff, rising from the beach. You angle the camera so that this line is one third of the way in from the side, while the setting sun disappears below the horizon at a position near the upper horizontal and the left vertical imaginary lines.

Attendant to the rule of positioning the subject near the center comes the question of what to put near the borders of the picture. A colonial mansion with its impressive columns can serve as the focal point of interest, while a sweeping lawn in the foreground forms a restful threshold. The winding driveway that leads to the house serves to further take our eye to the center of attention. To one side of the frame a huge magnolia tree rises majestically in silhouette, its branches tipping into our picture from the top. So much for the background. When our subject, let's say a small boy, comes running down the driveway and stops to see something off camera, he comes to a position approximately center, and slightly to the left, thus balancing with the tree at the right.

Foreground objects, such as trees, pieces of statuary, table lamps, and the like are called framing pieces and should not be strongly lighted so as to call too much attention to themselves.

Since the motion picture camera has the ability to change its viewpoint during a scene, the compositions become a series of flowing, moving canvasses, altering their shape and mass as the action progresses from one point to the next.

A well-composed scene may start with a mobile camera framing through the banister of a stairway and shooting down on the foyer of a stately mansion. A woman enters the shot, camera right, and starts down the stairs to the floor below. As the camera moves down with her and around the archway into the living room, it makes another composition with a foreground piece, a statuette, dimly lighted so as not to detract from the dramatic action. The lady pauses momentarily, then walking into a close shot (composed slightly off center so that she is looking toward the empty side of the shot). She hears the doorbell ring. Suspecting the identity of her caller, she reacts fearfully but is drawn to the door.

The camera moves with her, and as her hand falters on the doorknob the camera lowers to focus on the knob. The doorbell rings again, and the woman's hand turns the knob. As the door swings open, the camera tilts swiftly upward to disclose the looming face of the mysterious caller, composing a scene that gives dramatic emphasis to the sinister nature of the situation. In a continuously changing series of compositions, the camera has provided a variety of dramatic effects.

Composition of close-ups can be as important as the framing of more comprehensive shots. The extreme close-up, so common to television pictures, can be so unbalanced as to cause a feeling of restlessness among the audience. If the bottom frame line is too high, the subject's chin will disappear as soon as he speaks. Too much head room, that is, the distance from the top of the head to the top frame line, is another factor that can contribute to an unpleasing effect. Usually, in these large close-ups, if the subjects eyes are slightly above the imaginary horizontal center line, the rest of the face will be in balance.

Creating dramatic illusions through composition is just another use that the director can make of his knowledge of the camera. A typical example of this can be found where the illusion of height is to be created. Let's suppose that the script calls for an actor to be perched precariously on a ledge many hundreds of feet high. The studio art department has probably built a portion of this ledge on the stage, which matches an actual mountain location and which was used to film the long shots with the actor's double. You wish to establish this set, called an interior-exterior, taking advantage of everything you can to create a feeling of height. Shooting a point of view from below can help, but the real trick is to compose the shot so that the man on the ledge will be toward the top of the picture, and that a mass of rock fills the screen below. Normally unorthodox when the only dictate of the scene is pictorial, this composition aids the dramatic telling of the story. The opposite is true when other actors are to be depicted as being at the base of the cliff. Framing up, so that a mass of rock is above the actors, will do much to accomplish this feeling.

The technique of composing camera angles that are shot from below the subject has a tendency to emphasize the powerful, the dominating qualities of a character, while angles from high looking down create an opposite effect of weakness, helplessness, and even sympathy for the person.

Even the inanimate can take on another quality when viewed from below. I once had occasion to shoot a scene in which a piano was being hoisted from the sidewalk to a third-story window. Since this was a comedy and the piano was destined to fall in the picture, I placed the camera directly below and with a very wide-angle lens created quite a frightening shot as it was pulled slowly upward.

Aspect Ratios

No chapter on composition would be complete without a discussion of *aspect ratios*, the various frame sizes with which the motion picture business plagued itself some time years ago.

For fifty years the standardized proportion for framing movies had been a 3 by 4 ratio, the same standard that television adopted and uses. This is a pleasing, easy to balance frame, which still provides the best compositions under most conditions.

One of the most modern developments in studio cameras is the Panavision Reflex which allows the operator to view the action directly through the lens. Notice the absence of the finder, which always caused the problem of parallax. Director Richard Fleischer lines up a shot for Tora! Tora! Tora! *(20th Century-Fox)*

ASPECT RATIOS IN FILM

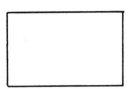

OLD 3x4

The original frame proportion of motion pictures from silent days through twenty-five years of talking pictures.
1.33 to 1

TELEVISION

Video projection cuts down on all sides but still conforms to traditional 3x4 ratio.
1.33 to 1

WIDE-SCREEN

The present "standard" of theatrical films, arrived at by cropping off top and bottom, then blowing up to larger screen.
1.85 to 1

CINEMASCOPE AND PANAVISION

The two most popular anamorphic processes project an extra-wide image from a 35 mm negative that has been "squeezed." Special lenses are required in projection.
2.35 to 1

TODD A-O AND SUPER-PANAVISION

Todd A-O is a 70. mm film process that results in a giant-sized screen image with unusual resolution. Super-Panavision achieves the same results by using a 65 mm negative.
2.21 to 1

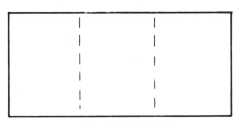

ORIGINAL CINERAMA

Although not currently used, the largest screen size ever developed was three-screen Cinerama. It took three cameras hooked together and three synchronized projectors in the theater to achieve gargantuan picture.
2.33 to 1

PROBLEMS OF ASPECT RATIOS

TWO-SHOT PHOTOGRAPHED IN ANAMORPHIC PROCESS

The above two photographs illustrate what sometimes happens when a theatrical feature made in a 2.35-to-1 ratio is released to television. If the director has not considered the future television exhibition problems and placed his actors at the far extremes of the frame, both actors can

SAME TWO-SHOT
PROJECTED ON TELEVISION

Two noses and a venetian blind.

end up "off camera," only their voices being heard. In these instances, special television prints are prepared by the laboratories that provide optical "pans" from one face to another, hardly satisfactory at best.

MOST DIRECTORS PROTECT TV SHOWINGS BY PROPERLY PLACING ACTORS.

NOTHING WILL BE LOST WHEN
SHOWN ON TELEVISION

SIDES OF PICTURE ARE FOR INCIDENTALS ONLY

SOME SHOTS ARE AWKWARD IN WIDE-SCREEN

When composed in the traditional 3x4 frame used by television, a more pleasing effect is achieved.

The near-vertical composition of man and horse does not lend itself to good use of Cinemascope or Panavision.

THESE SHOTS LEND THEMSELVES TO WIDE-SCREEN PROCESSES

THREE-SHOTS

This scene from *Gaily, Gaily*, directed by Norman Jewison, composes well in 1.85 to 1.

SPECTACLES

Hello, Dolly! made good use of Todd A-O, a 70 mm process which is higher but not as wide as the anamorphic processes. A 20th Century-Fox production directed by Gene Kelly.

There have been many attempts to stray from this 3 by 4 standard through the years, the most notable of which was Fox's Grandeur—a 70 mm film process—in which only a few pictures were produced. This occurred about 1929, but failed because exhibitors balked at the expense of equiping their theaters with larger screens and bigger projectors.

After Fox's first experiment with large film, nothing much happened to increase screen size for almost twenty-five years, and when they tried it again Cinemascope was born. This is an anamorphic process, which means that 35 mm film is used but that the image is "squeezed" in the theater by another lens onto a large panoramic screen. The ungainly dimensions of this Cinemascope screen, and the tendency toward a fuzziness of focus, have kept this process from becoming a standard—a thing that many people agree is necessary in a worldwide industry.

With 20th-Century Fox pioneering and staking all on Cinemascope, other producers followed their lead with processes and aspect ratios of their own. Paramount, for a while, exploited Vista-Vision, a wide-screen process that many agree was the closest answer to perfect projection. The other companies merely reduced the top and bottom of their projection apertures, shortened the focal length of their lenses to enlarge the picture and latched onto the aspect ratio of 1.85 to 1 as the desirable screen proportion. This may be the ratio that will stand the test of time, since films photographed this way are most easily projected on television, the complexities of which eliminate a portion of the top and bottom of theatrically designed films.

Todd A-O and Cinerama, both in the roadshow class, provide even additional aspect ratios and screen size, and today the deluxe theater that wishes to show all of the world's film product must equip itself with a variety of projectors, lenses, and screen and speaker arrangements.

Whether a motion picture is photographed on 35 mm or 70 mm film, whether it is composed in a 3 by 4 ratio or 1.85 to 1, whether it be in Cinemascope, Techniscope, Cinerama, or Panavision—the creation of film entertainment remains basically the same. Cameras are tools with which the director transfers the pages of a script onto a screen, large or small, in a theater or in a living room. A director could make his picture on 99 mm film, turn it sideways and call it "tall-screen" and still not impress his audience unless he is telling a story worth telling, filming it in style, without unduly calling attention to himself.

Mike Nichols, after directing *Catch-22*, let his views on this subject be known: "Frankly, I would hope I live never to see a zoom again, a long lens, any of the things available to the people making Pepsi-Cola commercials. It should all be stripped away. Techniques should serve the thing you're concerned with. The films that I most admire are those in which there is no apparent technique at all."

Lining up an unusual angle through the rear window of an automobile is director Ralph Nelson whose credits include Charly *and " . . . tick . . . tick . . . tick," as well as the award-winning television show* Requiem for a Heavyweight. (Metro-Goldwyn-Mayer)

The Multi-Image Screen

Although the technique of combining multi-images on a single screen is not new, it has reached an ultimate in complexity in films such as *The Thomas Crown Affair* and *Charly*. Like so many other techniques, the multi-image screen had its start with D. W. Griffith in *The Birth of a Nation*. He used several images simultaneously to make a single statement—soldiers rushing up the hill, the sacking and burning in the valley, and a leading character being helped up the hill in the foreground.

Ralph Nelson, who directed *Charly*, used the technique to enhance a scene between two characters seen just talking with one another. Rather than cut back and forth between the close shots of the two, he combined the shots optically onto one frame. The audience could see both the action and the reaction, in effect, doing its own cutting. In *The Thomas Crown Affair*, Norman Jewison effectively used as many as fifty-four duplicate moving images simultaneously, which enabled the director to cut a twenty-minute sequence down to four and a half minutes. In the polo sequence Jewison intercut his multiscreen images with single images with great effect. From a fifty-odd image shot of a player bearing down on the ball, Jewison cut to a huge single close-up of the ball being hit. The impact was much greater than if the sequence had been edited in the conventional way.

The multi-image technique can, of course, be overused but it has proved itself to be an effective way to combine action and reaction, to show parallel action simultaneously and to bring greater movement to an otherwise static situation.

Lighting the Scene

The director who has to rely on his own level of communication with the cameraman sometimes goes to the projection room and views a scene somewhat differently than the way he imagined it. More often than not this disappointment is because the lighting approach the cameraman used produced an effect unlike the one the director had in mind.

At least a rudimentary understanding of the techniques of lighting should be understood by every director, otherwise he will continue to be surprised from time to time during his career. The lights and their placement is the greatest single tool of the cameraman, and the great cinematographers of this industry have reached their place in the sun because of their knowledge of the intricacies of lighting. A cameraman not skilled in lighting is only a mechanic concerned with mathematical formulas of exposure, the theories of optics, and other scientific data. But when he moves his lights about, he truly takes on the status of an artist, just as if he had picked up a brush and pallet.

The glamour queens of Hollywood became that way because cameramen knew where to place the lights that flattered them. Because they needed special photographic handling, Lupe Velez and Merle Oberon had pieces of lighting equipment named after them—the "Lupe" and the "Obie."

Generally, there are three components to a properly lighted scene, the *key light*, or main source, the *fill light*, which opposes and balances the shadows created by the key, and the *back light*, which gives the actors a slight halo, or Rembrandt effect, making them stand out from the background. Added to this can be an *eye light* (for certain colors and qualities of eyes) and a miscellaneous assortment of *peanuts, babies, broads, juniors, seniors*, and *10 k's*. The *arc lights* usually provide the illusion of sunshine filtering in the doors and windows.

The arrangement and balance of this multitude of equipment is the cameraman's secret and is a knowledge he didn't acquire overnight. His usual approach to lighting is to first have the electrician light the walls of the background. Then the key light is positioned and a *meter-reading* is taken to bring the intensity of the main source of light either up or down to a proper *foot-candle* measurement. This intensity of the key light has previously been determined by the cameraman in relation to the *speed* of the film and the lens aperture, or *f. stop* he desires. Following this, the fill light is positioned, and this is balanced by eye through the *ground glass* of the lens. Then the back light, usually several units from the rim of the set, is directed toward the subjects and balanced for density. After this, the cameraman gives his attention to the electrical set dressing, the floor lamps, wall bracket fixtures, and so forth, and each is positioned and brought to its proper balance of illumination, and this is generally done by eye.

The director who appreciates what each light is for can, through practice and experience, determine what effect is being made on the film. He, too, can look through the ground glass of the camera and tell whether an object in the foreground is too "hot" and thereby distracting, or whether the moonlight coming through the window is too low in density to permit recognition of his actor. Thus, the more he learns of the effects of lighting, the better able he is to tell his story in the most effective way. And if he goes about "suggesting" to the cameraman a change in lighting here and there, no cinematographic feathers will be ruffled.

Cecil B. De Mille can be properly credited with introducing what is now referred to as low-key photography. In one of his early silent films, he had experimented with lighting and achieved a then startling result; only half of the actors' faces were lighted brightly, the other half falling off into deep shadows. This created a suspenseful mood to the picture, and De Mille had taken great pains in obtaining it. Many long weeks later, when the final print was ready and shipped to New York, his distributors viewed the picture with some misgivings, and wired De Mille in Hollywood that they were at a loss to know how to release the picture since they couldn't very well charge people full admission when only half the actor's faces were visible.

This disturbed De Mille, but he finally came up with the argument he needed to insure the picture's acceptance. He wired the distributors in New York: "What's the matter with you back there? Don't you recognize Rembrandt Lighting when you see it?"

Naturally, with this shot in the arm, the picture was released and became a big success. It was the start of mood lighting in motion pictures.

The lighting of subjects for the modern film is not solely an indoor sport. Much thought must go into the lighting of exterior scenes as well; when actors are involved in a scene the natural rays of the sun must be augmented or in some instances either filtered or completely replaced. Nothing has a more disastrous effect on a beautiful actress than improperly handled sunlight. It is much better, as a general rule, to let the sunlight act as back light, and provide by artificial means the key light and

Here is an example of effective mood lighting that highlights the main character of a scene while subordinating the lesser elements. Having the dominant figure stand apart and slightly above the others adds to the overall effect. This Rebel Breed, *directed by Richard L. Bare.* (Warner Bros.)

fill. Huge *scrims* are many times suspended over the foreground action to filter the harsh effects of the sun.

Cameramen use the word *balance* about as often as any other. The director who appreciates the full meaning of this word can quickly endear himself to his cameraman by not demanding camera set-ups that place an undue stretch on the range of light and shade. As an example, a director may be shooting a scene just inside a barn on location. The interior scene may be artifically lighted as any studio set-up would, but the director wants to pan an actor from some place in the barn to the open front door. This places too much of a strain on the balance of lighting, that is, the exposure for the incandescent portion of the shot is not consistent with the exposure for the glare of the sunlighted portion. If the director demands the shot, the cameraman (with plenty of time) can accomplish it. He will either build up the value of the light inside by the addition of arcs, or will reduce the value of the outside light, by placing a large scrim over the entrance to the barn. The cameraman may also balance his exposure in the pan shot by changing the shutter setting, which has an effect similar to changing the f. stop.

In the middle sixties, however, a complete disregard for balance in lighting began to come into vogue. When the new young director took the handheld camera and started using it himself, his own lack of knowledge created some interesting effects. Knowing nothing of the rudiments of photographic balance, he aimed his camera at the sun. Never having heard of the term depth of field, he started to make long shots with long focus-length lenses. Some interesting results came to light and new styles were introduced, much to the dismay of many old-time cameramen.

The camera is truly the director's prime tool, and through the motion picture's years of evolution it has never been underestimated. Just as no carpenter should attempt to build a house without first learning to saw a board or hammer a nail, the film director should thoroughly acquaint himself with the many tools placed at his disposal that the most imaginative and entertaining film may result.

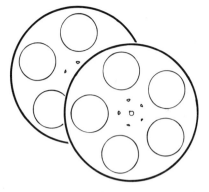

TELLING A STORY
WITH THE CAMERA

The Use of Transitions

I have won a few awards in my professional life, but the one that gave me the biggest boost in morale was the Paul Muni Award presented to me after a banquet and screening of *The Oval Portrait*, a 35 mm amateur film I made while a student at the University of Southern California. Since the picture was a silent film, and since I was writer, director, editor, and cameraman, I had the opportunity to proceed in autonomous fashion in working out interesting techniques of telling the story without sound and without subtitles.

The story had been adapted from one of Edgar Allan Poe's works and concerned itself with a painter who, in his intense devotion to his art, painted the very life out of his subject who happened to be his newly acquired bride. I employed the camera with the reckless abandon of a child with a new toy: I used a frog floating on the surface of the water of a rain barrel in a storm to denote the passage of time. I started him at the bottom, and after it had rained all night the barrel overflowed, and he hopped happily away. I used the burning down of candles to indicate how long the leading man had slept, and even allowed them to be snuffed out by a faint breeze from an open window to denote his death. I crammed every device, every cock-eyed camera angle, and every bit of inspiration I could muster at the age of nineteen into this picture; and for a nonprofessional attempt, it did much to demonstrate how a story could be told with the camera. It ran at Grauman's Egyptian Theatre on Hollywood Boulevard for a week and was reviewed glowingly by the *Hollywood Reporter* and *Daily Variety*.

Without violating my own personal rule that demands that the director place the emphasis on story and acting and not on himself, there are many techniques that often help to create more interesting scenes.

One that I used recently (and as long ago as *The Oval Portrait*) is as follows: to bridge an actor moving from one set to another without dissolving, fading, or following him all the way—simply have him pull out his watch in a medium shot, cut to a close insert of the watch and pull the camera back to disclose that the actor is now going through the same action but in another locale and at another time. This can be successfully accomplished by the device of taking out a cigarette, or a woman starting to powder her nose. It is simply the starting of an action in a medium shot and completing it in a close shot in another setting. In the college film, the transition was accomplished by the leading man proposing to his sweetheart. As he tentatively placed a ring on her finger, I cut directly to a large insert of the girl's hand with the ring continuing its movement on the finger. The camera dollied back, and our two lovers were disclosed kneeling before a priest in a marriage ceremony.

Norman Jewison has solved the problem of the low-angle shot: put the cameraman down into a manhole. Shown kneeling (left), Jewison is one of the newer directors who have made the successful transition from New York television to Hollywood movies. (United Artists)

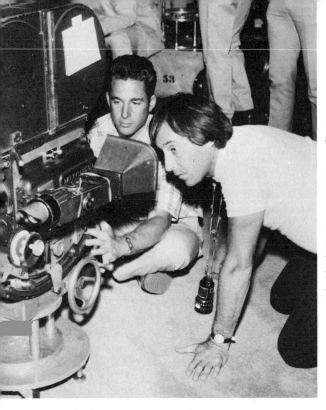

Paul Mazursky, who wears a director's finder around his neck, crouches to check a low-angle shot through the Mitchell BNC camera on a "high hat." Mazursky directed Bob and Carol and Ted and Alice, *his first try at directing, although he had co-produced* I Love You, Alice B. Toklas. (Columbia)

A character can be shown preparing for a big speech at his luncheon club. He starts to memorize his lines in his living room, reading from his prepared speech. Cut into a close-up and then pull back and we see the man is now speaking to the club members.

Any business or dialogue that, as a matter of story development, must repeat itself, can be handled in this manner—starting the action in a medium shot, then finishing the action in another location in a close shot.

Transition shots have been with us for a long time; one of the oldest cinematic clichés was the wheel-to-wheel dissolve: the camera pans down to a spinning roulette wheel that dissolved to a spinning automobile wheel.

The Angle of Approach

The *angle of approach* in filming a scene is of great importance, second only to that of the actors' performances. From what point the director allows the audience to view the action becomes vital in the telling of the story. Chaplin seldom took full advantage of the camera's infinite power, but, in one instance, he devised a gag that depended on the angle of approach for its effect. In *The Immigrant*, Charlie was aboard a violently rocking boat, with everyone feeling the effects of *mal-de-mer*. When Charlie was discovered, he was hanging over the side of the rail with his back to the audience, his body heaving to and fro, apparently in agony. Suddenly, he pulled himself up, turned to face the camera, and the audience saw that he had merely been fishing and had caught one with his cane as a pole.

The director who photographs his scenes from imaginative angles forces the spectator to take a keener interest in his work, one that goes beyond mere acceptance. Many times a production with an often-told story and no stars can be lifted by the director into a reasonably worthwhile film, simply by utilizing *style*. His style may be peculiar to his talents, or it may be in imitation of others, but this is unimportant if his film avoids the commercial, hackneyed, and perfunctory look so often seen in the cheaper features and television films. The directorial touches and the skillful manner in which the director handles the camera seldom add any cost to a picture's budget; rather it is indecision or confusion on the director's part that contribute to lengthy production schedules.

A German picture made many years ago introduced an actor in a close-up, standing in a courtyard and shaking his fists at someone behind the camera. The next angle, a full shot, showed the object of his wrath, a jail guard, but the camera had been placed on the other side of prison bars. Now, the audience received the full import of the scene, a man being released from prison, not all at once, and not in a conventional manner.

Another picture depicted the parting of two lovers as they stood on the deck of a luxury liner, a tender scene that had as its climax the young man leaving as the loudspeakers blared, "All ashore who's going ashore." As he moved away, the audience saw a heretofore hidden life preserver. On it was written the name of the doomed *Titanic*. What better way could there be to show that these young people would never see one another again. A thousand words could not have done it with the same impact.

A glamorous female spy has killed a Russian general in his study. Outside the door, soldiers knock peremptorily. The lady quickly manages to lift the general's body into his high-backed leather chair, and turn it so that the back faces the door. Then, she sits on the arm of the chair and calls, "Come in."

The soldiers enter, salute, and ask for orders. The lady spy, fondling the dead man's hand, turns to him and apparently asks him what he wishes the soldiers to do. She pretends to converse with the general, then turns to the soldiers and tells them that they are dismissed and that the general does not wish to be disturbed the rest of the evening. The danger

There was a time when this scene would have been shot inside a sound stage on a Hollywood lot instead of on a New York rooftop. But times have changed and realism is the word—even in the filming of musicals. David Swift (center) directs Robert Morse and Michele Lee in a scene from How to Succeed in Business Without Really Trying. Cameraman Burnett Guffey sits on stool. (United Artists)

When the horses gallop, the camera must go along too. Gregory Peck and Camilla Sparv handle the ponies while the camera crew hangs on for dear life on the "insert car." Director J. Lee Thompson is at extreme right. From Mackenna's Gold, a Carl Foreman production. (Columbia)

has been averted. The director, by staging his angle of approach to coincide with the soldiers' point of view, placed the audience in a position to receive the full impact of the situation and to understand how the soldiers might misinterpret what they saw.

Joseph von Sternberg, always one to devise unusual approaches, once shot a suicide scene without ever shooting the action from the conventional angle. The camera was set-up to shoot the water under a bridge. Nothing was in the shot except quivering water and the reflection of a woman, looking down and about to jump over the railing of a bridge. As she jumps, her reflected image races toward the lens, then enters the scene, splashing away her own reflection. The result of the indirect upon the direct can be startling and effective.

Another example of the indirect approach is in depicting the effect of a loud noise, such as a gunshot. Rather than photograph the gun going off, wouldn't it be more interesting to center on a group of birds, watching them take to the air as the shot is fired?

In today's motion picture and television scripts the writer usually concentrates on telling his story through his characters, what they do and what they say, with little regard for the visual powers of the camera as an adjunct to telling the story. The great directors of the silent pictures— Eisenstein, von Sternberg, Lubitsch, and Griffith—told their stories visually, not only because sound had not yet come into use, but because they understood the dramatic force of the camera's angle of approach. King Vidor, himself a top silent director, continued to use his unique handling of the camera on into talking pictures, while Federico Fellini and Ingmar Bergman display truly great understanding of the articulateness of the director's prime tool.

Modern stage directors are aware that one of the principal problems is the proper control of the *center of attention*. Taking *center stage* has always implied a position of importance, but because usually the full stage is in view at all times, there can be many things that rob a star of the center of attention. "Scene stealing" is as old as the theater itself, and an actor who scratches his beard at the wrong time can cause the audience's attention to be distracted quickly. Shakespeare solved this problem by having his other actors leave the stage while the important performer delivered a soliloquy.

The motion picture, through its ever shifting camera, provides the director with a complete control over the center of attention. When D. W. Griffith introduced the close-up, he locked in forever a rigid technique that forces an audience to look at what the director wants it to. Unlike the stage director, who must carefully balance all elements, the film director can bring any thing he wants center stage instantly through the techniques of cutting and camera angle.

The great majority of directors consciously attempt to use the camera advantageously, but there is one type of television production prevalent in Hollywood which, although shot on film with movie camera, completely ignores the basic concepts of the motion picture as an art form. This is the three-camera, live-on-film method common to the old *I Love Lucy* show, and used by many others since. Instead of a carefully lined up, single point of view approach to a scene, these comedies are filmed before an audience in a matter of a few hours, each camera getting its close-ups, medium shots, and long shots on a catch-as-catch-can basis. Effective lighting is an impossibility, and seldom can a director bring style to his shooting. I am inclined to exclude this type of filming from the category of motion pictures; rather, it would seem to me to be merely a visual record of a stage play.

Tricks of Illusion

Although it sounds trite to refer to "the magic of the motion picture," I continue to be amazed at what can be accomplished through *illusion* in telling a story. Practically any effect the director calls for can be produced on film, one way or another. Not so with the stage director who must come to grips with reality in creating his illusions.

A three-time winner of the Academy Award for best director, William Wyler has been nominated for the award on thirteen different occasions—ten times as a director and three times as a producer. His advice for would-be directors: "Have a knowledge of your craft and a passion for your subject." (Columbia Pictures Corporation)

The cowboy who takes the arrow into his chest right before your eyes did exactly that when the film was made; however, a two-inch board was beneath his shirt, and the arrow sailed down an invisible wire, safely under control. The director picked an angle of approach that would be most effective in heightening the illusion.

Another Indian draws his bow and lets an arrow fly, but this time the camera whips swiftly to the victim who is seen staggering backward, his hands clutching the arrow in his chest. This time no wire, no needless delay in lining-up the shot; merely a trick on the audience, whose eyes follow what they think is the arrow. When they see another arrow in the victim's chest, they assume it to be the same arrow that left the Indian's bow. Actually, the Indian shot his arrow some distance upstage of the intended target, but the illusion is perfect.

The screen, being flat and two dimensional, has an inability to reproduce depth in a scene, and many of the director's tricks depend on this photographic limitation. People who watch current television shows, especially the action and adventure variety, must wonder how those leading men take all those socks on the jaw. If the angle is just right, and the aggressive actor swings his fist across the screen with the receiver's jaw between the fist and the lens, he can miss by two or three inches and still create the illusion of a smashing blow. Of course, the addition of sound effects later help the final result.

The actor who is mauled by a lion is benefited by a double-barreled illusion. In the long shots, a stunt double, dressed in the same clothes, rolls and tumbles on the ground with the real lion, partially tamed for the movies. In the close shots, the actor duplicates the same action, this time clutching and wrestling with a stuffed lion's head. When the menacing sound of the animal's roaring is added, the audience truly sees its favorite movie star locked in mortal combat with the king of beasts.

The ability to stop and start, to shoot just what is needed, to throw out the bad and keep the good, is the film director's stock in trade. A synthetic tear placed on the cheek of an unemotional leading lady, or a few drops of movie blood spotted judiciously on the lips of the more robust members of the cast, can do much to create the right effect; and only in the medium of film can these be applied just when the director wants them.

Many of the illusions created in motion pictures are accomplished through the use of the process known as *rear projection*, and more commonly referred to as *process shots*. In simple terms, a process shot combines the foreground actors with a background that is either impractical to go to, or too costly or impossible to duplicate. For instance, the script calls for the leading man to be standing on the deck of a ship as it enters the Panama Canal. A film of the background, called a *plate*, is projected

THE INDIAN ARROW ILLUSION

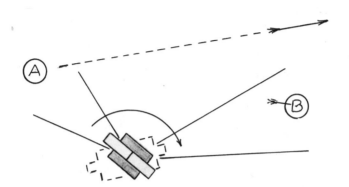

As actor A shoots arrow, camera whip-pans to actor B who already has another arrow lodged in a board concealed under his shirt. As he comes into view he clutches arrow, falls to ground. Real arrow sails harmlessly by on same level but camera's one-dimensional view does not discern the difference.

CREATING ILLUSION OF HEIGHT

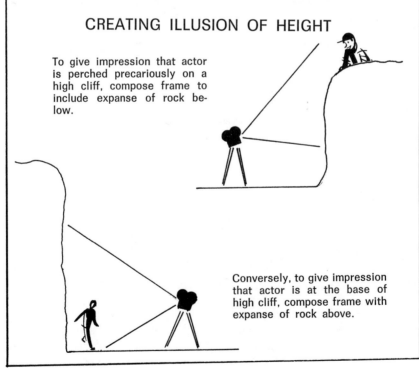

To give impression that actor is perched precariously on a high cliff, compose frame to include expanse of rock below.

Conversely, to give impression that actor is at the base of high cliff, compose frame with expanse of rock above.

This Air Force training film crew is shooting what some call "poor man's process," which supplies moving clouds on a background without using movie projection. When scene starts, camera is slowly moved forward and backward to give feeling of motion, and arc light (extreme right and top) is raised and lowered, casting movable shadows inside the plane.

onto a translucent screen, and is rephotographed with the actor standing in the foreground on a simulated deck.

Process has its limitations too. The angle of approach is limited to one that approximates ninety degrees to the rear projection screen. Camera movement is limited as well, and of course the movements of the actors are restricted according to the size of the screen in front of which they must work.

In 1969 a new type of process shot was introduced, *front projection.* A special projector shines the moving background onto a screen from the front, even on the actors themselves. But the projector light is so dim that the images on the actors do not photograph. The secret lies in the super-

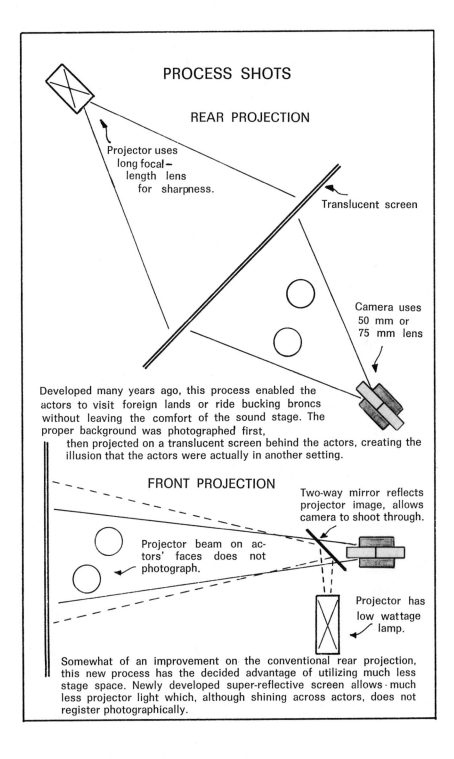

PROCESS SHOTS

REAR PROJECTION

Projector uses
long focal –
length lens
for sharpness.

Translucent screen

Camera uses
50 mm or
75 mm lens

Developed many years ago, this process enabled the actors to visit foreign lands or ride bucking broncs without leaving the comfort of the sound stage. The proper background was photographed first, then projected on a translucent screen behind the actors, creating the illusion that the actors were actually in another setting.

FRONT PROJECTION

Two-way mirror reflects projector image, allows camera to shoot through.

Projector beam on ac-
tors' faces does not
photograph.

Projector has
low wattage
lamp.

Somewhat of an improvement on the conventional rear projection, this new process has the decided advantage of utilizing much less stage space. Newly developed super-reflective screen allows much less projector light which, although shining across actors, does not register photographically.

reflective qualities of the background screen, which allows the camera to record the moving background as well as the actors in a much lower photographic key than ever before.

There are other methods of combining foreground action with backgrounds, such as *traveling matts* and the use of black light and fluorescent paints, but process remains the most inexpensive.

Most directors, in their desire for realism, prefer to shoot their films in natural locations, avoiding completely the use of process. When the actors are called on to converse in a speeding car, they do just that, much to the dismay of the cameraman and sound man who must record both action and voice under slightly difficult conditions.

Andrew Stone is one director who almost never shoots a picture in the studio. His film *The Last Voyage* is a masterpiece of realism with every foot of film shot aboard the *Île-de-France* while it was actually sinking. Stone, a stickler for practical locations, bought the ship from the salvage company who was about to dismantle it for scrap, and used it as his "studio" for many weeks.

Ring of Fire is another example of Stone's penchant for getting realism on the screen without the help of process or other studio facilities. In this film, he bought a sawmill, then proceeded to burn it down for his movie. Even a locomotive, which was required to push three passenger coaches through a flaming forest, actually moved through the fire accomplishing an excitingly realistic sequence for the highlight of the picture. Only scenes in which a small Oregon lumber town was burning down had to be faked by the superimposition of the flames. I'm sure Stone only resorted to this trickery after the city fathers refused to sell him their town.

Then there is the new school of directors who frown on the accepted tricks of illusion. They like to "tell it like it is" and give their films an honesty that defies the tradition of cutting from one shot to another, thereby allowing the director the opportunity to slip in some other piece of film or otherwise to indulge in fakery. They believe it is only the uninterrupted scene that can result in a total commitment to truth.

Perhaps the outstanding adherent to this philosophy is Mike Nichols who, in his *Catch-22*, conceived some of the most expensively uninterrupted scenes ever filmed, as truthful as they were. As Nichols puts it, "Every time a character says, 'Good morning, sir,' twenty-five planes take off." One scene involves two actors talking against a background of planes taking off. As the scene progresses, the actors enter a building and the same planes are seen through the window climbing into formation. As Frank Tallman, the chief pilot for the film, said: "Can you imagine the kind of timing and communication that takes? Every time Nichols tells us we have to do it again, we've got to land ten airplanes and line 'em up all over again."

Montage

No book on filmmaking would be complete without an analysis of the subject of *montage*, even though it is seldom seen in modern films. But taking into consideration the way cinema techniques seem to come and go, then come again, it is appropriate to evaluate all techniques. Montage, by way of definition, is a succession of individual, sometimes diverse, shots which, when viewed as a whole, create a unified emotional impression.

A typical montage sequence might cover a man's alcoholic downfall, first showing him taking a drink after being established as a reformed but shaky alcoholic. A series of different angles would depict the man taking drink after drink, then cocked angles of electric bar signs, with his face superimposed, drinking, drinking, drinking. Finally, his complete downfall is represented by his figure lying prone in the street on Skid Row. Weeks of imbibing is condensed to a minute or less of screen time.

Filmmakers have long looked on the montage as an expedient in favor of the production budget. Many sequences in screenplays have been condensed to a montage treatment, both to shorten the running time of the picture and to reduce the cost thereof. Yet, on a cost per foot basis, the montage can be the most expensive type of filmmaking, since a variety of sets and camera setups are used without accomplishing the shooting of an appreciable number of pages; a thing that any assistant director will always abhor.

Montages take many forms; sometimes a series of quick cuts, involving erratic camera angles. Other times, shots are blended together, one on top of another, in a succession of long dissolves. But whatever form a montage takes, it is usually designed to cover quickly, in terms of screen running time, a long period in the story in which an actor goes through a decided change of character or circumstances.

Norman Jewison, in his splashy film *The Thomas Crown Affair*, used the multi-image screen as a modern version of montage. The purpose was the same; to heighten the impact of a sequence and to shorten the running time of the film.

The new directors have borrowed many techniques from the masters of the silent days, but *montage* does not seem to be one of them. An exception to this would, of course, be the commercial directors who appreciate the value of condensing a succession of ideas into the shortest possible time.

Today's erratic tempo and cutting would seem to make a virtue out of handling our drunken actor's downfall in as abrupt a fashion as possible; one shot of him looking at a bottle, another lifting it in contemplation, while the last shot would have him unshaven and lying in the gutter. Perhaps a concession to today's more sophisticated audiences.

Director Robert Wise uses his director's finder to line up a shot for the cameraman. The small finder approximates the lenses on the camera and tells the director what he is going to get on film. Wise directed the all-time largest-grossing motion picture, The Sound of Music. *(United Artists)*

9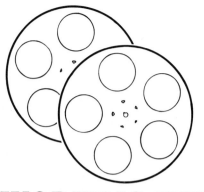

WORKING WITH
THE FILM EDITOR

The Editor as Extension of the Director

While shooting his picture, the director will from time to time confer with the film editor about the manner in which the scenes he has filmed should be treated in the cutting room. He will usually attend the *rushes* in the evening after he has finished the day's shooting, and view the film shot on the previous day. The director will make suggestions to the editor, explaining what he had in mind on the set, for the director must at all times while shooting visualize how the various shots will go together.

The director's work is far from finished when he has photographed and canned the last take of the picture. For now starts the sometimes long and arduous editorial process that includes the selection of the best takes and angles, the forming of the first *rough cut*, the trimming and tightening of the picture to improve the pace and tempo, the addition of sound effects, musical score, optical effects, such as *fades* and *dissolves*, titles, and the final *dubbing* that transfers as many as ten sound tracks to one. Then the *answer print* is made, and the picture is ready for the preview—an event in which the director is vitally interested.

The director's store of knowledge pertaining to the many facets of film production should include a thorough background in the techniques of editing. Cutting is just another extension of the director's ability to tell a story well, derive good performances from his actors, and in general to entertain. As he must know his camera, he must know the secrets of editing, for in the small fireproof cutting room lies an ever-present danger. Good actors can be made to look less than adequate, and a director's painstaking efforts toward style can be obscured, while pace and tempo can completely disappear. It is for these reasons the conscientious director will supervise the editing and make sure that his ideas are faithfully transformed into the *final cut* of the picture.

Although the Directors Guild has a firm agreement with all of Hollywood's studios which, on paper, insures the director's right to direct the cutting of the first rough cut, there is nothing to prevent the studio, or its representatives (usually the producer) from recutting the entire picture, and in some cases this has been done.

There have been directors who practically "cut in the camera"; in other words, they shoot the film so that the cutter has a minimum of editorial freedom. John Ford was a pioneer in this respect. Those who take this course had better be right, for many errors in shooting can be fixed in the cutting room, provided there is sufficient film shot, enough angles to enable some editorial latitude. While on this subject, it might be well to mention, that many an ordinary picture has been literally saved by an astute film editor who took an imaginative approach to the film and in a sense created what really wasn't there.

The first cut of *High Noon* was a disappointment to both its producer, Stanley Kramer, and its director, Fred Zinnemann. The film editor then started to experiment on his own. He took the final portion of the film, wherein Gary Cooper attempted to enlist the support of the townspeople in his pending confrontation with the killers, and condensed it to exactly one hour of screen running time, making it conform to the fictional time in the script. The effective cutting to various clocks in the town as time ran out served to heighten the tension and make the audience become involved with Cooper in his frustration.

In the sometimes hectic pace of television production, the director seldom sees a rough cut, if at all. He is usually engaged in filming another show at another studio when the rough cut is shown; so the right of the director seeing and approving the first cut is a theoretical one. Only on feature pictures can the director be assured of the opportunity to follow through in the various phases of editing.

The director who can pick a roll of film and its corresponding *sound track*, *sync* them together, then run them in the *Moviola*, is well ahead of the game, for this process is the mainstay of all editing. The various takes are viewed, selected, trimmed, and then spliced into the *makeup reel*, one at a time, and in their proper script sequence.

Sound in motion pictures has evolved through three separate and distinct eras: *sound-on-disc*, which came first, *sound-on-film*, which carried either variable area or variable density optical modulations, and the now almost universally used *sound-on-tape*, with its invisible magnetic impulses which reproduce sounds with amazing fidelity.

In editing, there is greater latitude in the cutting of sound tracks

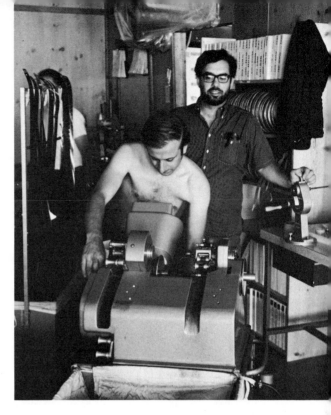

Francis Ford Coppola (right), an ex-student of cinema at UCLA, supervises the editing in the cutting room. The machine, called a Moviola, runs the separate sound track and picture in synchronization, runs forward and backward, and is the standard item of its kind in cutting rooms throughout the United States. (American-Zoetrope)

than the picture itself. A faulty reading on an actor's part can be fixed by substituting a sound track from another take and synchronizing it carefully over the best visual take. During editing, after shooting has closed down, a retake sometimes can be avoided simply by calling one actor back for a *wild line*, which is then matched to an over-the-shoulder shot that doesn't reveal the actor's lips.

Many times I have completed an intricate moving shot, which took an hour or so to line up and shoot, only to have the sound man come to me and say that one line did not record well. Rather than to shoot the entire scene over again and risk some other mechanical or human error, I have relied on the skill of the film editor and ordered a wild track of the single line that needed redoing. The actor simply reads his line into the microphone sans camera, and the tape is dispatched to the cutter with the proper notation.

Since editing involves the joining of scenes, the director should know the various methods involved and their time-space implications. Although some of the techniques of cutting have been passed up in recent years, old styles have a way of becoming new again. It is in this respect that the traditional methods are enumerated here. The *straight cut* is the basic manner of bridging one scene with the next and usually denotes consecutive or continuous action. The *fade out* and *fade in* (which involves the gradual going to black and vice versa) is used to denote the maximum passage of time or a complete disassociation with the preceding scene.

The *lap dissolve*, where one scene blends into the next, is usually used to eliminate unnecessary action, but also is substituted for the fade-in and fade-out, simply as a device to maintain the forward movement of the picture. In simpler terms, the fade-out is the director's period mark; the dissolve, his comma.

The lap dissolve has found many tricky variations, and each can have its special significance. The *wipe*, a sharp line moving across the screen to make the transition from one shot to the next, usually brings the feeling of accelerated pace, while the *flip-over* blends one scene with the next much in the manner that a page in a book is turned. There are at least fifty variations of the trick wipe, each of which causes the audience to be reminded that here is a mechanical trick interloping into their consciousness that would much better be served by being trained on the story.

Wipes and dissolves and other similar optical effects to denote the passing of time or the elimination of unnecessary action have all but disappeared in the modern motion picture. Today's filmmakers use the *direct cut* to bridge two sequences, completely disregarding the traditional use of optical effects. The technique, strangely enough, was born out of the advent of color to television. Optical effects in color were much too expensive, so producers started releasing their films without any. The crisp, abrupt style caught on and now major motion pictures (which can well afford dissolves and wipes) use direct cuts with mixed results. As in any technique, there is a time and a place for its use.

The mark of good editing is to put the many takes and scenes of a motion picture together in such a manner that the smooth flow of the dramatic action is not interrupted, and the audience's attention is not diverted to the editing itself.

Perhaps the most basic of the many techniques involved in film editing is what is known as *matching action*, or splicing two pieces of film together in such a manner as to cause the splice to be unnoticed. Let us suppose we wish to join a medium shot of our leading man with a close-up of the same action. We will view the two pieces of film on the Moviola, and search for a place in the action that is common to the two takes. For instance, the actor may have reached for a cigarette just before he spoke his line in one angle, while in the other angle he spoke the line, then reached for the cigarette. (A good script clerk would not have allowed this to happen). The two pieces of film are closely scrutinized, and finally a place is found on each that will make a smooth cut—in

THREE EDITORIAL TRANSITIONS

STRAIGHT CUT

LAP DISSOLVE

FADE-OUT (IN)

The most elemental of the editorial transitions is the straight cut, and yet it is used most in the modern motion picture. When the industry went to color almost exclusively, dissolves and other optical effects became too expensive, and filmmakers found that the straight cut gave films a "new" look.

The lap dissolve for years denoted the elimination of unnecessary action. In the above illustration, dissolving eliminates the carousers going home and takes the audience directly to next day's luncheon club meeting. Today's no-nonsense cutting technique would do the same thing in a direct cut.

Up until the mid-forties, the fade-out and fade-in were used to denote the passing of time, but this tended to slow down the action. Fades were replaced by dissolves and now are almost completely confined to the very beginning and end of a film.

other words, the actor's head, lip, and body movements match between the two scenes. The film is snipped, the takes joined together with paper clips (awaiting the assistant cutter's job of splicing), and then wound up on the reel.

A director should understand thoroughly the problems that can arise in the editing room. He should learn at once the fact that a smooth cut is achieved by *cutting on movement*. This means that, other things being equal, the editor would splice the two takes somewhere during the actor's action of taking out and lighting the cigarette. Or, he would cut on the actor's movement as he rises or turns or in some way causes movement.

The director who wishes to win the respect of his film editor will always *overlap* his action from one camera angle to the next. For instance, our leading man has sat on the couch in a medium shot and has carried on a conversation with the leading lady. He has reached for a cigarette and lighted it, and the editor has chosen this spot to cut to a close-up to smoothly make the transition to the closer angle. The actor, after a page of dialogue, rises and heads for the door, and the editor accordingly *cuts back* to the medium shot at the spot where the actor starts to rise, again choosing a place in movement to join the two scenes. Unless the director has the actor rise out of each shot, both medium and close-up, the overlapping of action will not occur; and the editor will not be able to find a common spot in movement between the two pieces of film so that a smooth cut can be made. He may have to resort to a *cut-away* shot, provided the director has made one. A cut-away is any shot that can be used to divert the audience's attention and is sometimes used to avoid a direct mismatch of action.

The casual visitor to a movie set sometimes hears the director turn to the script clerk after a take and say, "All right, print that—and we'll *pick it up.*" What he is saying, in effect, is that the scene was good to a point and that only the balance of the action need be done again. So the actors return to their positions, the director tells them from what point in the dialogue or action they will start, and the camera turns. But, here lies danger, lurking silently, only to show itself later in the cutting room— unless the director remains alert.

There are only two ways in which a scene can be picked up and expected to cut in with a previous take. First, the director must provide a shot that will *bridge* the action, such as a close-up to be inserted between the last part of the preceeding take and the first part of the succeeding take. Second, the director must change his angle or picture size on the pick-up shot to allow the film editor to splice it to the preceeding take in case there is no logical bridge shot. This follows the rule that no two shots made from the same identical point of view should be cut together.

IMAGE SIZE IN CUTTING

In editing the various pieces of film in a given sequence, only shots that vary image size sufficiently will cut together smoothly.

Assuming camera remains in one place, these lenses will provide enough change in image size to make good cuts:

From	To
18 mm	30 mm
30 mm	50 mm
35 mm	50 mm
40 mm	75 mm
50 mm	75 mm
75 mm	100 mm

THESE SHOTS WILL CUT SMOOTHLY:

50 mm

75 mm

40 mm

75 mm

SO WILL THESE:

30 mm

50 mm

35 mm

50 mm

BUT THESE SHOTS WILL NOT CUT SMOOTHLY:

30 mm

35 mm

35 mm

40 mm

Many times a scene plays perfectly in "one"; in other words, the movement of actors and camera around the set makes unnecessary the insertion of close-ups. The problem arises, then, of how to make a pick-up and properly bridge the parts of two different takes. A simple solution is to first determine at what point the two takes should be cut together. If at this point the preceding scene is in a medium shot, all that is necessary is to move the camera into a close-up of one of the actors, then as the succeeding scene gets under way, dolly back to the medium shot and resume. If, in the preceding scene, the camera was in a close-up of one of the actors, the succeeding scene should start either in a close-up of the other actor or in a medium shot of both.

Although the subject of lenses is covered more thoroughly in a previous chapter, their use in relation to editorial techniques should be mentioned here. Since it has been established that cutting from one shot to another without changing angle or picture size makes for an awkward *jump cut*, there are two ways to vary the angle; one, to move the position of the camera itself, and two, to change lenses.

Let's say that a scene is being made with a 40 mm lens and the director wishes to pick-up without otherwise cutting away from the scene. If he wishes to increase the size of the subject, that is, bring it closer, he must resume shooting with a 75 mm lens. Cutting from a shot made with a 40 mm lens to one made with a 50 mm lens will not sufficiently change the angle to make a smooth cut. Similarly, if the director is using a 35 mm he must follow with at least a 50 mm to provide the proper change in screen size.

A full understanding of the film editor's problems will cause the director to avoid mistakes on the set that can not be rectified in the cutting room. Many shots are put aside and never reach the screen because the editor finds it difficult to fit them together with their counterparts. An instance of such a shot, which is doomed to end up on the cutting room floor, is the one where the only logical point to make a cut is in the middle of a dolly movement. Let's say our leading man is about to read a key line to our leading lady, casting suspicion on her for some ignominious deed. For dramatic emphasis, the director decides he would like to dolly in on the leading man just as the accusation is made, forgetting the dictates of the scene as a whole. The shot of the man is made, and the camera dollies in at the proper moment. Then, the corresponding reaction shot of the leading lady is made and the sequence is complete.

The director will discover his mistake soon enough, either as he views his dailies in the projection room, or when he becomes involved with the editor in the putting together of his first rough cut. It will be obvious that he dollied in to the leading man at an inopportune time, because for the scene to play properly, the lady's reaction shot must be cut in immediately after the man makes his accusation. But, because the camera was in movement at the precise moment that the audience should see the lady's reaction, an awkward cut must be made or the reaction shot dropped altogether.

Sometimes this situation is compounded because the director has ordered the camera to dolly on the reaction shot as well. The director must fully visualize the proper sequencing of all his shots *as he makes them,* particularly in the matter of camera movement. He must decide where effective camera work should be utilized, and confine it to scenes that do not call for the cutting away to other shots. He should literally "cut in the camera" in relation to camera movement as he builds his scenes one by one throughout the shooting of a picture, but he should not fail to *cover* himself, that is, to provide the editor with more than one take of each scene. This is a protection of which every professional director avails himself, for many things can go wrong between an okayed take on the set and the assembling of a rough cut. Purely technical matters, such as a scratched negative in the camera or a damaged piece of film in the laboratory, can completely eliminate the use of any given take. If the director only shot the scene once, and from only one angle, a costly retake must be made. Many times a director has ordered a print on a scene, has rushed forward to congratulate the actors on their performances, and has then turned to the crew and said, "Now, let's do one for protection."

Directors, such as John Sturges, Mark Robson, and Robert Wise, have one thing in common; their pictures have a slick craftsmanlike look to them, composed of a succession of perfectly balanced shots, flowing gracefully from one to the other, and containing smoothly coordinated camera movement. These three men were top notch film editors before becoming directors, and they have never forgotten the importance of what they learned years ago in the cutting rooms.

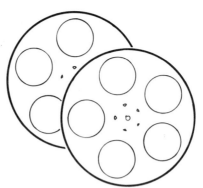

THE DIRECTOR'S INFLUENCE
ON PERFORMANCES

The Director's Medium

Films have been called the director's medium.

The theater has been called both a playwright's and an actor's medium.

Unlike a stage director who, in lengthy rehearsals, guides his actors through a series of sustained performances, the film director must do his job in bits and pieces, fitting them together like a giant jigsaw puzzle. He may be required to shoot the end of his picture first, and he may shoot several sequences that are at opposite ends of the emotional spectrum all on the same day. In the theater, the director builds his drama gradually from beginning to end, and watches it emerge as a total creation; but in motion pictures the director, as he creates each shot, each scene, must know how it will fit in with the one it follows or the one it precedes. He, and he alone, is held responsible for the correct level of performances, characterization, and mood in each of the hundreds of nonconsecutive bits that he fashions up one by one. He does not depend on the actors to give him a sustained performance, but rather they depend on him to *construct* a performance, which will appear sustained.

Charlton Heston is one actor who agrees with this: "I believe that the stage director is less important [than the film director]. On a stage, no matter how much the director gives you or how talented he is, on opening night he goes across the street and gets smashed because there is nothing he can do once the curtain goes up. Very few directors can bear to watch the whole thing through because it can be an agonizing experience. On the screen the director is practically the whole picture. When an actor realizes the way film is made and the way an actor's performance is used, it becomes clear that he must depend on the director in a far more complete sense."

Heston firmly believes that in films the actor depends on the director so completely that there must almost be a father relationship. An actor can assess his performance on the stage, but in films he cannot always tell whether it is working or not. Therefore, declares Heston, an actor must trust his director's taste, intelligence, experience, and judgment.

Two Kinds of Acting

To gain a proper insight into the profession of acting, especially as it relates to direction, the director should familiarize himself with the two major styles of acting, the *method*, and the *technical*. An actor who is called a technician has as his heritage the thousands of years of the theater itself. His main concern is to portray the character the way the author created it; and this technique probably reached its peak during the days of the traveling stock companies, wherein an actor would be called upon to do a variety of roles each week, changing back and forth from character to character, and portraying each one with conviction and skill. Modern television has been compared with the days of stock, since its insatiable appetite provides a variety of roles to Hollywood's more competent performers.

The method actor approaches his assignment from an altogether different viewpoint. He doesn't just want to act the part, he wants to *be* the part. He relies on improvisation and the inspiration of the moment. He must be *in the mood* before he can do a scene. He can't *turn it on and off* the way the technician does.

The great Stanislavsky, director of the Moscow Art Theatre, developed the method style of acting and directing over sixty years ago, but it did not become popular in America until sometime in the 1930's. Following it, came a rash of "method" plays—all down beat, all about the "little man," each consistently unromantic and realistic. As these plays began to reach the screen, Hollywood became aware that there was another kind of actor besides Clark Gable and Errol Flynn. Marlon Brando and James Dean arrived on the scene and were instant successes. Flynn's romantic flourish and Gable's manly stride were replaced with Brando's slouch and stammering speech. Soon the *method* influenced the direction of pictures, and Elia Kazan turned out the startlingly realistic *On the Waterfront*, which was made on natural locations in New York with method actors and some nonprofessionals. The film was an instant success at the box office and won several Academy Awards for its artistic merit.

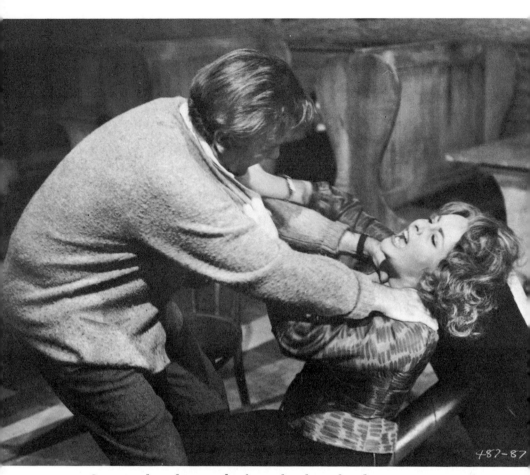

Scenes such as this must be directed and acted with great care to avoid "hamminess." Here Richard Burton vents his anger on Elizabeth Taylor in a drunken domestic quarrel in Who's Afraid of Virginia Woolf? *Directed by Mike Nichols. (Warner Bros.)*

With Hollywood rapidly forming sides in the preference of acting styles, it becomes more apparent that certain directors are better at one thing than another. The romantic, the escapist, and the fanciful have their proponents, while the realistic and downbeat themes attract other directors.

When I directed *This Rebel Breed*, for Warners', I found myself in a sea of youthful method actors. The film, a hard-hitting realistic exposé of crime in high schools with an overtone of juvenile racial intolerance, had

Sometimes directors "jump right in" with the actors. Director Blake Edwards (in trunks) shoots a scene for Experiment in Terror. *Stefanie Powers has just received an imaginary blow from her unseen assailant. Here is an ideal place for the handheld camera.* (Columbia)

for one of its highlights a rather shocking scene. Three youthful gang members had captured a Negro teenager, a member of an opposing gang. The white leader ripped the Negro's shirt off and said, "You guys are all talkin' about integration—well, we're goin' to integrate ya." With that, he dipped a large brush into a can of white paint, and while the Negro struggled futiley, he was painted white, body, hair, face, and all.

When the scene was over, the actor who had so worked himself up to hate the Negro in order to give a realistic performance dashed off to his dressing room. Ten minutes later, he was still sobbing.

"I feel so ashamed," he said, uncontrollably.

I tried to explain to him that *he* didn't hate Negroes, that it was only the character he was playing. It took an hour to bring him back to reality. While shooting, he had literally become the character of the race-hating gang leader.

In This Rebel Breed, *three white gang members capture a rival black gang member and "integrate" him by painting him white. This scene caused one of the white actors to break down from a sense of guilt. The actor had literally "become" the race-hating character he was portraying, an extreme example of method acting. Directed by Richard L. Bare. (Warner Bros.)*

Dealing with Emotion

Someone once said, "If you want me to weep, first you must grieve." The audience will not be *moved* by a picture unless the actors feel strongly the emotions of the screenplay they are performing.

For a director to reproduce emotion in a scene and to thereby stimulate the emotions of his audience, he must be an individual so constituted as to be himself *moved* by a good dramatic work. The man who has gone to the movies and has not shed a tear at one time or another is certainly not the one to try to make others cry.

The writer may cause an audience to become interested in a character, but the director must make the audience *care* about him. It is this state of *caring* that causes the emotional reaction known as *empathy*, otherwise described as the complete understanding of another's feelings.

When William Wyler made *Ben-Hur*, he demonstrated his skill as a director. He took a multimillion dollar pageant and, by telling a story of human beings in personal terms, created an empathic response in the audience. He made galley slaves, leprosy, and chariot races seem as familiar to the audience as if they were watching events in the twentieth century. A similar picture, *The Ten Commandments*, reached lavish heights of production and told a similar story; but it lacked the emotional vibrations that helped the audience find identification with the characters on the screen.

Whether an audience will receive an emotional response to a film depends on many things—the general character of the script, the sensitivity of the actors, and, of course, how adroitly the film is directed. Unfortunately, a thing as delicate as emotion cannot be measured, since the very stimulus of the emotion may mean different things to different people. A simple expression, "I don't want to die," can vary in emotion from one actor to another. What sounds right for one can be "overboard" for another. How can the director tell when the line is properly read?

A scene may call for one character to scorn another, or there may be a situation where a father grieves over his dead son. Attempting to achieve genuine emotion, the director may only extract "corn." What, then, can guide the director in this delicate and elusive area?

He cannot learn how to achieve emotion from reading books on film directing. He cannot learn it from watching others act or direct.

It is akin to the ageless question, "What makes one painter better than another?" Both may paint the same scene, use the same paints and canvas, but one picture will bring an emotional reaction from the viewer, while the other is just a painting. So it is with the art of directing. The mechanical techniques of picture-making, the basics of dramatics and playwrighting can be mastered by the would-be director; yet unless he is born with or develops a high degree of taste and sensitivity, he will never become a fine director.

Occasionally an actor will be cast in a key role, and it will become apparent that he lacks the ability to create emotional values. The director may be a sensitive individual himself, but his problem remains how to transfer his feelings to the actor. Émile Franchel, the well-known teacher of hypnosis, tells of instances in which inadequate actors gave emotionally moving performances while under the spell of a hypnotist. Linda Darnell once used the services of a hypnotist to facilitate the memorization of many sides for a stage performance in Chicago. She had been called on to do the show on short notice, and this method apparently aided her to absorb the voluminous dialogue. But, short of becoming a Svengali and hypnotizing his actors, what can the director do to stimulate the actor into feeling a scene?

George Stevens once went to a great deal of trouble to bring genuine emotion to a scene while he was directing *The Diary of Anne Frank*. Anne and her family had been hiding for some time in Nazi-occupied Holland when they were to look through their window and see an American plane, their symbol of hope, blasted out of the sky.

One of the biggest earners among child stars, Jackie Coogan benefited little from his money. Legislation called the Coogan Law forced parents of other kid actors to preserve their wages and hold them in trust. Jackie was bounced around in another way, too. When his director wanted Jackie's tears to flow, he would tell him that his dog had just been killed.

Stevens told his players that here was a friend, trying desperately to help them; and that when it was shot down by the Germans, they should not feel sorry for themselves, but rather, they should think of that flyer as a human being with a wife and children, dying for the cause of freedom. The prop man rigged up a cut-out silhouette and when projected on a large backing, the outline of a small plane moved across the sky. A flash bulb would explode to indicate the plane being hit by antiaircraft, and the image of the plane would sink toward the ground. None of this, of course, was in view of the camera; it was merely to stimulate the actors. When Stevens was ready to make a take, the actors were well conditioned to the mechanics of the scene and were ready to let their emotions go. But Stevens hadn't told them everything. As the take progressed, and the plane fell, the actors heard something other than George Stevens's voice as he told them the story of the lone Yankee flyer. A carefully hidden record player was filling the sound stage with "The Star-Spangled Banner." The actors were suddenly moved, and the tears flowed copiously. They were playing Dutch Jews, but they reacted as Americans, and Stevens got his scene.

Jackie Coogan told me what his director did to him when he was a five-year old in early Chaplin pictures like *The Kid*. Just before he was expected to cry, the director walked up to Jackie, holding an opened telegram, and said, "Jackie, I'm afraid I have bad news. Your dog, Spot, just got run over by a car."

Jackie, of course, broke out into tears, and the camera ground out true emotion. Manufactured somewhat cruelly by the director, genuine feeling came across to the audience, and little Jackie Coogan endeared himself to millions.

Establishing emotional values in actors can be easy, difficult, or impossible, depending on the person involved. Some respond quickly, while others need much help from the director. Stanislavsky maintained that we know only the emotional experiences that we have lived, and the actor may recall these and apply them to the role he is doing. He called this method the *memory of emotion*. If the scene calls for the actor to mourn for a relative, he may be able to transfer a similar past emotional experience from his real life to that of the character he is playing, and the director can do much to effect that transference.

How many times have you come out of a theater or moved away from your television set saying, "I don't believe it"? You may have been impressed by many things in the production, but there was something about the performances that didn't quite ring true. What probably was at the root of this trouble was a lack of *sincerity* or the presence of *false emotion*.

It is the director's job to inspire truthful performances, to make his actors *really believe* the character and scene they are portraying; for if the actor fails to believe it, the audience certainly won't.

The director must be a sounding board, ever vigilant for the first sign of insincerity. Inexperienced or incompetent actors display insincerity by tending to overact, and the director's only defense against such an actor is to somehow manipulate him into underplaying. The most often-used phrases by directors who find themselves in this predicament are,

"Try the line again, completely flat," or, "Do it once more, simply, ever so simply." One prominent television actor is a genuinely sincere person in real life, but as soon as he hears the director call "action," one eyebrow lifts and he starts to "act." He has not yet discovered the all-important key to sincerity in performing.

Working with Actors

Each director has an individuality just as each actor does. In every walk of life people meet people they like—and do not like. The matter of *chemistry*, as it is sometimes called, can become a great factor in the rela-

Anthony Quinn (left) and director Stanley Kramer discuss the script during filming of The Secret of Santa Vittoria. *After an initial setback with his first production, Kramer went on to become one of the Hollywood "greats" with* The Defiant Ones, Judgment at Nuremberg, *and* Guess Who's Coming to Dinner. *(United Artists)*

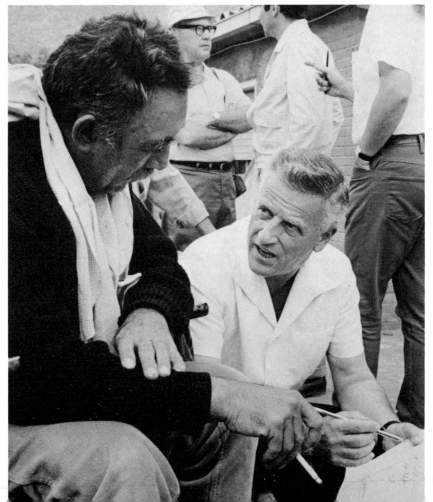

(ABOVE, LEFT)
The Wild Bunch, *directed by Sam Peckinpah, was a high point in movie violence. Death scenes were explicit and gruesome, almost to the point of being sickening. Here an actor is about to jump on a blood-soaked victim for good measure.* (Warner Bros.)

(ABOVE, RIGHT)
Violence in motion pictures is not always faked. Richard Rust does a realistic stunt in This Rebel Breed, *which points up the hazards of acting.* (Warner Bros.)

tionship between the director and his actors. When two people hit it off, great achievements can result. When they do not, the achievements may occur, but it most certainly will involve greater effort.

When the director begins to work with an actor, he must first size him up as a human being. In the theater, this process of analyzation may continue over several weeks. But, in pictures and television, the director must appraise his actors' personalities quickly, often within moments on their first meeting. Similarly, actors go through the same procedure, for they, too, must discover as quickly as possible a common meeting ground with the person who will be directing their performances. Methods that work with one person will not work with another. Some people are outward, expansive, and approach the job of acting in a businesslike manner. Others are introverted, childlike, and sensitive to small hurts. One can be talked into a performance, the other must be inspired to give one. Some can be given instructions so the whole crew can hear, others must be taken off to one side for an intimate discussion. It is the director's duty to determine what kind of personality he is working with, then decide how to handle it.

When the preliminaries of getting acquainted are over, the director can devote his attention to the problem at hand, transferring the author's word into film. First, he must make sure that the actors understand thoroughly the meaning and purpose of the story, that they understand that each scene and character are there for a reason. With the leading players, this early indoctrination comes with office meetings or prepro- duction rehearsals, but the exigencies of television filming may find the director and his principals getting acquainted, discussing the roots of the story and rehearsing the first take simultaneously.

The director must see to it that each actor knows the interrelation- ships of the central characters and especially what his role contributes to the whole. He must instruct the makeup man in the use of any special character makeup, and be certain that the wardrobe provided fits in with the general feeling of the scene.

Above all, in cases of shooting out of continuity, he must make sure that the actors understand fully just where the scene they are doing fits in the story.

While we are on this point, one of the pitfalls that can plague the new director concerns his own understanding of the juxtaposition of the individual scenes. Sometimes a director will shoot a scene without bothering to even reread the scene that will play just prior to the one he is filming. The attitudes, physical condition, and the like of the perform- ers must match from the end of one scene to the beginning of the next, and unless care is given to this detail an unevenness will result.

During the rehearsals just prior to filming, it will become apparent to the director whether he is working with Hollywood picture actors long used to the microphone, or whether New York stage actors have been hired for the job. When too much *projection* or playing to the balcony occurs, the director must caution his actors to use a natural, intimate voice level. With other inexperienced types, usually female, he must bring their voices up to a proper recording level lest the sound man complain.

By the time several takes have been made and the best one printed, it will have become apparent whether the director has cast his actors correctly. If an actor is right for the part, emotionally and physically, the director will receive his reward. He may have selected the actor after hearing just a few lines read and instinctively felt that this was the person for the role. Of course, his judgment is not confirmed until the actor has fully gotten into character and with makeup and wardrobe completed the visual impression. Even in character roles that do not demand the addition of makeup or even wardrobe, the true actor will *look* the part after he has started to *feel* the part. This getting into character by a stage actor is usually done as he stands in the wings preparatory to making an entrance. In films, a different set of circumstances prevail, too often to the detriment of the player. Attempting to get into character, the film actor searches the floor for his chalk mark, dodges the assistant cameraman's tape measure while bells ring frantically, the assistant director shouts for quiet, and the sound slate claps loudly right under his nose. The director calls "action," and the actor is expected to make you believe that he is truly shaken by the news that his wife has left him for another man.

Early film directors gave instructions to their actors by using the word *register*. "Register surprise," they would say, and the actors would respond promptly with quivering nostrils, raised eyebrows, and popping eyes.

Today, the good actor gets to the root of the emotion, imagines the mental and emotional processes that the character would go through. His face and eyes will show a change all right, and not with a superficial expression, but with something real. He doesn't register, he creates.

Sometimes a leading role will be filled before the director has been assigned and if there has been no time for rehearsals or preproduction conferences, a player will walk on the set with a preconceived idea of characterization not in accord with the author's, the producer's, or the director's.

Roy Huggins, whose success with *Maverick* at Warner Bros. catapulted him into the vice-presidency of Twentieth Century-Fox television, had fashioned a political satire and I had been assigned to direct. Before starting to shoot *How Does Charlie Feel?*, which starred Cliff Robertson and Diana Lynn, Huggins and I had discussions about the pitfalls in this kind of comedy; the actors were to play it straight, right from the heart, just as they would in a drama. The situation would provide the humor; the actors should at no time try to be funny.

After the first day's shooting, it became apparent to me that Miss Lynn was not in tune with our philosophy. Although a capable and talented dramatic actress of considerable experience, she was playing it strictly for farce. After each take, I tried different ways to convince her that we were not making a wacky comedy and that a more honest approach to her characterization was in order. Miss Lynn, a beauteous but strong-willed leading lady, seemed to agree, but still when the cameras rolled each successive take, her performance changed but little.

That night, I pondered for a way to get her to change her concept, since the next day her truly important scenes would be coming up. It has never been my nature to create "scenes," to harangue or to direct in a dictatorial manner. Causing angry exchanges on the set can only lead to production delays—a thing no television show can afford. So, having a showdown was out. I had to find some subtle way to bring her into accord with the dictates of the script. I finally decided on writing myself a note, ostensibly from producer Huggins. The note would point out the trouble with Miss Lynn's performance and order several scenes retaken. I called Huggins at home, and he agreed to this method and even the forging of his name on the letter.

The next day, the assistant director, who also got a copy of the note, showed it to Miss Lynn. It pointed out that if, in comedies of this nature, the actors were having a ball, it was a certainty that the audience wouldn't. The retakes were made and Diana gave the performance that she had always been capable of. After that, whenever there occurred a tendency to slip back into her previous style, I merely alluded to the fact that I was sure that when Mr. Huggins saw the dailies another retake would be ordered. It worked fined and Diana Lynn was both attractive and sympathetic in the part. No actor enjoys having his scenes reshot while the other members of the cast and crew stand by watching.

Although it has long been a practice in the legitimate theater not to correct line readings until full memorization takes place and the character begins to take shape, it works in reverse in motion pictures. Perhaps the reason for this is due to the brief rehearsal period, sometimes less than five minutes before an actor must "go on." Whatever the reason, correcting misreadings and mispronunciations in early rehearsals seems to prevent the eventual forming of small mental blocks while filming a take. Many times the misreadings are due to a lack of understanding of the content of the scene and can be corrected easily. Other times, an actor may continue to misread a line because he believes that way to be the right one, or it may be because he is *tone deaf* and lacks the proper *ear* to hear the line any other way.

Many actors resent being given line readings by the director who then expects them to imitate him. Sometimes correcting a misreading by demonstration is simply an expedient, but more often, if the director will make use of his vocabulary in explaining the reason behind another reading, he will maintain the actor's good will and perhaps inspire him to give a better performance.

I have never seen a script so perfectly written that it justified the

George Stevens instructs Edgar Buchanan, Jean Arthur, and Ronald Coleman in their action preparatory to making a shot with one of the film industry's largest camera cranes. The huge device not only raises, lowers, swings in and out, but dollies along the special track at left. From Talk of the Town. *(Columbia)*

producer demanding "not a line be changed." The fact that an actor transposes, interpolates, or otherwise changes a line does not in itself become a violation. Only when he changes the meaning behind the line, or disrupts the next actor's cue, is it time to insist on "sticking to the script." Many times a better performance will result when the actor puts the thoughts expressed by the line into his own particular phrasing. The producer who disallows this freedom on the part of director and performer does himself a disservice, for restricting the actor in this respect hampers the free flow of creativity so important in the obtaining of a perfect scene. It will be perfect not because every word is delivered as the author wrote it, but because the idea behind the words is interpreted in a way natural to the character.

I have known actors who, because of their own lack of concentration, couldn't retain even the idea behind the dialogue. The more they would "blow" a line, the angrier they would get, and the first and logical target to attack was the writer. Invariably they use the same lines in expressing their vitriol, "How can anybody remember stupid words like these?"

It is true that well-written lines are learned quicker than cumbersome or *non sequitur* dialogue, but just as often these attacks on the writer are defensive maneuvers on the actor's part designed to cover up his own inadequacy.

Sometimes actors can remember pages of dialogue but have trouble with one small line. I have known of instances where they will write the line on a little slip of paper and hide it behind a vase or some other object on the set.

Actors study their lines in many different ways. Some stay up half the night, pacing the floor while being cued by a friend or relative. Others get up early in the morning, and with a fresh and rested mind, absorb dialogue with ease. Many actors never look at their lines until

Director Blake Edwards poses with his whipped-cream-covered cast after the pie-throwing sequence of The Great Race. *Almost identifiable are: Tony Curtis, center, in white; standing on table, left to right, Jack Lemmon, Natalie Wood, and Peter Falk.* (Warner Bros.)

they are seated in the makeup chair before the day's shooting, and then there are the lazy ones who wait until they can walk the rehearsals with the script in their hand.

The quickest study I ever worked with is John Carradine, who reads a script just once and remembers every line, word for word. He is blessed with a so-called "photographic memory" and can digest pages of dialogue with great facility.

A few years ago on *Dragnet*, Jack Webb made what he considered a virtue of the problem of memorization. He simply banned it. No actor was permitted to learn his lines, rather, Jack preferred him to read it off a machine called the Teleprompter, which contains a large roll of paper on which is printed the dialogue. The machine is controlled by an operator and the lines appear in front of the actor at whatever speed he chooses to deliver them.

Webb accomplished one thing with this technique. He was able to lop off many hours of shooting time through the virtual elimination of successive takes. In less skilled hands, this technique can produce stilted performances and many actors cannot adjust at all to the Teleprompter.

There is an axiom among people in show business that holds performing for the movies isn't acting, it's *reacting*.

The actor who merely stands, frozen faced, waiting for his cue, and then speaking his line, is only doing half the job he is being paid for. *Listening* can be one of the most important single techniques in the actor's repertoire, and he must *listen in character*. During rehearsals he has listened for his cues, listened to the remarks of the director and cameraman, but once the camera starts to turn, he must listen to the other actors' words as if he is *hearing them for the first time*. This is important, for unless he can accomplish this the scene will not carry with it the illusion that it is being performed in reality, or in other words, for the first time. If a player steps out of character while another is speaking and doesn't properly react through listening, the scene will result in a disjointed one-sided affair. Conversely, if he listens as if he is interested and hearing something for the first time, then thinks over his own reply before he delivers his line, a well-executed scene will result. An axiom of the drama is to "pick up your cues." However, sometimes too much emphasis can be placed on this rapid-fire delivery, and the scene suffers because the actors don't seem to be *listening*.

The alert and sensitive director will be quick to recognize when an actor *anticipates*. Since all drama is based on the premise that what is transpiring is happening for the first time, the actor who turns his head in anticipation of a sudden sound, or opens the door as if he knows who is on the other side is guilty of anticipation.

A scene that "plays," in other words comes alive with vitality or emotion, is usually a *master shot*. The actors were all in the same shot together and received the benefit of contact with one another. But, the demands of the film business require that the director *break it up*, or *cover* with additional shots, usually closer angles. When this happens, he comes to grips with a very real problem, that of re-creating the same spark from his actors when perhaps only one of them is on camera at a time with the others reading their lines off camera. In the master, there was no problem with *overlapping*, that is, picking up cues so fast that one actor starts to speak before the other actor finishes. But now the sound man cautions the director just as he goes into each close-up, "No overlaps, please." The director explains to the neophytes that the film editor can not make clean cuts on the sound track unless there is a separation of the spoken lines. This can change the flow of the scene considerably, and can result in shots that lack the vitality of the master. One way to solve this is to design the shooting in such a manner as to film fast moving and overlapping dialogue with a fluid camera, getting the entire scene in one continuous shot. If the actors are moved about, constantly changing positions and with the camera dollying in and out accenting first one and then another in close-up, many times a much better scene will result.

The director may determine that a key line of dialogue is worthy of emphasis, and in that event, will suggest that the actor pause just before delivering the line. Or, he may place emphasis on the line by having the actor rise or sit or walk toward the camera into a close-up. There are many ways to emphasize a line—by repetition, raising volume, lowering volume, or making it an exit line—and the director should decide which is appropriate to the scene.

If the locale of the film being directed is a foreign country, the question of accents will arise, usually in conferences with the producer before the start of the picture. Hollywood has always tended to require its actors to "flavor" their speech with the accent indigenous to the country that is being depicted. Yet, how wrong this seems when one reverses the situation and imagines German actors doing *A Streetcar Named Desire* in German with an American accent. A better rule to follow is this: when English-speaking actors portray characters in their native land, let them speak a neutral Standard American diction.

Stanley Kramer, who produced and directed *Judgment at Nuremberg*, solved a touchy translation problem in an imaginative way. As each witness was called to the stand and started speaking in German, the camera traveled inside the translation booth where his words were heard in English as spoken by the translators. As the camera moved back to the witness, he continued to speak, but this time in English. Audiences ac-

In directing television comedy, anything goes, just as long as all of *Eva Gabor's* charms are covered with soap bubbles. A scene from Green Acres, *directed by Richard L. Bare.* (Filmways)

cepted the device, grateful not to have to read the translation on subtitles.

Although every player should be well trained in the rudiments of acting, he may not be experienced in the mechanics of film acting, especially if he is from the theater.

An *on-camera* turn means that the actor makes his turn with his face nearest the camera. An *off-camera* turn means turning in front of the camera with his face upstage or away from the camera.

In crossing, for an actor to maintain strength, he crosses in front of the other actors or makes a downstage cross. If the director wishes him to be dominated by the other players, he makes an upstage cross. When two characters cross during dialogue, the upstage (and more important) actor walks slightly ahead of the other player.

In vaudeville, there was a stage area known as *in one*. It was as far downstage as the actors could get without stepping into the footlights. When two actors stand almost shoulder to shoulder in a two-shot facing the camera instead of each other, the *in one* feeling is reproduced. Comedy scenes are often filmed with this camera treatment. When one of the characters in this shot decides to make an exit, he should make a *long* side exit, with the camera slowly centering on the actor who is left behind. The actor who pops out of a scene on the short side of the frame actually gets away too fast, unless the camera pans with him.

Opening and closing doors sometimes can be awkward even for experienced stage actors. The ability to glide gracefully through a door is still one of the hardest for actors to master. If the door is on one side of the set, an actor making an entrance should grasp the knob with one hand, swing the door open, then pass through, and, without breaking the rhythm, grasp the knob with the other hand and close it behind him.

Phone conversations have a preferred technique peculiar to movie making. When photographing two people having a telephone conversation, each in close-up, they should be looking in opposite directions, so that during the intercutting of shots the impression will be strengthened that they are talking to one another. Most actors seem to make a habit of dialing all small numbers to get the business over with, I suppose, and some even forget to make that seventh revolution. Audiences pick up on small things and these inattentions to detail can mar an otherwise good scene.

The staging of a love scene, especially if photographed in full figure, should seem easy and natural, and skillful players usually have no difficulty. But with players less than skillful, the director should strive for a graceful and believable scene. The two actors embracing should stand close to one another; any other position would appear awkward. The position of the feet must be predetermined to avoid sudden collisions upon embracing. When the director shoots the same embrace in close-up, he must decide who's face is to be featured at the moment of the kiss or full embrace. The scene should be unhurried, with the accent placed on anticipation of the actual kiss, longing in the eyes, hands moving slowly upward to touch the shoulders or neck. And when the kiss is finished, it should not end too abruptly, but the players should linger again with their eyes, hands withdrawing slowly.

Rhonda Fleming, who has been kissed by Hollywood's top stars, said once: "Since you're usually kissing another star, it must be decided who's face is going to be shown in the camera, and then there's another problem. If you turn slightly to the right because you feel it's more complimentary (and if the leading man has the same idea) you're faced with a head-on collision of noses. And the worries still aren't over. The leading man is divine: strong, masculine, but two inches shorter than I am. I fall into his arms and gaze soulfully into his eyes, and I must admit he looks marvelous—even if he is standing on a box!

"Let's consider the ingredients that make any kiss romantic, forgetting the leading man, for the moment. A soft June night, a full moon, a quiet country lane—and solitude. In pictures, you have the full moon and the country lane, even though plaster of paris and plywood. But solitude? If you don't count the director, the cameraman, six grips, and twelve electricians, you might say you're alone."

If Miss Fleming thought she had a problem during the days of her reign as a Hollywood sex goddess, what do the female stars of today think about the lovemaking that is expected of them on the screen? Unless an actress can take her clothes off in full view of the crew without batting an eye, she has not reached the fountainhead of professionalism.

In the staging and direction of death and murder scenes, great care must be given to avoid the overemotional and the "hammy." Although expert direction and performances coupled with a convincing story can lull an audience into a sense that they are watching reality, no one for a moment believes it when a player dies or gets killed, therefore the director should strive for truth. If an actor has been shot and the script calls for him to be in great pain, his vitality should be at low ebb, for nothing mars a death scene as an actor speaking his last words in full voice or gesticulating with energy.

If he dies in bed, he should be immobile, his voice barely audible, his speech broken. When death comes, the head should relax and fall slightly to one side. Sometimes in a color picture, the cameraman will alter the light on the face from a natural skin tone to a grayish hue. Even in black and white, a slight dimming of the keylight only in the area of the face can give the illusion of life flickering out.

When a western character takes an imaginary .45 slug, he should either spin out or topple over backward. One may think the spin has been exaggerated by the movies, but in truth those western bullets crashed into a human being with tremendous force, sometimes knocking a man five or six feet. One has only to remember the bloody death scenes in Sam Peckinpah's *The Wild Bunch* to realize how far it is possible to go in depicting the horrors of death on the screen.

Every actor will appreciate the director's help in devising bits of business to go with the dialogue. The average television script has been so hurriedly written, that many times the writer only bothers to set down the dialogue, and it is incumbent on the director to provide pantomime action to further characterize his players. When I directed the pilot of *77 Sunset Strip*, I told Edd Byrnes, who played "Kooky," to comb his hair during one of the scenes. Six years later, it was still his trademark and even the subject of a popular record.

Perhaps the most difficult actors to direct are those who have become directors themselves. Because they know the director's secrets, they are more inclined to have opinions of their own regarding staging, camera treatment, and even of the performances of the other actors. One exception to this is Cliff Robertson, who worked with me after he had written, starred in, and directed a television show. Never once did he overstep the line that separates the actors from the director, and accordingly gave a superb performance. His concentration was on the character he was playing, not in the problems that beset the director.

As a last word regarding the director's relationship with actors, beware of the "close-up actor." He's the one, usually an old-time Hollywood player, who knows all the tricks. He has been known to fluff his lines deliberately in a group shot when sharing honors with several others, because he knows that is one way to force the director to cover his performance in a close-up. Strangely enough, he is always letter-perfect when the camera comes in close. Fortunately, among the thousands of actors in the movies and television today, the fellow who stoops to this kind of chicanery is in the minority.

Generally speaking, the director and his actors provide a solid superstructure to the foundation of the picture, the story, and with mutual admiration and respect can work together to create the ultimate in dramatic achievement—entertainment.

The Serious Field of Comedy

Years ago when this business was in its infancy, some harried producer uttered the now classic remark, "Our comedies are not to be laughed at!" What he meant was that turning out comedy film is a serious and exacting affair.

Although my own career started in comedy and I have directed more than three hundred of them, when I think of writing a chapter on the subject I realize how little can be put down on paper on the subject. The director who doesn't already *know* how to do it shouldn't attempt it. Unless it's within his unconscious nature to construct the tricky flow of comedy action, perfectly timed and properly staged from the correct angle of approach; unless he possesses a personal sense of humor and an appreciation for *all* humor, the director should stay in another field. However, there are several basics that can be passed on to the newcomer.

The pace of comedy is, of course, faster than in drama, but it should never be so frantic that there is no time for reactions. The funniest part of a Laurel and Hardy comedy was Ollie's reactions to Laurel's antics, and vice versa. Laurel scratched the top of his head and Hardy fussed

Working with animals is not the easiest of the director's multitude of chores, although Arnold of Green Acres *is one of the most accomplished four-footed actors in Hollywood. "He's a method pig," says director Bare.* (Filmways-CBS)

with his necktie while reacting to some nonsensical bit of slapstick. When an actor reads a funny line, it is funnier if another actor can play off the line, rather than going on with his own line. In television comedy these reactions are mandatory to provide the spaces for laugh tracks.

Normally, a good comedy director avoids long walks by his actors. Instead of the door opening and the actor making his entrance and walking across the room to the fireplace, camera panning, it is better to take one shot of him coming through the door and exiting the shot, then setting up at the fireplace and letting him enter this shot. What has been eliminated is five to ten seconds of unimportant movement and a consequent slowing down of the story. A staccato treatment in cutting is helpful in giving the scenes the pace they need, but not so frantic that they shorten the reactions of the people.

An iron-clad rule of comedy is that the comedians should never laugh at their own jokes. Play it straight, the experts maintain. And yet many television comedies do just the opposite, especially if the characters are portraying modern sophisticated types. Almost every funny line that Paula Prentiss and Dick Benjamin uttered in the charming television show *He and She* was followed with a slight laugh, which meant, "Of course, we're only kidding." The cast of *The Governor and J.J.*, with Dan Dailey, also followed this technique with apparent success. Perhaps the fact that these shows were not long-run successes can be traced to the audience's subconscious disapproval of the actors' apparent lack of sincerity. A comic situation in its total construction closely resembles a tragic one, and for the actors to be convincing, they must take it seriously.

Schopenhauer's theory of laughter maintains that we laugh when there is a sudden incongruity between concept and percept. This is important to remember, especially the word "sudden." Almost all comedy depends on the sudden incongruity to tickle our funny bones.

Suppose an actor enters a restaurant, goes to the counter, and sees a sign: "Our Food Untouched by Human Hands." He then looks beyond the counter and into the kitchen and sees a huge gorilla making hamburger patties. The laughter comes with the *sudden incongruity*. The secret is to not show the gorilla in the long shot that brings the actor into the restaurant.

The degree of ridiculousness of the incongruity determines the amount of laughter. I once shot a scene that had an actor carrying on a conversation with his friend at a lunch counter. He was eating a piece of pie, when the waitress came along and cleared the dishes, his partly eaten pie with it.

"Hey, I've only had one bite out of that!" the actor exclaimed.

With that, the waitress reached in the pie display, took out a fresh piece, took one bite out of it and placed it on the counter. The secret was not to tip to the audience what the waitress was about to do. She had to act like she was going to give the man a new piece of pie. When she took the bite out it had to done quickly so the incongruity between concept and percept would be sudden. It was a belly laugh in the theater.

The modern philosopher David H. Monro in his *Argument of Laughter*, has compiled a list of ten familiar circumstances which will produce laughter:

Schopenhauer's theory of laughter maintains that we laugh when there is a sudden incongruity between concept and percept. In this scene, the incongruity came when the above shot followed insert of a sign, "Our Food Untouched by Human Hands." (Warner Bros.)

1. Any breach of the usual order of events such as eating with chopsticks when one is accustomed to forks.

2. Any forbidden breach of the usual order such as belching in public.

3. Any indecency, such as a man caught outside his house in his underwear.

4. Any importing into one situation that which belongs in another such as a drunk at a funeral service.

5. Anything masquerading as something it is not, such as two men in a horse costume.

6. Plays on words, such as puns, spoonerisms, etc.

7. Nonsense, such as television's *Laugh-In.*

8. Minor misfortunes, such as a man who slips on a banana peel.

9. Any incompetence, such as the paperhanger who gets tangled up in his paper.

10. Veiled insults. (Wife: "To you marriage is just a word." Husband: "It's more than a word, it's a sentence.")

Although Monro can tell us the things we laugh at, he cannot with any accuracy tell us why we laugh. He concedes that to analyze a joke, or to track a comic situation to its source, is to make it disappear.

Many times a comedy writer will write a funny line of dialogue and yet when it is delivered by an actor it fails to get a laugh. This sometimes can be explained by showing that the actual laugh or the highpoint of the line is buried in the middle instead of at the end where it belongs. Here the director, by inverting the line, that is, placing the word or combination of words that provoke the laughter at the end of the line, cannot only insure the laugh, but in the case of television comedy, prevent the canned laugh track from covering the dialogue.

The full execution of comedy is not a simple matter. Many times an actor—the first time he has rehearsed the scene—will come up with marvelous nuances of expression or mannerisms. By the time the camera starts to roll, he has already lost some of the freshness he had in the first rehearsal. That is why I never over-rehearse a comedy scene, and if at all possible, I will print the first take. It takes an exceptionally skillful comedy technician to bring spontaneity to the eighth take.

It is important for the director to keep a relaxed atmosphere on the set. The director who goes around with a scowl on his face and who won't allow some levity among cast and crew has no place in comedy directing. The actors, particularly, must relax and enjoy their work otherwise the scene will lack the brightness and life so necessary to the playing of good comedy.

Working with animals is a part of directing comedy. Almost every television situation show involves a dog, monkey, or some kind of animal. For five years I directed the most difficult, the most temperamental, and the "hammiest" animal actor ever to gain stardom in Hollywood— Arnold, the pig. The creation of Jay Sommers, the producer of *Green Acres*, Arnold has found his way into the hearts of millions of television fans. His mail, believe it or not, is enormous. And warranted. Arnold signs his name with a crayon. Arnold turns on the television set. Arnold plays the piano. He's worn dark glasses, a French beret, and a World War I helmet and goggles. He laughs, cries, and carries his books to school, where I believe, he's in the third grade.

Directing animals requires infinite patience and a thorough knowledge of how to trick a performance out of them, in other words, making the animal appear to be giving a human response. I've dangled a live mouse in front of a dog to inspire an alert expression. Other times I've used a small rubber squeaker to make a kitten sit up and cock its head. But, with Arnold, my approach is on a higher level—I bait him with caramels and then whisper two words in his ear, "Oscar Meyer."

11

CREATING A JOB FOR YOURSELF

From Student to Professional

The aspiring director can read books such as this one, can take courses in cinema and dramatics at a university, can make superb amateur films, and then come to grips with a most perplexing question, "How do I get a job as a director?"

He may be armed with contacts, have letters of introduction, or be endowed with such a forceful personality that he obtains on his own interviews with producers and even heads of studios. And he will no doubt exude self-confidence as he articulately presents a formidable case for himself, maintaining that he will bring rich and imaginative skill to his directing assignment—if he could only be given the chance. He will also, no doubt, hear a time-worn phrase, "Get a little experience, then come back and see us."

How can he get experience if nobody will give him a job?

This is the problem and it is a serious one. But, it is not insurmountable, as I found out years ago. In fact, when I made the leap from amateur to professional, it was perhaps at the worst possible time in terms of the economic condition of the motion picture business. Today, with the tremendous output of television films, more directors work every week than ever before when only theatrical pictures were being made. The opportunity for the director to get his first chance is much simpler today, due to the less rigid demands for perfection that television has brought about. It is one thing to take a chance on a new director with a $75,000 film as one of a series on television against gambling from $250,000 to several million by entrusting him with a feature picture.

As I outlined in a previous chapter, people become directors in a variety of ways. They are elevated from other jobs within the industry itself; they come from the legitimate stage; they distinguish themselves in college film production; or the just simply create a job for themselves.

Dennis and Terry Sanders, while in school at UCLA, produced a twenty-three-minute 35 mm dramatic production, *A Time Out of War*. Dennis directed and Terry photographed. When it was completed the brothers arranged to have it exhibited on television. This led to a theatrical distribution deal with Universal and to date, Dennis and Terry Sanders have made better than twenty thousand dollars profit from their labor of love. The film won an Academy Award for the best theatrical short subject and won a similar honor at the Venice Film Festival.

A producer saw the film and promptly hired Terry to direct a second unit of *Night of the Hunter*. The boys had writing talent as well and went to work for Paul Gregory doing the screen play for *The Naked and the Dead*.

Steve Broidy of Allied Artists heard about the Sanders brothers and decided to back them in *Crime and Punishment, U.S.A.*, which they produced and directed.

Paul Wendkos has had a strong interest in films since his days at the University of Pennsylvania. After graduation he studied film courses at Columbia University, then started making documentary films for the State Department. His first attempt at commercial filmmaking came when he directed *The Burglar*, which Columbia later acquired. He considers this film a failure resulting from too much ambition combined with too little experience, but from it he began to develop a style that carried him through a score of feature films such as *Guns of the Magnificent Seven* and *Angel Baby*, the latter receiving festival showings at Venice and Berlin.

Sydney Pollack studied acting under Sanford Meisner then served as his assistant for five years, an apprenticeship that has given him a keen insight into the sensitivities of actors. He appeared in several Broadway productions and the old *Playhouse 90* series. This led to a lasting friendship with director John Frankenheimer who encouraged him to go to Hollywood where he got his first chance to direct a television western. He later won an Emmy for *The Game* on the Chrysler Theater program. His first feature assignment was *The Slender Thread*.

Stuart Rosenberg majored in literature and drama at New York University, graduating with a PhD, making him perhaps the only Hollywood director entitled to be addressed as doctor. But teaching couldn't hold Rosenberg and soon he was an apprentice film editor with a New York firm making television commercials. He soon worked up to full fledged editor, then he was given the chance to direct on the series

Sam Peckinpah likes to have his chair available when he's ready to sit down—which seldom happens on pictures such as The Wild Bunch. Peckinpah, a writer-director, is known for his hard-hitting, gutsy westerns. (Warner Bros.)

Russ Meyer, who graduated from 8 mm amateur films to 35 mm "nudies," makes final adjustments on fig leaf in Beyond the Valley of the Dolls, his first million-dollar film. (20th Century-Fox)

Decoy, starring Beverly Garland. After he switched to the *Defenders* series, he won the Emmy for best television director. Now exclusively a feature film director, Rosenberg comments: "The joy I experience directing for the big screen is not just the liberation from the necessity of the many close-ups, but the big thing is the sense of involvement with the audience. In television you never really know how your thing goes over. It's great to sit in a theater and feel the audience move with what you've created."

One director who made the transition from student filmmaker to professional came by way of developing a thorough background in the arts. Irvin Kershner studied painting under Hans Hoffman in Providence and music at Temple University. After transferring to the University of Southern California, he decided to concentrate his interests in the field of cinema. Already an accomplished still photographer, his work became an integral part of a book illustrating a collection of rare musical instruments. The artistry of the photographs caused more interest than the instruments themselves and soon young Kershner had a job shooting documentary movies overseas for the United States government. This led to a combined director-cameramen's job on a local television show in Los Angeles called *Confidential File*. But Kershner had higher ambitions so he and Andrew J. Fenady promoted thirty thousand dollars and turned out a black and white feature picture, *Stakeout on Dope Street*. Warner Bros. promptly bought it outright for a handsome profit to the youthful producer and director. Today, after many films, including *The Hoodlum Priest* and *Loving*, his sound artistic, photographic, and musical background clearly shows in all of Irvin Kershner's films.

Hubert Cornfield couldn't get anyone to give him a job as a director so he decided to become one anyway. He made a twenty-minute short called *The Color Is Red*. He did all the camera work and the editing as well. He financed the cost himself, did his own advertising campaign, and conducted his own sales deals direct with the theaters. A few years later he was directing films like *Sudden Danger* and *Pressure Point*.

Michael Sarne started his career as a professional actor in England while still attending London University. During his final year he recorded a "pop" record that became number one on the British hit parade. But Sarne had ambitions to become a film director so he made a short subject, *The Road to St. Tropez*, which won a prize at a film festival. An executive of 20th Century-Fox saw the short and this led to his being assigned to direct his first feature, *Joanna*, a picture which was both an artistic and financial success. After this Fox brought him to Hollywood where he was assigned to write and direct Gore Vidal's explosive best seller, *Myra Breckinridge*.

Mark Rydell was a jazz musician who tired of the night life so decided to become an actor. His fellow students at Lee Strasberg's Actors Studio were Steve McQueen and Sydney Pollack. When Rydell came to Hollywood, Pollack introduced him to a producer of television and soon he had his first chance to direct. After forty television shows, he was given his first feature film, *The Fox*. When Steve McQueen saw what his former classmate could do, he welcomed him as director of *The Reivers*.

John Cluett and Harry Mastrogeorge got together and produced a $60,000 mini-feature called *Cabbages and Kings*, which starred New York model Samantha Jones. Cluett, who produced, played one of the leading roles, and Mastrogeorge directed, having been Cluett's teacher at the American Academy of Dramatic Arts in New York. They hired a young graduate from UCLA's cinema department as their cameraman and got all the actors and crew members to work for practically nothing. In a time when sex scenes are more than explicit, there was no nudity in *Cabbages and Kings*.

Russ Meyer, who made a name for himself as "King of the Nudies" and who recently went respectable, budgetwise, that is, with a million-dollar Fox movie, started out as a boy camera fiend. At the age of fourteen, Meyer badgered his mother until she bought him a movie camera. A few years later he had made a documentary film about Catalina Island and won a prize in an amateur film contest. During World War II he became a combat cameraman for the Signal Corps. Later Meyer got an idea that there was money in shooting sexy scenes about sexy women. His first film, which he wrote, directed, produced, and photographed (a true *auteur*) was *The Immoral Mr. Teas*, a 16 mm film that cost in the neighborhood of twenty-five thousand dollars. The picture went on to gross a small fortune and Russ Meyer was established as the only director of sex films who showed some taste and imagination in his work. After a few years of turning out similar films, which included the highly sensational *Vixen*, 20th Century-Fox offered him the directorship of *Beyond the Valley of the Dolls*. Meyer, a personal filmmaker, refused much of the help the studio placed at his command preferring to "do his own thing."

Richard Rush, director of the Columbia film *Getting Straight*, studied cinema at UCLA. After graduation he worked in Hollywood as messenger boy, recording engineer, and still photographer. Then he went to an advertising agency, where he got his first chance to work with film on commercials. A few years later he owned his own commercial production company, which led to feature filmmaking. He produced, directed, and co-wrote *Too Soon to Love*, which was shot in record time and cost only $50,000. When he showed it to Universal they promptly made a deal that netted Rush and his backers some $200,000.

The youngest member of the Directors Guild of America, Steve Spielberg made 8 mm films at the age of twelve. He crashed the gates of Universal Studios by donning executive garb and waving at the gateman. By the time he was twenty-two he was directing Joan Crawford. (Universal)

Rush has this to say to the graduating film student: "If you want to be a director, direct. That's not so difficult nowadays. Working in 35 mm film is expensive, but 8 mm isn't. And the things that cost the most in a studio—actors, sets, scripts, etc.—are free to the amateur. The only cost is camera and film. When I started out, the goal of most filmmakers was to become the successful director of the commercial style movie. But that's all changed. For the first time, the commercial film is the art film. So now the film student can aspire to a much loftier goal—that of being an artist."

George Lucas, producer-director of Warner Bros. *THX 1138*, was a student of cinema at USC. He made a short film, also called *THX*, and won the National Student Film Festival Grand Prize in 1967 and was catapulted into the professional film world through a contract with Warners. It was only natural that he should adapt the film that brought him attention into a feature film.

Sometimes recognition comes when an amateur filmmaker takes his first step toward professional movie making. Take the case of Steve Spielberg who started early in his chosen profession and, as this book is written, is twenty-two years old and well on his way to success as a film director.

Steve knew exactly what he wanted to do in life from the moment he borrowed his father's 8 mm movie camera and took his first home movies. He made his first film complete with story and actors at the age of twelve after the family moved from Cincinnati to Phoenix, Arizona. He followed this with a five-minute western and got his photography merit badge in the Boy Scouts. By the time he was thirteen he had copped first prize in a film contest with a forty-minute war film, *Escape to Nowhere.*

"I really didn't have any formal instruction," recalls Steve, "I just started shooting, making over-the-shoulder shots, dolly shots, and everything I had seen on television."

When Steve reached sixteen and was in high school, his grades went down as his craze for filmmaking went up, for he had gone Hollywood in his ambitions. He turned out a 140-minute epic entitled *Firelight*, which

---

(LEFT)
Sydney Pollack explains what he wants to Burt Lancaster during the shooting of The Scalphunters, *a surprisingly good western that was made on a modest budget. Once an actor himself, Pollack came to Hollywood to direct Television and made the switch into features after winning an Emmy for his direction on the Chrysler Theatre.* (United Artists)

took a year to make and was complete with fancy titles, a music score, and a dialogue sound track. Even the budget was of astronomical proportions for Steve, a walloping five hundred dollars. The film was exhibited at the Phoenix Little Theatre with searchlights in the sky and all the hoopla of a Hollywood premiere. When Steve counted the money there was over five hundred dollars profit. He promptly put the money in his pocket, for he had financed the production entirely with his own funds earned while whitewashing the trunks of fruit trees.

Later at California State College at Long Beach, the enterprising young filmmaker turned out five more films, one in 35 mm. But he was itching to get inside a Hollywood studio. He had made a guided tour at Universal Studios but was not allowed to see much in the way of actual movie-making. So he conceived a daring idea. He had noticed while making the studio tour that the Universal executives all wore basically the same clothing, a Brooks Brothers charcoal suit and a black tie. And they had short, establishment-type haircuts. After a trip to the barber shop and a haberdashery, young Spielberg was the picture of a youthful executive. Armed with a briefcase, Steve walked right through Universal's main gate and waved at the guard. The guard waved back. Steve nosed around the office buildings and found an unoccupied office that he promptly took over. For months he walked in and out of the studio several times a week. Then, tiring of the long walk to the outside parking lot, he went to a sign shop and had a small sign made which read, "Mr. Spielberg," and placed it opposite a vacant studio parking space. After that Steve drove onto the lot, the guard on the gate waving even more friendly than before.

When people on the lot would ask him just what it was he did there, he would reply that he was an "official observer." Studio workers, thinking he might be the boss's nephew or some important stockholder's protégé, warmed up to the personable young man. He watched Universal's biggest pictures being made from close range. He talked with top writers, directors, and producers and everyone gladly answered his questions about movie making. Then one day a studio payroll employee walked into Steve's "office" and asked him just who he was, his name was nowhere to be found on the studio records. Steve, who had absorbed about as much as he was going to from merely observing, told the payroll man the truth, expecting to be summarily tossed off the lot if not arrested. When the studio bigwigs heard the full story, they were impressed with the young man's audacity and promptly gave him a bigger office in the Executive Tower. But Steve had seen all that there was to see at the valley studio so moved his activities over to Columbia Pictures, where he proceeded to walk in the studio gate, waving to the guard, and looking ever so much like he belonged there.

Youthful George Lucas, who assisted Francis Ford Coppola on The Rain People, *got his start as a director on the science fiction* THX 1138. *He made a two-hour documentary on the filming of* The Rain People, *which Coppola candidly admits "may be better than the picture." Here he relaxes with the French Eclair camera.* (Warner Bros.)

The trend toward youthful film directors is not exclusively American. Here Claude Lelouch, director of the exquisite French film A Man and a Woman, *explains a scene to his actors, one of them being Jean-Paul Belmondo. Lelouch, who started to make amateur films at the age of ten, made short subjects when he was seventeen.* (United Artists)

With his observing days over, Steve raised $18,000 and started on his first professional film, *Amblin'*, a twenty-minute short about two hitchikers. When his former friends at Universal saw the film, they signed him to a director's contract. At the age of twenty-one, Steve Spielberg was the youngest member of the Directors Guild and was directing Joan Crawford in a World Premiere feature film for television. Spielberg says of this experience: "I expected hostility when I started on this film but no one called me, 'Hey, kid.' As a matter of fact, the older people on the set were the first to accept me. The only ones I had conflict with were the kids my age who thought maybe they could direct as well as I could."

The young director should not shy away from exercising his authority just because of his youth. There was a time when most actors sought the "father image" in his director and this worked when the director was older or of comparable age. It was rare that a valuable star's reputation was put into the hands of a new, unproven director. But today things have changed . . . considerably. Most theatrical films are made for a youthful audience. It is entirely fitting that they be directed by young directors.

Noel Black took cinema courses at UCLA then created his own showcase for the professional film world by directing and co-producing a two-reel short *Skaterdater*, which received an Academy Award nomination. Black raised the money for *Skaterdater* ($19,000) by forming a limited partnership, then giving each investor an 8 percent interest. His partners included a junior agent, the owner of a Chinese restaurant, a pottery maker, and two men from the electronics business. Soon after his short received acclaim, he was offered his first feature film, *Pretty Poison*.

Claude Lelouch, one of France's newer and better directors, started filming with his father's amateur movie camera at the age of ten, a self-taught cinema student. A movie buff, he attended the cinema three times a day, shunning his classrooms. He bought his first camera at the Flea Market and started turning out ten minute films. When he was seventeen, his father sent him to New York in connection with the family textile business. While there, Lelouch purchased a 16 mm camera and turned out two short subjects that he sold to television back in France. At eighteen he was a full-fledged television news reporter, writing and directing his stories. After a career in television commercials, Lelouch entered feature film production and after several films, turned out the sensitive *A Man and a Woman*, which won the Grand Prix at the Cannes Film Festival as well as garnering the Academy Award for his direction.

At least one student filmmaker turned his college cinema class into a production center for films with calculated commercial possibilities.

Francis Ford Coppola takes over operation of the Eclair Camera as he directs a scene from The Rain People. *Coppola was given carte blanche on this production, which he calls a personal film.* (Warner Bros.)

Martin Scorsese was too sickly as a child to engage in sports so his father encouraged him to go to the movies. After seeing his first western movie he was hooked; after seeing *Citizen Kane* on television he started to understand what a director could do. When Martin got to college he enrolled in every cinema class NYU had to offer and soon was making his own films. His first one was a nine-minute, black and white comedy, *What's a Nice Girl Like You Doing in a Place Like This?* The short film won four first prize awards including the National Student Film Award of 1963. His next project, the two-reel *It's Not Just You, Murray!*, not only won more prizes including the Jesse L. Lasky Intercollegiate Award of the Screen Producers' Guild, but was distributed commercially. Scorsese, encouraged by the reception given his first two shorts, then decided to make a feature picture. Having graduated from NYU meanwhile, the young movie maker promptly enrolled in the college's Graduate School of Arts for the purpose of providing himself with a base of operations for his projected film. He wrote a script, then in January 1965 started shooting it in 35 mm, a new milestone in his picture-making activities. Shooting on weekends, Scorsese soon ran out of money. But he had seventy minutes of film in the can.

"The total cost of those 70 minutes was $6,000," says Scorsese. "I got this money by taking out student loans and my father taking a few bank loans (he's a ladies' garment presser). After we ran out of money, we printed up what we had even though we knew it wasn't quite ready to be shown. This was an error. I figured I would show the 70 minutes around and raise money to finish the film, but instead many of the people who were excited by 'Murray' were turned off when they saw the half-completed film. The experiment was a total loss, no feature, no jobs and no money."

For fifteen months Martin Scorsese did odd jobs with New York film companies including one as a film editor that netted him $350 for two months' work. He had practically written off the idea of ever finishing his feature picture. As he recalls: "Finally, at the end of 1966, my past professor from NYU, Haig Manoogian, formed a movie company with Joseph Weill. They felt that my picture (which was called *Dancing Girls*) had some scenes in it and that if the original script was revised a bit we would have a good picture. We started with $5,000 and finally wound up spending another $30,000 in cash. Most of the cast and crew deferred most of their salaries. We began shooting the new scenes in February of 1967 and finished four weeks later. The picture was now titled *I Call First*. While we waited for acceptances from foreign film festivals (which never came) I worked as a news film editors at CBS. Ten months later the picture was accepted into the 3rd Chicago Film Festival."

This was the impetus young Scorsese needed. Roger Ebert of the *Chicago Sun-Times* called the film "A new classic . . . abolutely genuine, artistically satisfying and technically comparable to the best films being made anywhere."

Of course, the title would have to be changed, and a few scenes added. The final title became *Who's That Knocking at My Door?*.

Finally, in March 1969, four years and two months after he started shooting at NYU, Martin Scorsese's first feature had its world premiere in Chicago. The press were almost unanimous in praise. *Time* magazine said, ". . . introduces a young director who just may turn out to be one of the brighter talents of this eager new generation." The *Chicago Tribune* added, "Made by 25 year old Martin Scorsese, the film is a sharp, rewarding, often witty film highlighted by incredible tuned in dialogue," while the usually reserved *New York Times* commented, "Scorsese is obviously a competent young filmmaker . . . he has composed a fluid, technically proficient movie, more intense and more sincere than most commercial releases."

One would think that a film that survived the agonies of postponed production and then went on to critical acclaim would, in turn, recompense its makers for their efforts.

"It didn't," says Scorsese, "the picture opened in New York at the

Carnegie Hall Cinema and in several other cities. The film got good reviews but didn't make money."

Scorsese went back to NYU as an instructor in cinema. Two years later Roger Corman remembered seeing *Who's That Knocking at My Door* and got in touch with Scorsese and offered him the director's job on *Boxcar Bertha*. This time the boxoffice was as good as the reviews and now Martin Scorsese is firmly established.

An outstanding success story of student turned professional in recent years is the one that tells of Francis Ford Coppola. He earned his master's degree at UCLA by making a commercial movie as his thesis. He wrote a script called *You're a Big Boy Now*, raised the money to shoot the picture (some $800,000), and produced and directed it himself. The film gained an Oscar nomination for its star, Geraldine Page. Soon after, Coppola was directing *Finian's Rainbow*, a $3,500,000 super-musical for Warner Bros. After that he was offered a contract that gave him complete autonomy; he did not have to obtain the studio's approval of stories. He wanted to return to making the "personal" film and his first was *The Rain People*. He shot his film in *cinéma vérité* style, following his actors across the United States with a company of twenty and a truck that carried all of the highly mobile camera and sound equipment. Coppola says, "I use what you could call a relentless camera—a single shot for as long as eight or ten minutes. The camera just stays and watches; when you are scrutinizing a human thing you don't have to cut."

Francis Ford Coppola has temporarily abandoned his personal film making plans for a return to the big studio where his direction of *The Godfather* has reestablished him as a top film director.

Truly, an exponent of the *auteur* theory, Coppola can claim to be the central force behind his films. Certainly Richard Brooks, who wrote, directed, and produced *Happy Ending* was the author of his film. John Schlesinger achieved total artistic freedom during the making of *Midnight Cowboy*, as did Mike Nichols on *Catch-22*. It is quite possible that, despite all the opposition to it (mainly by writers), that the facts have finally caught up with the *auteur* theory.

The Long Road to Success

Since my own entrance into the motion picture business was a result of academic training, and not by either one or the other routes, I will recount my own experiences leading up to receiving that first paycheck.

Although I had created the most pretentious college film of its day and had received a banquet attended by leading luminaries of the film capital who watched me receive an impressive plaque, it still took me seven years to get a contract with a major studio. Seven long years of frustrating effort to convince a bona fide employer that I was the talented young man I thought I was.

My first fascination with the movies came at the age of ten in Modesto, California, when my father bought me a small projector and I proceeded to charge pins as admission to my basement theater. Soon after the first show, I discovered that nickels were as easy to extract from the neighborhood kids as pins.

As I matured, and with the principles of projection firmly established, I became the grammar school projectionist, running the study films once a week, and even projecting the religious movies the Presbyterian Church occasionally presented.

What really jarred me on the way to a chosen profession was when my father presented me with a movie camera on my fourteenth birthday. This was no 8 mm toy, or even a 16 mm outfit. It was a genuine DeVry 35 mm professional motion picture camera, the kind that was commonly used by newsreel men, but the cost of which was moderate.

I wasted no time in mastering its operation but my exposure left something to be desired. That was when I decided to study motion picture photography by correspondence. Before I had even received my high school diploma, I had sold three newsreel stories to Universal Newsreel at a dollar a foot, and had almost fallen out of an airplane in the process.

This is as good as any place to touch on the subject of what an intense desire to accomplish can do for the young person bent on a particular career. I feel that possessing an undeterred drive to reach a goal is two-thirds of getting there, that talent or ability makes up the rest. The old saw about the formula to success, "Take one part inspiration, two parts perspiration and mix well with your fellow man," still applies.

The drive leaves a person soon enough; he should develop and nurture it in himself when it is in full bloom. Nothing should stand in his way on the long road to achievement.

I soon got a job in a gas station to be able to afford my hobby, shooting movies. I convinced the manager of the local theater that a home-produced newsreel would more than pay for itself at the box office. Whether it did or not I'm not sure, but I had lots of fun shooting the film.

By the time my junior year in high school came around, I was ready to add a dramatic dimension to my amateur filming. With my pal, Bud

Shoemake, who was equally as interested in picture making as I was, I embarked on a two-reel western picture, *West of the Rio Grande*. The cast was recruited from the high school dramatics class, props and costumes were rounded up, and with a borrowed truck we traveled to "location" each weekend. Modesto, being only a few miles from the heart of the Mother Lode country, provided easy access to some remarkable and picturesque backgrounds, and for eight months our student group maintained its initial enthusiasm for completing the picture.

When it was finally finished and edited, we had spent $480, and now we were ready for the big test. Would anybody come to see it?

We had some circulars and window cards printed, put an ad in the *Modesto Bee*, and promoted a local sign painter to put up a large banner that extended across the main street—all on credit. When the night came for the running, Bud and I, who were running the projectors, looked through the portholes into a jam-packed high school auditorium and received the thrill of our lives. The show went off without a hitch, and at the end of the performance on the last night we counted the money. We had not only got our production cost back, but we made enough money to pay our advertising costs. Not always an easy thing to do in professional picture making.

After a summer vacation in Hollywood, during which I managed to get into a studio and get a job as a five-dollar-a-day extra, I came back to my senior year all pepped up somehow to make talking pictures. Bud and I spent many hours in our attic "studio" rigging parts from an old phonograph and hooking it in sync with a new camera I had acquired. We selected a part-singing, part-monologue record and had a friend of ours memorize the words to the record. When he was word perfect we put some makeup on him, then stood him up before the camera, and started to turn the crank. The camera mechanism turned the record, and the actor heard the voice. He mouthed his memorized words in perfect sync and, when the film was developed and the record attachment hooked onto the projector, we had accomplished our first talking picture.

After graduating from high school, I enrolled in the University of Southern California. It was the only college on the west coast that had a cinema department.

My camera, although an inexpensive but professional-looking instrument, was a big hit with the professor of the department as well as the other students, and I was soon chief cameraman for the Campus Newsreel. Warner Bros. studio decided to sponsor a film contest and provided a trophy to be awarded the student who, during the year, made the best amateur film. The contest was open to all colleges, and the studio, seek-

The author (top left) was barely sixteen when he and his high school buddies organized the Cinema Arts Picture Corp. and started shooting the two-reel West of the Rio Grande. *The 35 mm camera came with the last lesson by correspondence from the New York Institute of Photography.*

No shot was too difficult for the high school filmmakers. When they needed a close-up of the leading lady as she fought to control a runaway horse and buggy, they mounted the movie camera in the rumble seat. When West of the Rio Grande *was presented at the school auditorium, it made all its cost back in three nights.*

ing to further the career of one of its leading stars, named the trophy the Paul Muni Award.

With this as an inspiration, I was supercharged into action. I adapted an Edgar Allan Poe story "The Oval Portrait" and proceeded to gather a student cast and crew to film what I was sure would be the most colossal college film ever made. I found a colleague, Evan Shaw, whose enthusiasm matched mine, and who, parenthetically, could hold up his end on the financing side. It seems that the matter of the budget plagues all picture makers, amateur and professional alike. In this case, my new associate, a young divinity student, secretly shared a desire, it seems, to be an actor. He had a classic profile, a deep resonant voice, the body of a young Apollo, and was captain of the polo team. After a few hours with me he was convinced that he should star in *The Oval Portrait* and put up most of the cash money needed as well. I say cash money because I had already talked Metro-Goldwyn-Mayer into lending us stage space, standing sets, wardrobe, and so forth. Eastman Kodak Company donated 10,000 feet of negative, and Consolidated Film Laboratories agreed to do our processing. Later, I was to convince Pacific Title and Art Studio that main and end titles by them would further the cause of education at the university, and RKO Studios to make all of our optical effects, fades, and dissolves. So, the actual expenditure was small and covered things like gasoline, lunches for location, and the few small items of rental that were impossible to promote.

When directors like King Vidor insist that a single point of view makes the best films and that the director should control the production from the inception of the idea to the final editing of the film, they have a champion in me, for I learned early the practical application of this theory. I had written the script, adapting it from a Poe short story. I owned the camera, so naturally I did the photography. I directed. I produced, and I edited the film in my room at the fraternity house. I even ran the projector at the banquet when the film was first unveiled. I wasn't yet twenty.

Filming spanned a three-month period. After shooting our interior scenes at MGM, we labored on weekends shooting our outdoor scenes in and around the Palos Verdes hills.

When the big night came at the Roosevelt Hotel, *The Oval Portrait* had already been selected as the winner of the college contest and was shown to an audience of Hollywood notables and the Los Angeles press.

I was given the Paul Muni award, a handsome plaque, which I was sure would be my *entrée* to any studio in town.

A few weeks later, the picture opened a two-week run at the Egyptian Theatre on Hollywood Boulevard and received glowing notices:

USC students shooting The Oval Portrait *at the Metro-Goldwyn-Mayer Studios in Culver City. Producer-director Bare needed a haunted-house set, so he telephoned Walter Wanger who arranged for the students to shoot on the lot. Eastman Kodak donated the film, Consolidated Film Lab donated the processing.*

"Picture beautiful to look at . . . exquisite proof of the camera's potential art," said the *Hollywood Reporter. Daily Variety* came forth with, "Production showed sound fundamentals in screen technique and directorial promise by Richard L. Bare." The now defunct *Los Angeles Post-Record* said, ". . . a cleverly directed costume drama, and should refresh the jaded appetite for celluloid. Raises the movie to the realm of art."

All this, of course, had its profound effect on me. As I moved about the campus on the few remaining days of the semester my feet barely touched the ground. At nineteen, I had apparently arrived. My schooling was behind me, and I had the rest of the summer to call on the various studios and pick and choose the place I wanted to work. I was armed with letters of introduction, a photo of my award, copies of my reviews, and an unbridled enthusiasm to crack the business once and for all. One by one, I called on the executives of each studio. Nobody seemed to need a young genius to direct their pictures. They weren't interested in taking on any new assistant directors, or even second assistants. In fact, they didn't need any prop men, furniture movers, or even any messenger boys. How about a job as an observer with no pay? No—not at this time.

When the summer was over, my illusions of fame and success in the movie business had been replaced with more practical appraisals of the situation, and I took the first offer that came my way in three months of hounding the studios for a job. A director I had met arranged for me to pile lumber on the back lot at Paramount for twenty-one dollars a week. Admittedly a letdown, I was nevertheless grateful and plunged into my duties as a laborer with virgin zeal, hoping to be noticed by someone in production that I was obviously superior to the job I was doing.

I piled lumber harder and faster than any other man on the gang. This seemed to upset the foreman, and I was told to slow down as it made the other men look bad.

I would work for eight hours, then drop into my bed at the YMCA completely fatigued. The phone would ring at eight o'clock, and a voice would say, "You want to work the night shift?" When I began to hedge, the voice announced they could easily take me off the list since I was a new man. One night in particular, after having worked a day shift, I got up, put on my clothes, and trudged into the studio to answer a call for night work. I was herded onto a truck with a gang of other souls, and driven to the Paramount Ranch at Calabasas. There we shoveled all night

The Oval Portrait *was the first University of Southern California film production. The author, at the age of nineteen, is shown with script in hand, directing fellow student Evan Shaw, in full character makeup. This early venture won the Paul Muni Award.*

long to level the side of a hill so that von Sternberg could lay a dolly track for a shot he would be making for *The Scarlet Empress*. I was bawled out for working too fast. The next day I quit.

My next employment was as an assistant cameraman on a six-day "quickie," and although elated at my good fortune, I soon found out why I had been selected over more experienced men. I was willing to defer my twenty-five-dollar salary until after the picture was completed. I deferred, and I waited. I never got paid.

With my funds depleted, I went home to Modesto somewhat in defeat. It looked like I was never going to get a job in Hollywood. But, then something came into my life that was to renew the spark and even kindle the old flame again.

I ran across an ad in the classified section of the *San Francisco Examiner* that read, "ASSOCIATE WANTED. Film director wants to meet party with small amount of capital to produce western picture. Box 616–A."

When a battered old Lincoln drove up to my father's house, and an unimpressive-looking fellow introduced himself as Denver Dixon, I was frankly disappointed in what I saw; but then I was not about to let slip away any chance to become involved in the making of a Hollywood movie.

Dixon explained that he was actually Art Mix, the silent movie western actor, and had recently made a contact with a New York distributor who was interested in releasing a series of westerns in which he would star as well as direct. All he needed to get the first picture made, which was to be a two-reeler, was the small sum of twenty-five hundred dollars. He explained that he had many friends in Hollywood who would help him and that he could get a cast and a cameraman who would wait for their money, and he knew a laboratory that would extend him credit. He already owned the story, so that was no problem.

I rose to the bait like a hungry trout, and told Denver, as he preferred to be called, that I could get him the money provided there was a responsible position for me. Eagerly, he offered me the position of producer, an equitable arrangement, I thought.

Remembering my money-raising abilities with such amateur projects as *West of the Rio Grande* and *The Oval Portrait*, I tackled some good friends in Modesto. Within a week, we had formed a company and I was headed for Hollywood, this time, I was certain, for good.

Denver had gone on ahead and rented a small studio on Santa Monica Boulevard, and had lined up a flea-bitten cast of old western cronies who had worked in the old Art Mix silents. I soon got better acquainted with Denver. He was a one-man outfit, a pioneer along poverty row, which was the area around Gower Street and Sunset Boulevard, and a promoter who took a backseat to no one. He had for years managed to raise the capital to make westerns, exacting his livelihood out of the production money in the form of salary, for very little ever came back from the distribution of Art Mix westerns. His screen credits were a classic of deception. They always read, "Victor Adamson presents————Art Mix starring in————Directed by Denver Dixon." But they were all the same man.

Years before, he had come by the name of Art Mix during the period when Tom Mix was the giant of all western stars. Knowing the value of a name, he always controlled his billing on the one sheets outside the theaters, so that the name "MIX" was oversized, while the name "Art" was infinitesimally small.

A few years before I met Denver Dixon, Fox Film Corporation filed a large damage suit against this man who was capitalizing on the name of one of their top stars and who, they claimed, was misleading the public.

Denver, never a man to run from a good scrap, frantically looked around for a legal loophole. His agile mind soon came across one. He learned from a lawyer friend that if Art Mix was his legal name, the Fox people wouldn't have a leg to stand on. Quickly, Denver sprang into action. He looked in the phone directory until he came across an Arthur J. Mix. He called Mr. Mix for an appointment and went out to see him. A half hour later, and with the promise of a fifty-dollar payment, Arthur J. Mix agreed to adopt the middle-aged western actor, and thereby to legalize the name of Art Mix. Fox Film Corporation dropped its suit, probably deciding it wasn't worth it anyway.

My first professional screen credit as a producer was on a two-reel western entitled *The Double Cross*, starring Art Mix, but nobody got a chance to see it. It was never released. I guess it was a new low even for Adamson–Dixon–Mix.

Again, I went back home, this time more sure than ever I was a perpetual failure. It seemed the only films I could make that people would pay to see were amateur ones. So, temporarily, I shifted my energies toward another direction in show business. I found a vacant theater in Carmel, California, and started showing foreign films. The venture was an instant success.

This theater was to sustain me for the next three years, while I was carefully studying the work of the world's leading picture-makers, secretly making plans for another frontal assault on Hollywood.

I formed a corporation in Carmel and raised capital to make a color short subject based on Robert Edgren's newspaper syndicated cartoons,

Miracles of Sport. The picture cost $5,000, and we sold it to Warner Bros. for $2,500. But it was a good film, and people saw it in theaters, even if the stockholders didn't fare so well. I was moving up.

The theater business was getting so good in Carmel that my fame as an entrepeneur of foreign films spread to Southern California. I was invited to run a newly proposed art film theater in Claremont, with the capital to be supplied by local citizens. Knowing that I would be closer to Hollywood, I made the move from Carmel to Claremont and invested all my savings in the new project. In one year, I was broke again, the victim of a combination of underfinancing and poor clearance, which means the pictures I could get were only old ones.

Determined never again to go home to Modesto, I slipped into Hollywood, and by a stroke of good timing, managed to get a job as assistant cameraman with George Pal, who was then hiring nonunion cameramen for his Puppetoon shorts.

This was the turning point in my then young career. After a year of experience as a cameraman actually being paid to do the job, I was ready to pursue photography as my life's work. I applied to the cameraman's local 659, I.A.T.S.E., and was summarily turned down. As I look back, I can only be grateful, for it pointed my energies toward a more lucrative profession—directing.

About this time I had made the acquaintance of Warren Scott, who had succeeded Boris Morkovin as head of the Cinema Department of USC. News of my mild flurry of campus fame a few years previous had sifted down to Scott who was in need of additional instructors in the art and techniques of filmmaking, so I became an addition to his staff.

For the first semester, I taught photography; then, I joined forces with William Keighley in a class in film directing.

Although I had come quite a way from my lumber piling days at Paramount, I was still far from my goal, which was to have a studio contract in a creative position. Even my close association with Keighley opened up no doors, for there was still no established route for an academically trained picture-maker to become a major studio employee. I knew—I had tried everything. It was at this time that I formulated the plan that inspires this chapter. If there were no jobs, I would create one.

Two years before in Carmel I had written a short subject script entitled, *So You Want to Give Up Smoking*, and had sent it to Pete Smith, who was then making his short series at MGM. Pete sent it back with a note saying he had enjoyed it very much, and even tried to get it passed by the studio. But, since it dealt with methods to eliminate the smoking habit, he felt that it would alienate too many powerful tobacco companies.

Now I had a script. Warren Scott needed projects, actual productions that could be made at the University that would serve as practical training grounds for the students. It took little persuasion on my part to get Scott to see the obvious benefits of shooting such a moral script as one that dealt with the evils of nicotine.

With ample funds available, I gathered together some of the best students from the photography and directing classes and turned out a professionally slick two-reel short. For the smaller roles, friends and university students were used, but for the major part, a professional actor was persuaded into donating his services for the cause of education. His name was George O'Hanlon, and he suspected not that this was the start of a fifteen-year association with the fellow who at that time was known to him as "teach."

When the film was completed, and the students had received the benefit of the experience gained from working on a production, it worried me that all this effort in turning out a genuinely entertaining picture was going to repose quietly in a can, unappreciated by millions of theatergoers throughout the world.

The evils of tobacco made an appropriate subject for a university-financed student production, so Richard L. Bare wrote, produced, and directed So You Want to Give Up Smoking *for USC. When Warner Bros. saw it, they wanted to buy it. That was the start of Bare's professional career.*

With the success of So You Want to Give Up Smoking *behind him, Richard L. Bare went on to make sixty-five more subjects, each titled* So You Want to———. *Most theatergoers knew the series by the title* Behind the Eightball, *as that was the trademark for the series of one-reelers. Here, in one called* So You Want to Get Married, *the bride's mother raises her daughter's hand in victory as the minister pronounces Joe McDoakes a married man.* (Warner Bros.)

So, one day, acting completely on impulse, I took it out to Warner Bros. studio and showed it to Norman Moray, then head of short subject distribution. When the lights came on after the screening, he asked me what I wanted for it. Completely off guard, I stammered out a price, "Twenty-five." Moray, without batting an eyelash, wanted to know was I referring to thousands or hundreds. Hundreds, I assured him.

Without any more small talk, he stood up and asked me to come with him to the legal department where contracts would be drawn right away. As I walked down the corridor, a horrible thought occurred to me. Here I was about to sell something that didn't really belong to me. I could tell Moray the whole story, confess how the film was made to educate students, and that the negative belonged to the University and that in all likelihood it would frown on any such commercial exploitation of the film. And, if I did tell him all this, he, being a very busy man, would turn his attention to other available shorts on the market and buy up the year's quota of outside product. I could see my big opportunity for a

So far as is known, it has never happened before or since: a student-made film sold to a major company and becoming the prototype for a series that ran for ten years. Here Director Bare and Star O'Hanlon pose in their first personal chairs, symbol of Hollywood success. (Warner Bros.)

studio affiliation postponed another seven years. So, I took a chance. I went through the preliminary motions of getting the contracts started, and then dashed out to the University to see Scott.

I hedged for five minutes, trying to present to him what I had done in a way that wouldn't make him think of me as some scholastic Ponzi. Just when I thought that he would veto the whole thing, he came up with a solution to my dilemma. He, perhaps, could turn the negative over to me for safekeeping, since the University had no fireproof vaults of its own. And then, since I was a true-hearted and loyal Trojan, I might want to make a donation to the University, say of a thousand dollars? I quickly agreed that this was, indeed, a wise solution. I delivered the negative to Warners, picked up the twenty-five-hundred-dollar check, then endowed USC with one thousand. Not bad for all concerned.

A month later, Warner Bros. asked me to make another; and this time it was, *So You Think You Need Glasses.* I hired O'Hanlon again, and this time he was paid in cash, as well as brought up to date on the smoking picture. When this one was completed, I signed O'Hanlon to a personal contract, calling for seven years of services with options, of course. Warner Bros. looked at my second picture, and I was invited to join the short subject staff under Gordon Hollingshead as a writer.

Seven years had rolled by since I had received the Paul Muni Award. I was now in the door. Under contract! It wouldn't be long before I was a director. But fate intervened again, this time in the form of the sneak attack on Pearl Harbor. My remorse was close to agony, as I had been finally assigned to direct my first short subject at a major studio. My career, it seemed, was to be postponed a while, maybe forever.

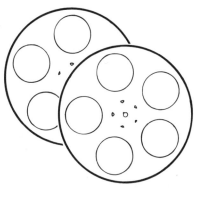

12

THE DIRECTOR'S REQUIREMENTS AND RESPONSIBILITIES

The Directors Guild of America

When the war was over, thousands of film technicians, writers, directors, and actors returned from the service to resume their careers in the motion picture industry. I was fortunate to have used up only eight months of a term contract that still had some time to go, and accordingly I found a job waiting for me when I returned to Hollywood.

The four years of service were not wasted, as far as filmmaking went. I had directed more than thirty-five training and morale films for the Air Force and had matured considerably from the young man who had bounced into Hollywood direct from university production.

More than that, I appreciated the full meaning of the word *responsibility*. The Air Force had entrusted me with well over a million dollars, and I made pictures from Saipan to the Texas Panhandle.

Now that I was back at the studio, I must become a member of the Directors Guild to impress the front office that I possessed full requirements for a position as a staff director. The Directors Guild, at that time, was composed of only a few hundred members and the initiation was nominal. The bylaws defined just what a director was, as follows: "A director is one who directs the production of motion pictures as the word *direct* is commonly used in the industry, and the fact that he may also render services as a producer and/or writer shall not take him out of the classification of director."

A director who worked for the minimum scale in 1946 got $312 per week, and he worked on Saturdays. It cost him $250 initiation fee and nominal yearly dues to belong to the Guild. Today, with over twenty-two hundred senior directors (as differentiated from assistant directors), the director who works for union scale receives $1,000 per week if he works in feature pictures. If he works by the film in television his minimum salary is $1,100 per half-hour show, $2,200 per hour show, and $4,400 per ninety-minute show.

To join the Directors Guild of America, it will cost $2,000 initiation fee and annual dues computed at 1 percent of the director's income, up to $1,000 dues maximum.

The Directors Basic Agreement, currently in force and signed with the various studios in 1968, covers the usual bargaining agreements such as Article II, the Guild Shop provision, which provides that any director employed by the producer shall be or become a member of the Guild within thirty days of his employment. The minimum preparation time and cutting time the director gives to his employer is spelled out. A starting date, with a one-week latitude either way, must be given the director at the time of employment, and any location travel must be in transportation "first class or the best obtainable."

If production of a motion picture, after once closing down, is resumed again, the director may be called back but only paid for the actual time worked; in contrast to the actors who must be paid "carry" time if they have not completed their roles. Elizabeth Taylor's much publicized illness on *Cleopatra* resulted in many hundreds of thousands of dollars paid to actors as carry pay.

On a *term contract*, a period of employment not less than twenty-six weeks, a director may be given *layoff*, usually not more than six weeks in each twenty-six week period. During layoff, the director is, of course, not paid. A director under term contract can be *loaned out* to another company, even for more money than is called for in his contract, and the difference pocketed by the director's employer.

A director may be *suspended* for reasons that run the gamut from mental or physical incapacity to *force majeure*. Naturally, the director agrees to conduct himself with due regard to public convention and morals, and, in the words of one studio's contract, ". . . not to commit any act that will tend to degrade him in society or bring him into public hatred, contempt, scorn, or ridicule, or that will tend to shock, insult, or offend the community."

The director, according to the Guild Agreement, is to be consulted regarding cast before the assignments are made, with the exception of any cast members assigned before he, himself, has been assigned.

When it comes to editing, the director is to be consulted and allowed to express his opinion, although the final cut rests with the production company. It is the producer's obligation to notify the director of the time and place of all "sneak" previews.

Further clauses relative to editing give the director the right to express his editorial ideas directly with the company executive in the event he and the producer don't see eye to eye. But, all final decisions are to be the producer's: "The producer's decision as to all cutting and dubbing shall always be final and nothing herein contained shall be so construed as to prohibit the making of such changes as the producer may deem fit."

There is nothing in the Basic Agreement to prevent a Zinnemann, a Stevens, or a Wise from making other arrangements with the studio, and of course, they always do. Like all union agreements, the Director's Basic is to protect the average director, not the giants whose services are always sought and paid for at premium prices and working conditions.

Screen credits have always been a controversial subject in Hollywood, and the Guild has covered it this way: "The director shall be given credit on all positive prints in type not less than 40% of the size of the title and no other credit shall appear on such card, which shall be the last title card appearing prior to principal photography."

In television, the director's credit may be as outlined above, or it may come at the end, being shown directly after the last commercial and before any other credits.

There is an additional compensation to directors of television, and the Basic Agreement states:

> The salary paid to the director for his services in a television motion picture shall constitute payment in full for the telecasting of such motion picture once in each city in which any television broadcasting stations are now located.

> *Amount for reruns:* If the producer desires to telecast any televison motion picture for more than one run, the employment contract of each director engaged therein shall contain a separate provision for additional compensation for re-runs, which shall be *not less than* the following amounts:

	30 min. films	60 min. films	90 min. films
2nd run	550.	1100.	2200.
3rd run	440.	880.	1760.
4th run	275.	550.	1100.
5th run	275.	550.	1100.
6th run	275.	550.	1100.
7th run	165.	330.	660.
8th run	165.	330.	660.
9th run	165.	330.	660.
10th run	165.	330.	660.

In addition, on those films which are shown on television outside of the United States, the director shall receive:

HALF HOUR

On initial showing	82.50
at $7,000 gross	55.00
at $10,000 gross	55.00

ONE HOUR

On initial showing	165.00
at $13,000 gross	110.00
at $18,000 gross	110.00

90 MIN.

On initial showing	330.00
at $18,000 gross	220.00
at $24,000 gross	220.00

These rerun payments, referred to as *residuals,* are the popular topic of conversation among Hollywood television groups and are paid to writers, directors, and actors who are lucky enough to work on television shows that get more than one showing. I knew one director who fondly named his boat the *Residual,* since it was from this source the cost and upkeep of his hobby came.

The theory of rerun payments, as established by the leading talent guilds, maintains that every time a film is reshown it has taken a creative job away from someone. The residuals are a form of penalty to the producer, and sometimes turn out to be a windfall to the guild member.

If a director is called on to do a television *pilot* (first sample show of a proposed series) he must be paid double the minimum, if he works by the day his salary is $250, and if his job requires him to go up in an airplane or down in a scuba suit he must be paid an additional $50 per day.

The many feature films butchered by television stations has caused the inclusion of a clause in the Basic Agreement that insures that the director will be consulted before any cutting is done on his picture shown on television.

The Directors Guild was one of the first union organizations to recognize the danger of a producer's making a motion picture for one medium and then exhibiting it in another. Strict regulations are in effect now, but I can remember when I directed the first hour-long television film ever made in Hollywood and for a very small fee, since television was just getting started. A month or so after its showing on a leading network, I saw the picture advertised in a downtown Los Angeles theater. All my protests and those of my attorney could do nothing to persuade the producer that he had done anything illegal or immoral. But, when bargaining time came around again, the Guild put teeth in the language that would prevent this from ever happening again. Parenthetically, when I directed the pilot film of 77 *Sunset Strip*, which was made as a ninety-minute theatrical feature, I was paid a theatrical salary under the terms of the Basic Agreement. Later, when it was rerouted from the theaters directly to its premiere as an ABC Network program, I was paid again, this time for directing a television film.

Many years ago, the practice of *deferring* salaries got started in Hollywood, and in some cases, is still around today. The Directors Guild Basic Agreement specifically prohibits its membership from postponing their salaries, but it allows them to make better terms for themselves if they can.

While the minimum salary on a half-hour television show is $1,100, established directors usually command $1,250 to $2,500. The hour-show producer will pay a director from $2,500 to $3,500 and up, while scale is $2,200. The television director, who works regularly on a free-lance basis, can easily chalk up $50,000 in a year, with residual payments from previous years adding another $5,000 or $10,000 to that. Of course, the top feature men make from $100,000 to $300,000 per picture, plus percentages and part ownership.

Yes, a rewarding business, this—from many standpoints.

The Directors Guild of America provides many so-called fringe benefits to its members through its liberal pension plan and group insurance program.

The DGA-Producer Pension Plan provides that the producer contribute 7½ percent of the director's salary in theatrical films up to a maximum of $100,000 per member per picture, and in television films, to contribute 7½ percent of the director's salary up to an amount equal to double the minimum scale.

Retirement for the director may come at age sixty or sixty-five, at his election, provided he has 180 or more months of credited service as a director.

A director who retires at sixty-five will receive $175 per month for life, plus 60 percent of the actual contributions that have been made by him toward the plan. The total can run as high as $400 per mouth.

The Group Life Insurance Plan of the Guild provides $1,000 automatically with additional coverage available. There is a complete schedule of hospital and surgical benefits for both the member and his dependents available at small cost to the director.

One of the most controversial points ever discussed in Hollywood labor meetings has been the one in which the three talent guilds (directors, writers, and actors) demanded additional payment for their members' services on those theatrical motion pictures made after 1948 that were shown on television. As a result of years of negotiations, on feature pictures made after April 30, 1960, the producers have agreed to contribute to the DGA 2 percent of their gross television receipts, after deducting a flat amount of 40 percent of total gross receipts for distribution fees.

The Basic Agreement now provides for the eventuality of pay television, that much heralded medium which has been so long in arriving. In the event that such a system is established and that the producer's film rentals are materially increased, the Directors Guild may reopen negotiations relating to the theatrical minimums then payable. But, the producers have carefully provided a clause that reads, "Theatrical exhibition shall be deemed to include any form of pay television." However, since the last director-producer negotiations were held, the word *cassette* has entered Hollywood's vocabulary, and one can make book that if and when this new form of home entertainment becomes a reality, all the film unions will demand a share of the revenue.

Through the Guild's Benevolent Fund, members may receive financial aid in time of stress, and many contributions are made to nonindustry charities through this branch of the Guild's activities.

Each February the membership gathers, usually at the Beverly Hilton Hotel in Beverly Hills and the Waldorf-Astoria in New York, to have a social evening and applaud the winners of the Directors Guild Achievement Award for the year. The feature picture director who has, in the opinion of the members, distinguished himself during the year is presented a gold medallion, and similarly the best television director of the year receives equal honors. The awards have a true significance, since the winners have been adjudged by other directors who are in a position to best evaluate a director's contribution to a film.

Housed in its own handsome building on Sunset Boulevard in Hollywood, the Directors Guild of America has come by its new name (formerly, Screen Directors Guild) through combining with the New York Directors Guild and the Radio and TV Directors' Guild.

The objectives of the Guild are stated, in part, in its bylaws: "To represent and coordinate the activities of the various individuals now or hereafter engaged or employed as directors in the motion picture and television industries—to help its members secure equitable compensation and better working conditions—to establish and enforce standard minimum contracts—and to adopt, promulgate and encourage the observance of a code of ethics for its members and those similarly engaged or employed."

A new member will be admitted upon the payment of $2,000 initiation fee and first-quarter dues, provided he has obtained the written recommendation of three director members and can qualify as having landed himself a job.

Although the Guild may take strict disciplinary action against a member who, in the opinion of the board, may be guilty of any act that may be prejudicial to the welfare of the Guild, there has been a conspicuous absence of directors or assistant directors who have behaved in a notorious way or have brought discredit upon themselves or the motion picture and television industries. In the main, the men who have chosen directing as their life's work have brought a dignity and stature to their profession that has few parallels among the guilds and unions of the vast entertainment industry.

Restrictions and Censorship

Since the beginning, the motion picture business has been controlled by some form of censorship. In silent days, when producers got somewhat out of hand, local censorship boards sprang up all over the nation, each with a different set of rules. A producer, not wanting his films slashed to pieces, found it difficult, if not impossible, to outguess the many censorship boards as to what would be acceptable in the various areas. New York might object to one thing, while Boston another. This dilemma caused the formation of the Hays Office of the Motion Picture Producers and Distributors of America, and brought into being the Production Code Administration, which was a self-censoring body controlled by Hollywood's producers. Most local censorship boards disbanded shortly after that, although certain cities still maintained them for years.

When television came into existence, a similar need was apparent, and the TV Code was devised and administered by the National Association of Broadcasters.

In recent years, changing public morals and tastes have caused a relaxing of the restrictions of the feature film code, mainly in the area of sex and violence. In television, in addition to the Code of the National Association of Broadcasters, each network has its censor which protects its own interests as well as those of its sponsors.

There are many restrictions placed on the television director that are outside the sphere of normal good taste, and these are the commercial censorship rules. For instance, the cigarette sponsors never allowed a character to smoke a cigar, nor would they allow a cigarette butt to be tossed away irresponsibly or crushed into an ashtray in anger. One large cigarette company struck the word "oasis" out of a line of dialogue because that happened to be the name of a competing cigarette company.

Tennessee Ernie Ford was invited to make a guest appearance on a Chevrolet program, but was blocked from appearance by an advertising agency, which decided against giving their biggest rival a free plug.

The television director must be ever vigilant not to allow profanity or obscenity to creep into his dialogue, although in theatrical films these former bars have been let down considerably. And one network once refused to televise any film if an actor used the word "crazy," since mental insitutions the country over use television as a part of their therapy treatments.

To illustrate the recent changes in Hollywood's (and the nation's) moral sense both the former and the present motion picture production code should be compared:

THE OLD CODE

1. Crime shall never be presented in such a way as to throw sympathy with the crime as against law and justice, or to inspire others with a desire for imitation.
2. Suicide, as a solution of problems occurring in the development of screen drama, is to be discouraged unless absolutely necessary for the development of the plot, and shall never be justified, or glorified, or used specifically to defeat the ends of justice.
3. There shall be no scenes of law-enforcing officers dying at the hands of criminals, unless such scenes are absolutely necessary to the plot.
4. Pictures dealing with criminal activities in which minors participate, or to which minors are related, shall not be approved if they tend to incite demoralizing imitation on the part of the youth.
5. Murder:
   (a) The technique of murder must not be presented in a way that will inspire imitation.
   (b) Brutal killings are not to be presented in detail.
   (c) Revenge in modern times shall not be justified.
   (d) Mercy killing shall never be made to seem right or permissible.
6. Drug addiction or the illicit traffic in addiction-producing drugs shall not be shown if the portrayal:
   (a) Tends in any manner to encourage, stimulate or justify the use of such drugs; or
   (b) Stresses, visually or by dialogue their temporarily attractive effects; or

    (c) Suggests that the drug habit may be quickly or easily broken; or

    (d) Emphasizes the profits of the drug traffic; or

    (e) Involves children who are shown knowingly to use or traffic in drugs.

7. Stories on the kidnapping or illegal abduction of children are acceptable under the Code only (1) when the subject is handled with restraint and discretion and avoids details, gruesomeness and undue horror, and (2) the child is returned unharmed.

Sex:

The sanctity of the institution of marriage and the home shall be upheld. No film shall infer that casual or promiscuous sex relationships are an accepted or common thing.

1. Adultery and illicit sex, sometimes necessary plot material, shall not be explicity treated, nor shall they be justified or made to seem right and permissible.

2. Scenes of passion:

    (a) These should not be introduced except where they are definitely essential to the plot.

    (b) Lustful and open-mouth kissing, lustful embraces, suggestive posture and gestures are not to be shown.

3. Seduction or rape:

    (a) These should never be more than suggested, and then only when essential to the plot. They should never be shown explicitly.

    (b) They are never acceptable subject matter for comedy.

    (c) They should never be made to seem right and permissible.

4. The subject of abortion shall be discouraged, shall never be more than suggested, and when referred to shall be condemned.

5. The methods and techniques of prostitution and white slavery shall never be presented in detail, nor shall the subjects be presented unless shown in contrast to right standards of behavior. Brothels in any clear identification as such may not be shown.

6. It is permissible under the Code for the Production Code Administration to consider approving references in motion pictures to the subject of sex aberrations, provided any references are treated with care, discretion and restraint, and in all other aspects conform to the Code.

Obscenity:

1. Dances suggesting or representing sexual actions or emphasizing indecent movements are to be regarded as obscence.

2. Obscenity in words, gesture, reference, song, joke or by suggestion, even when likely to be understood by only part of the audience, is forbidden.

Blasphemy and Profanity:

1. Blasphemy is forbidden. Reference to the Deity, God, Lord, Jesus, Christ, shall not be irreverent.
2. Profanity is forbidden. The words "hell" and "damn," while sometimes dramatically valid, will if used without moderation be considered offensive by many members of the audience. Their use shall be governed by the discretion and prudent advice of the Code Administration.

THE NEW CODE

This code is designed to keep close harmony with the mores, culture, the moral sense and change in our society. The objectives of the code are: (1) to encourage artistic freedom, and, (2) to assure that the freedom which encourages the artist remains responsible and sensitive to the standards of the larger society.

In furtherance of the principals stated above, the following standards shall govern the Administrator in his consideration of motion pictures submitted for code approval:

1. The basic dignity and value of human life shall be respected and upheld. Restraint shall be exercised in portraying the taking of life.
2. Evil, sin, crime and wrong-doing shall not be justified.
3. Special restraint shall be exercised in portraying criminal or anti-social activities in which minors participate or are involved.
4. Detailed and protracted acts of brutality, cruelty, physical violence, torture and abuse shall not be presented.
5. Indecent or undue exposure of the human body shall not be presented.
6. Illicit sex relationships shall not be justified. Intimate sex scenes violating common standards of decency shall not be portrayed.
7. Restraint and care shall be exercised in presentations dealing with sex aberrations.
8. Obscene speech, gestures or movements shall not be presented. Undue profanity shall not be permitted.
9. Religion shall not be demeaned.
10. Words or symbols contemptuous of racial, religious or national groups, shall not be used so as to incite bigotry or hatred.

11. Excessive cruelty to animals shall not be portrayed and animals shall not be treated inhumanely.

12. In further recognition of our obligation to the public, and most especially to parents, we have extended the code operation to include a nationwide voluntary film rating program which has as its prime objective a sensitive concern for children. It is our intent that all motion pictures exhibited in the United States will carry a rating. These ratings are:

G—SUGGESTED FOR GENERAL AUDIENCES
(acceptable for all audiences
without consideration of age)

P-G—SUGGESTED FOR ALL AGES
(parental guidance suggested)

R—RESTRICTED
(persons under 17 not admitted unless
accompanied by parent or guardian)

X—PERSONS UNDER 17 NOT ADMITTED
(not suited for children because of treatment
of sex, profanity or violence)

A comparision of the old code to the new one introduced and adopted in 1967 manifests one thing: the trend is away from censorship, both governmental and self-regulated. Even the present code is interpreted in an extremely liberal fashion judging by some recent films that have received code seals.

But Jack Valenti, president of the Motion Picture Association of America, is not sure that the line of permissiveness in filmmaking is good for the industry as a whole. He maintains that the producer or director who inserts senseless violence and useless sex in his film so that he can lure voyeurs into the box office is a faker and should be so labeled. "What one can do in the privacy of his home," says Valenti, "may be something he ought not to do in the lobby of the Waldorf. Blood and brutality, entwined nudity, foul language—these are the last, gasping cries of the inept filmmaker as he drowns, talentless, in a sea of mediocrity."

While the Television Code in general follows the pattern of the old Motion Picture Code, it goes much further in its restrictions. For instance, the subject of sex aberrations, approved for theatrical presentation, may never be shown on television. The television profanity clause, in contrast to the Picture Code, reads: "Profanity, obscenity, smut and vulgarity are forbidden, even when likely to be understood by only a part of the audience."

Divorce, while acceptable in theater films, is not a proper subject in television: "Respect is maintained for the sanctity of marriage and the value of the home. Divorce is not treated casually nor justified as a solution for marital problems."

Gambling, which finds no restrictions in motion pictures, is the subject of a specific clause in the TV Code. "The use of gambling devices or scenes necessary to the development of the plot or as appropriate background is acceptable only when presented with discretion and in moderation, and in a manner which would not excite interest in, or foster, betting nor be instructional in nature."

The TV Code goes on to restrict exhibitions of fortune telling, occultism, and astrology unless they are specifically required by the plot, while legal and medical advice and treatment will only be permitted when they conform to ethical and professional standards. The use of "subliminal perception," or transmitting messages below the threshold of normal awareness, is strictly prohibited.

Another clause reads: "Televised drama shall not simulate news or special events in such a way as to mislead or alarm. Expletives such as 'flash' or 'bulletin' and statements such as 'we interrupt this program to bring you . . .' should be reserved specifically for news room use."

One only has to recall the famous Orson Welles radio incident during the thirties to understand why this clause is now a standard part of the Code. Welles simulated a news broadcast describing the invasion of space enemies and threw a large portion of the public into a virtual panic.

Recognizing New Talent

One of the requirements of a director is to possess the ability to recognize new talent. Hollywood and New York are literal stock pens of undiscovered actors just waiting for someone to come along and give the needed boost. The director, whoever he is, is able to react somewhat emotionally to this situation, since he became a director through the same process—someone took a chance on him.

One director I know met a young girl at a lunch counter on Sunset Boulevard. He was immediately struck by her long, honey-blond hair, unmarred by harsh bleaches. She had a wholesome, natural beauty, wore practically no makeup, and what she did wear was in excellent taste.

My friend introduced himself to the girl, telling her that he was a director at a major studio, and inquired if she had thought about picture work. She replied that she, indeed, had thought about it, was in fact an actress from the East, and had recently arrived in town. The director took her to the studio and arranged to give her a screen test. The head of the studio heard about the girl, and although he didn't meet her in person, ordered the red carpet treatment.

When word got around the studio that "the chief" had ordered the finest possible test, the various department heads got busy. The makeup people swarmed around her, deciding that her face could be remodeled by the right application of shadowed makeup. Oversized false eyelashes were added and her eyebrows were shaved and then painted on to give her a more "provocative look." The hairdressing department decided that her natural honey-blond locks were too dark and wouldn't photograph right and that a glamorous new hair style would enchance her chances. The wardrobe department disdainfully rejected the idea of her wearing the appealing sweater and skirt she wore to the studio the first day. Her dress must be a tight-fitting, sequined evening gown. The studio dentist looked her over and made a porcelain jacket to fit over a small space between two of her teeth.

When the director made the test, he hardly recognized her as the same girl he met at the lunch counter.

When the head of the studio ran the test, he hotly demanded to know why the director and talent head had wasted his time and money. "She looks like just any other Hollywood starlet," he said.

Perhaps this is more indicative of a bygone era when studios were run like large factories, although it happened less than ten years ago.

Talent still lurks in lunch counters, on both sides of the counter, in Schwab's Drugstore, and on street corners.

One night I was in a small, rather "divey" bar on the Sunset Strip that was a familiar hangout of bit players and stunt men. I was introduced to a young man by the name of James Bumgarner and learned that he was a new actor in town having just come off the road in *The Caine Mutiny Court Martial.* There was much levity and libation in the place that night and little consideration was given to the future of the motion picture business.

The next day, Bill Orr of Warners' suggested that we find some new faces for some of the smaller parts in the first episode of *Cheyenne.* We had already signed Clint Walker, an unknown, for the lead, and now he wanted more unknowns. I remembered the tall, handsome fellow in the bar of the previous evening, so I called the place and got the bartender. No, he didn't remember the fellow. Then, I remembered actor Bob Lowery had introduced us, so I rang the bar again, this time for Lowery's phone number. The bartender didn't have his number but said he'd probably be be seeing Lowery that night and would give him my message. I told him to be sure to have him call me at the studio. Three days went by but finally Bumgarner called. I told him if he wanted a job in television he'd better get out to the studio right away. Within an hour, he arrived at my office and I gave him a scene to read, the part of a young army lieutenant.

Bill Orr, who listened in on the reading, agreed with me that this handsome fellow was no Barrymore, but that he did come across with some personality. Was he good enough for the part? Orr decided to take a chance with me, and we shot the picture. The next day, Warner Bros. signed the new young actor to a seven-year contract and changed his name to James Garner. *Maverick* made him a star, and when his contract was up he abandoned television for features. His salary grew to $400,000 per feature film, and he soon became one of the hottest bets in pictures.

While on the subject of having an instinct for talent, I must admit that it hasn't always been this way. I missed picking one bigger than Garner.

I was testing six actors one day, looking for an actor for a part in a Technicolor western. One of the candidates was Rock Hudson. I thought he was the worst of the lot. I selected someone whose career was so short-lived, I can't recall his name.

Another time I was having dinner alone in the Cock N'Bull on the Sunset Strip. I noticed a beautiful young lady at a nearby table. I gathered my courage, moved over her way, and introduced myself, wanting to know if she was interested in getting into pictures.

"Not anymore," she cooed. "My name is Kim Novak."

At that time, she had starred in at least two important films. And I was ready to "discover" her.

The Director's Responsibilities

From the time a film is scheduled for production until the final shot is in the can, the director's life is one decision after another—all under the tremendous pressure of time and temperament, of budgets and blueprints. Before shooting begins, he is called on to be a master strategist, planning the production with all the skill of a military chief of staff. Once on the stage, he must become an instant tactical expert, confidently meeting an infinite variety of daily problems, while calling all signals with the flexibility of a major league quarterback.

Although there always will be many different kinds of directors, no one should attempt this profession without possessing infinite patience and the stubbornness of a bull; he must be strong of heart and body, schooled in the use of words, lest he misunderstand the author and mis-

The author met James Garner in a bar one night and gave him a small part in a television film at Warner Bros. Within a year he was starring in Maverick *at the same studio, which was also directed by the author. Shown here with Jack Kelly who played Maverick's brother, Garner (left) graduated from television and now makes only theatrical films.* (Warner Bros.)

lead the actor. He must be decisive, yet cooperative; imaginative, yet truthful in his art. He must be a psychologist, analyst, teacher; captain, teammate, baby-sitter; artist, craftsman, bookkeeper; thinker, dreamer, workhorse; storyteller, magician, and *showman.*

The film director has many responsibilities:

To the author—to augment, to strengthen, and give life to the written word.

To the players—to guide and inspire them in interpreting the story in terms of their personalities, not his own.

To the producer—to use the money he has been entrusted with wisely, striking a delicate balance between quality and cost.

To the audience: to tell the story with honesty, neither talking down from lofty heights nor underestimating the perception and taste of the public—and, above all, to *amuse* and *entertain*.

A Last Word to the Aspiring Director

Where can the student filmmaker, when his academic training is completed, go to find employment in his chosen field?

There was a time when the talented student seeking employment stood face to face with a wall as impregnable as the Rock of Gibraltar. The old-guard studio establishment, while proclaiming a never-ending search for youthful talent, offered few opportunities for the amateur who was ready to turn professional.

Fortunately, a new and more youth-oriented regime is in control of Hollywood's film companies and at least three firms have publicly announced a desire to help the student find employment.

Warner Bros. Pictures is the most conspicuous of the major companies to involve itself in a training program designed to enlist the college film student, and it is no secret that they expect to uncover some directorial and writing talent and place it under exclusive contract. Under the supervision of sales executive John Whitesell and creative affairs Vice President Fred Weintraub, a liaison with the National Entertainment Conference comprising 450 colleges and universities has resulted in a film festival with prizes ranging up to $500 and summer job scholarships at the Burbank studio. The training program has offered a lecture series by established directors as well as courses in camera, sound, and editing. And, of even greater importance, the Warner organization has instituted an annual workshop program wherein selected students will write, direct, and produce a short film for nontheatrical release.

Universal Studios has announced a program in connection with the USC Division of Cinema whereby graduate students will be given credit for courses partially conducted at the studio. That the company will keep its eye open for promising filmmakers is a foregone conclusion.

One of the first independent producers to hold out hope for the aspiring director is Roger Corman, producer-director of such diverse films as *The Wild Angel, Fall of the House of Usher,* and *Bloody Mama.* Corman, from time to time, has actually sought out cinema students and has paid them modest sums to turn out pictures for him that he finances himself. It was Corman who first employed Francis Ford Coppola while he was still at UCLA. Coppola sold Corman a script for $250 and then became his assistant at $400 per week doing odd jobs such as dialogue director, cameraman, and assistant director. Corman later financed Coppola's first solo film, *Dementia 13*, which launched the ex-student as an innovative director. Corman has also financed Bruce Clark, a former UCLA cinema graduate, in a film called *Naked Angels*. Clark went on to direct *The Ski Bums* for Avco-Embassy Productions and is now solidly well on his way. Such fairly well-known names as Bernie Kowalski, Curtis Harrington, and Irvin Kershner all at one time or another in their halcyon days received both guidance and financing from Corman.

Stephanie Rothman, a woman director of four feature films, and a vice president of Dimension Pictures of Hollywood, has an open door for qualified female film makers.

"There's no area in which I would hesitate to use women in production," she says. "And that goes for directors, cameramen, gaffers, art directors, etc. I would consider them on their merits and not on their sex." Miss Rothman remembers her own start on her way to professionalism. While a student at USC, Miss Rothman won a Directors Guild fellowship. Later, when she became a director, she hired a female sound mixer on *The Student Nurses* and a female art director on *The Velvet Vampire*.

Jeff Young studied cinema techniques at the American Film Institute in Beverly Hills but got his real education as a trainee with Arthur Penn on *Alice's Restaurant*. Penn, enthusiastic about the idea of helping newcomers, said: "To put it succinctly, I would have hired him had I the good fortune to have known him before." Not long after, young Jeff Young was signed by Paramount to direct his first feature film, *Been Down So Long, It Looks Like Up to Me*.

Even Irvin Kershner, previously a cinema student, has lent a helping hand to trainees, his most recent being Mathew Robbins who observed the director firsthand on *Loving*.

George Seaton, who directed *The Country Girl*, *Miracle on 34th Street*, and the high-grossing *Airport*, is still another port in the storm for young, aspiring filmmakers. He was one of the first in the industry to bring trainees on the set while he was shooting a picture, assigning each one a rotating task until every trainee had experience on a variety of jobs connected with film direction. Seaton has helped cinema students, mostly from UCLA, as far back as 1954, and many have gone on to important jobs in the film industry. Jerry Krell and Alan Rossman served their apprenticeship on a Seaton picture, then went on to join the film production staff of the United States Information Agency. Jim Bruner observed the Seaton technique and now owns his own company making commercials. Jack Ferrucci was a top student at UCLA when Seaton took an interest in his talent and showed him the practical aspects of making movies. This led to a cameraman's job on a Disney nature film, *Hurricane Hannah*, and today he is vice president of John Sutherland Productions. Daisy Gerber is another Seaton ex-protégée and is currently the only female assistant director in the Directors Guild. Her credits include *The Killing of Sister George* and *Topaz*.

Seaton once was invited to view several student films at a Los Angeles television station. One film, a seven-minute subject by Richard Miller, did not impress Seaton as much as some of the other films. On the way out of the screening room, Miller collared the veteran director and wanted to know why he didn't like it. Seaton obliged the young man, but in discussing the film with him he detected a sincere desire to work and learn the film business. Seaton telephoned George Stevens, Jr., at that time director of the United States Information Agency, and recommended Miller for a job. Stevens hired the ex-student and gave him a chance to improve his technique by sending him to several foreign countries where he directed many films. Today he is back in Los Angeles, active in commercial and documentary production. "I cannot speak too highly of Mr. Seaton," he says. "He gave me the boost when I needed it."

George Seaton comments on the subject: "I was one of the first directors to take an interest in helping young people. They come out of the cinema schools filled with theory; what they really need is some good practical experience. I will always try to help the serious student find a start in the motion picture industry."

It is not difficult to get an audience with Warners, or Corman, or Seaton, provided the aspiring director has made his film. They and many other companies will screen a newcomer's work, hoping to discover a fresh new talent. But what of the film itself? Where can the youthful producer-director find a release for his finished product?

There are several concerns which specialize in handling experimental films, insuring distribution and exhibition and in some case even a return on the filmmaker's investment.

Genesis Films, Ltd., headed by Reg Childs, himself a former film student, has been organized as a commercial venture devoted to the distribution of student and experimental films. The audience for these films are the several hundred colleges throughout the nation, and the producer of a film that gets a Genesis release can count on at least $500 as an advance against 50 percent of the profits. In some cases, Genesis Films has advanced the production money when a promising script has turned up. Colin Higgins, UCLA cinema graduate, made two films, *Opus 1* and *Retreat*, which he turned over to Genesis for distribution. This attracted attention to his work, and Paramount signed him to a contract as a writer-director.

Universal Studios has formed an Education and Visual Arts division, devoted to the distribution of avant-garde short films and has become an exclusive distributor for the better student films made at USC. EUVA has announced through its president, Peter McDonald, that it will advance from $500 to $1,000 to students with promise, provided they have a script which will be, in their opinion, popular with conventional audiences.

Stanley R. Jaffe, who at twenty-nine became Paramount's chief operating officer, made the following statement in *Life* magazine: "Five years ago a kid with an idea for a film couldn't get through a studio door. That's not true nowadays. We're not interested in what a person has done in the past. We're interested in what he has in mind and how he expects to bring it off." That would suggest that Paramount, also, is a haven for the would-be director.

Another possibility for the student filmmaker seeking financial underwriting is the American Film Institute, now permanently lodged in Greystone, the old Doheny mansion in Beverly Hills. Worthy experimental projects are financed through grants, with the accent on the film producer's talent, not the specific subject matter of the film project.

There is no question that combined efforts of the film industry and the more than three hundred college cinema departments have provided an atmosphere for the novice director unparalleled in the history of motion pictures. It is only for the student to accept the invitation extended him by making the finest, most original, and technically excellent film he can possibly create. When that is done—if he has achieved his goal—the film companies will roll out the red carpet of opportunity for him.

If you want to be a director—*be one*. Find ways to prove your worth. Master your craft before attempting art. Rules must be learned before they can be effectively broken. Prepare yourself for the job of directing, then *stick to your goal*, no matter how many disappointments come your way. For, with this philosophy, you must succeed. Talent will out, and you will be given the chance to guide the production of a motion picture—you will have arrived; you will be the director.

A PARTIAL LIST OF
UNIVERSITIES OFFERING FILM COURSES

University of Alabama
American University
Antioch College
University of Arizona
Auburn University
Bennington College
Bob Jones University
Boston University
Brandeis University
University of California, Los Angeles
University of Cincinnati
Columbia University
Cornell University
Creighton University
University of Denver
Emerson College
Florida State University
Fordham University
Goddard College
Hampshire College
Harpur College
Humboldt State College
Hunter College
Indiana University
University of Iowa
Ithaca College
University of Kansas
Louisiana State University
Loyola University
Marlboro College
Maryland Institute
Memphis State
University of Miami

Michigan State University
Montana State University
University of New Mexico
New Mexico State University
New York Institute of Technology
New York University
University of North Carolina
Northwestern University
Oberlin College
Ohio State University
Ohio University
University of Oregon
University of Pennsylvania
Pennsylvania State University
Philadelphia College of Fine Arts
Richmond College of New York
Rochester Institute of Technology
San Diego State College
San Francisco State College
University of South Dakota
University of South Florida
University of Southern California
Southern Illinois University
Southern Methodist University
Stanford University
Stephens College
Temple University
University of Texas
Texas Christian University
Washington State University
University of West Virginia
University of Wisconsin
Xavier University

DIRECTORS GUILD OF AMERICA
AWARD WINNERS FOR
THEATRICAL DIRECTION

1948—Joseph Mankiewicz   *A Letter to Three Wives*
1949—Robert Rossen   *All the King's Men*
1950—Joseph Mankiewicz   *All About Eve*
1951—George Stevens   *A Place in the Sun*
1952—John Ford   *The Quiet Man*
1953—Fred Zinnemann   *From Here to Eternity*
1954—Elia Kazan   *On the Waterfront*
1955—Delbert Mann   *Marty*
1956—George Stevens   *Giant*
1957—David Lean   *The Bridge on the River Kwai*
1958—Vincent Minnelli   *Gigi*
1959—William Wyler   *Ben-Hur*
1960—Billy Wilder   *The Apartment*
1961—Robert Wise/Jerome Robbins *West Side Story*
1962—David Lean   *Lawrence of Arabia*
1963—Tony Richardson   *Tom Jones*
1964—George Cukor   *My Fair Lady*
1965—Robert Wise   *The Sound of Music*
1966—Fred Zinnemann   *A Man for All Seasons*
1967—Mike Nichols   *The Graduate*
1968—Anthony Harvey   *The Lion in Winter*
1969—John Schlesinger   *Midnight Cowboy*
1970—Franklin J. Schaffner   *Patton*
1971—William Friedkin   *The French Connection*

DIRECTORS GUILD OF AMERICA
AWARD WINNERS FOR
TELEVISION DIRECTION

1953—Robert Florey — *The Last Voyage*
1954—Roy Kellino — *The Answer*
1955—Don Weis — *The Little Guy*
1956—Herschel Daugherty — *The Road That Led Afar*
1957—Don Weis — *The Lonely Wizard*
1958—Richard L. Bare — *All Our Yesterdays*
1959—Phil Karlson — *The Untouchables*
1960—George Schaefer — *Macbeth*
1961—Ernie Kovacs — *A Study in Silence*
1962—David Friedkin — *The Price of Tomatoes*
1963—George Schaefer — Shaw's *Pygmalion*
1964—Lamont Johnson — *Oscar Underwood Story*
1965—Dwight Hemion — *My Name Is Barbra*
1966—Alex Segal — *The Death of a Salesman*
1967—George Schaefer — *Do Not Go Gentle into That Good Night*

1968—George Schaefer — *My Father and My Mother*
1969—Fielder Cook — *Teacher, Teacher*
1970—Lamont Johnson — *My Sweet Charlie*
1971—John Rich — *All in the Family*

GLOSSARY OF MOTION PICTURE
AND TELEVISION TERMS

ACTION. The business or movement by players or objects within a scene. The command given by the director to start acting.

AIRIFLEX. The most popular hand held camera used today. A reflex type camera that allows the operator to view the action as it is being filmed through the lens.

ANGLE, CAMERA. What the camera takes in. This angle may be drawn by projecting two straight lines from the center of the lens to the two outside edges of the scene as photographed.

ANGLE OF APPROACH. The point from which the director allows the audience to view his film.

ANIMATION. 1. Screen cartooning photographed frame by frame to give the illusion of movement. 2. In acting, to give life to, make lively, gay or vigorous.

ANSWER PRINT. The first trial composite (sound) print of a completely edited, dubbed, and scored motion picture.

APERTURE. Lens; the round iris diaphragm that allows light to pass through. Camera; the square opening that frames the picture being taken.

ASPECT RATIO. The shape (not the size) of the frame of a motion picture. From the old standard of 1.37 to 1, to Cinemascope's 2.35 to 1.

ASSISTANT DIRECTOR. One who handles strictly production problems; does not concern himself with the art of directing.

BACK LIGHT. The so-called Rembrandt lighting where strong light is thrown on the actors from the back of the set, rimming them in a kind of halo that gives the appearance of relief to the picture.

BALANCE. The relationship of the light and shade in a picture. The cameraman usually measures the brightest portion of the light with a meter, then balances the shadowed portion by eye.

BARNEY. Soundproofed blanket used when shooting sound with a silent camera.

BLIMP. The soundproofed casing around the motion picture camera.

BLOW-UP. 1. An enlargement of a scene magnified on the optical printer. 2. The "fluffing" of a line by an actor.

BNC. The standard sound camera manufactured by Mitchell Camera Company.

BOOM, CAMERA. The cranelike device that holds the camera and gives it completely vertical, horizontal, lateral, and diagonal mobility.

BOOM, MIKE. The adjustable pole that holds the microphone and extends out over the actors' heads.

BREAK IT UP. The filming of other angles of a master scene, usually close-ups.

BRIDGE. A close-up, insert, or other angle, which is made to insert between two sections of the same scene and camera angle.

BUSINESS. A definite bit of action, as "business of unpacking suitcase."

CAMERA LEFT. The left side of the camera. Opposite of stage left.

CAMERA RIGHT. The right side of the camera as the cameraman stands looking toward the action to be photographed. Opposite of stage right.

CENTER OF ATTENTION. In motion pictures, that which the camera is focused upon.

CLAP STICKS. The black and white sticks attached to the slate that are clapped together to make a visual and sound impression to facilitate the editor "syncing" the scene.

CLOSE-UP. An individual shot of an actor, usually taking in his head and shoulders, and not showing anything below the top button of his suit.

COMPOSITION. Arrangement of various objects or choosing the point of view in a picture so that the whole will be pleasing.

CONTINUITY. The detailed plan of a motion picture containing action and dialogue in the order in which they are to be shown.

CONTRAST. The degree of difference between the shadows and highlights of a photograph.

COVERAGE. The amount of close-ups or other angles the director shoots in addition to his master scene.

CRAB DOLLY. The camera perambulator that eliminates the use of metal tracks and permits the camera to be moved in any horizontal direction. It has a vertical movement of approximately five feet.

CRANE. See camera boom.

CREDIT TITLES. The announcements at the beginning or the end of a film that give the names of the various artists and craftsmen.

CUT. 1. Stop the camera. 2. Stop the action. 3. To edit or shorten a scene by cutting the film. 4. The end of the scene.

CUT AWAY. The act of filmically going to another subject.

CUT BACK. Where two lines of action take place simultaneously, the secondary action is shown in cut backs. The alternating between two parallel pieces of action.

CUT IN. Any close-up or insert that is added to a scene between the beginning and end of the scene.

DAILIES. The film of the previous day's scenes just as they have come from the laboratory.

DAY FOR NIGHT. Shooting in the daytime but resulting in a night-time quality on the film. Accomplished with filters.

DEFINITION. The sharpness or clearness with which objects are photographed by a lens.

DENSITY. The degree of darkness of a negative determined by the amount of opaque silver deposit on the film. The brightness of the light in a scene.

DEPTH OF FIELD. The range in which objects are sharply in focus by a given lens.

DIFFUSION SCREEN. A screen or spun glass placed in front of a light source of lens to reduce the harshness of the lighting. Used in varying strengths on women.

DISCOVERED. A term used to denote that an actor or object is already in the scene when it commences.

DISSOLVE. The gradual transition, or melting, of one scene into another. Accomplished by overlapping a fade out with a fade in.

DOCUMENTARY. A film that depicts actions or events as they are, with no attempt toward dramatization. Usually made in natural locations with nonactors.

DOLLY. The camera perambulator.

DOLLY SHOT. A moving shot accomplished by pushing the camera dolly about the set.

DOUBLE EXPOSURE. A composite picture made by exposing the same piece of film twice, either in the camera or in the optical printer.

DOWN SHOT. A shot taken from a high point looking down.

DRIVE MOTOR. The motor that operates the camera and sound recorder in synchronization.

DUBBING. The process of rerecording several sound tracks onto one composite track.

DUPE NEGATIVE. A duplicate negative made from a fine-grain print.

EMPATHY. The complete understanding of an audience for a character's feelings.

EXPOSURE. The length of time the light is allowed to act upon the emulsion, or the amount of light allowed to pass through the lens.

EXPOSURE METER. An instrument that determines exposure by measuring the intensity of light.

EXTERIOR. Any scene shot outside the stage.

EXTRAS. A term used to indicate the nonspeaking actors usually performing in the background.

EYELIGHT. A small light used near the camera to bring out a sparkle in an actor's eyes.

F. SYSTEM. The method of calibrating lens diaphragms in terms of exposure.

FADE IN. The beginning of a scene that gradually comes from complete black to full in.

FADE OUT. The end of a scene that gradually disappears to complete black.

FEET PER MINUTE. Pertaining to standard film travel speeds. Silent speed 60 feet per minute, sound speed 90 feet per minute, slow motion 180 plus per minute.

FILL LIGHT. The weaker light used to balance the shadow side of a subject.

FILTER. Any glass or gelatin used in the camera to change color values, balance, or to create night effects.

FINAL CUT. The final polished and reedited film ready for dubbing and scoring.

FINDER. An accessory that shows the approximate field embraced by the lens. Always attached to the camera, sometimes used "wild" by the director and cameraman in lining up a shot.

FLARE. A fogged spot on the film due to reflection of a strong light on the lens surface.

FLATNESS. Lack of brilliance or contrast in a print or negative. Also, in lighting, caused by having the key light too close to the camera.

FOCUS. The plane in which a lens produces a sharp image.

FOG. A veiling of the image caused by unwanted light falling upon the exposed film.

FRAME. 1. An individual section of film that includes one separate exposure. 2. To compose a scene.

FRAMES PER FOOT. 35 mm film has 16 frames per foot of film. 16 mm has 40 frames per foot.

FRAMES PER SECOND. Silent speed, 16 frames per second; sound speed, 24 frames per second.

FULL SHOT. A comprehensive shot that takes in the actors in full figure.

GATE. The two metal plates that hold the film in place as it receives its exposure in the camera.

GLASS SHOT. A scene in which the camera shoots through a glass on which is painted a part of the background that is impossible or too costly to build.

GOBO. The black boards used to shade light off of walls, or to keep it from hitting directly into the camera lens.

GRAIN. Visible granules of metallic silver in a negative.

GRIPS. The carpenters on a set who move wild walls, handle gobos, and operate the camera dolly.

GROUND GLASS. The focusing screen in the camera that is on the same plane as the film and that is brought into view by the process known as "racking over." When the director looks through the eye piece he is looking at the scene exactly the way it will appear on film.

HALATION. A kick-back of reflected light which shines too strongly into the lens.

HALF-TONES. The various tones between highlight and shadow.

HARD LIGHT. The arcs used to approximate sunshine on a set.

HEAD. The top of a piece of film. When film is wound ready for projection it is known as being "heads out."

HIGH KEY. Lighting with few dark tones. Used in comedies and light entertainment.

HIGHLIGHTS. The lightest part of a scene or print. The darkest part of a negative.

ILLUSION OF REALITY. The quality of a scene that purports to be real or actually happening.

IMAGINARY LINE. An imaginary line that corresponds to the proscenium in the theater and over which the camera should not move when making close-ups in order to maintain a consistent direction of looks.

INFINITY. An indefinitely great distance away from the camera.

INSERT. A close-up of letter, gun, etc., used to call attention or to identify the object.

INTERIOR. Any scene photographed inside a building or stage.

INTERLOCK. A condition arising out of perfect synchronization between the camera and the sound recorder.

INTERMITTENT MOVEMENT. The mechanism that pulls down the film in a camera or projector one frame at a time.

JUICER. A slang name for electrician.

JUMP CUT. The effect of splicing two pieces of film together photographed from the same angle without bridging them with a close-up or other angle.

KEY. A length of background film that is projected from the rear onto a process screen (also *plate*).

KEY LIGHT. The main, and usually most intense, light in a scene. Used to model the subject's face with.

LAP DISSOLVE. Same as dissolve.

LEADER. The length of film that preceeds the actual photography on a reel.

LENS MOUNT. The device that holds a lens onto the camera.

LINE CUTTING. The act of eliminating speeches through editing, either on paper or on film after the scene has been shot.

LOCALE. A locality or environment in which a scene takes places.

LOCATION. Any place away from the studio used as a background.

LONG FOCAL-LENGTH LENS. A lens at least 75 mm in length that shortens and tends to make out of focus the background.

LONG SHOT. A shot made from a considerable distance from the subject.

LOOPING. The process whereby an actor recreates his dialogue on the sound stage in sync to the picture. This is done to replace faulty dialogue recorded under noisy conditions such as factories, airports, or busy streets.

LOW KEY. Photography wherein lighting is held to a minimum, or lighting with many dark tones.

MAGAZINE. The light tight container that feeds and takes up the film in a motion picture camera.

MASTER SHOT. A continuous take that covers all or a great part of a scene.

MATCHING ACTION. In cutting, the act of selecting two pieces of film that contain an overlap of action, then selection of the spot where the cut will be the smoothest.

MATT BOX. The device that extends forward of the camera lens, used to hold filters and matts.

MEDIUM SHOT. A shot that is a waist figure or has two or more people in it; somewhere between a close-up and a full shot.

METER READING. Measuring the intensity of the key light to determine the f. stop to be used on the lens.

METHOD. A style of acting introduced by Stanislavsky of the Moscow Art Theatre that helps the actor to *be* the character, not *play* the character.

MINIATURE. Small scale sets or props used to represent actual settings. Used to reproduce train wrecks, ship sinkings, explosions, and the like.

MITCHELL. The motion picture camera that has become the standard of the film industry.

MONTAGE. A series of individual shots which, when viewed together, form a unified story impression.

MOVEMENT. 1. Camera; the intermittent mechanism in the camera that pulls down the film a frame at a time. 2. Dramatic; changing place or position of actors, backgrounds, camera. Also accomplished in editing.

MOVING SHOT. Any shot made while the camera is in motion, either on a dolly or other moving vehicle.

MOVIOLA. A small viewing machine that reproduces both picture and sound. Used in the cutting rooms.

NC. An earlier Mitchell camera, now used for wild shots without sound, or with a barney.

NEGATIVE. The raw film that receives its exposure through the camera and when developed has its images reversed, light for dark.

NEUTRAL DENSITY FILTER. An optical glass or gelatin that reduces the amount of light reaching the film.

NIGHT FOR DAY. Shooting actually in the night, but resulting in the film being lighted for day.

OPTICALS. Fades, dissolves, blow ups, or other trick effects made in the optical printer.

OUTLINE. A synopsis of a story, usually what the writer starts with before developing characters or scenes.

OUT TAKE. Takes that are completed, but not printed because of mechanical error or of low quality performances.

OVERCRANKS. Operating the camera at above normal speed to produce slow motion effect.

OVEREXPOSURE. Allowing too much light to travel through the lens and onto the film. Results in a light, washed out print.

OVERLAP. 1. Action; when shooting a scene from two or more angles, the overlapping of action to facilitate the cutter making a smooth cut. 2. Sound; when shooting a close-up of one actor and the actor off camera picks up his cues too quickly, causing an overlap on the sound track.

PAN SHOT. A shot made while the camera swings on its tripod in a horizontal arc.

PANTOMIME. Action in which the actors express themselves without words, using gestures.

PARALLAX. The difference in the way a scene is viewed through the finder from that of the lens.

PARALLEL ACTION. Two lines of action that occur simultaneously, shown to the audience via the cut back.

PICK IT UP. The order to continue with a scene not completed from the same spot it went bad, without changing camera angle.

P.O.V. Point of view. Usually a view seen by an actor.

PRINT. Order given when a take is satisfactory. Also, the positive film.

PROCESSING. The developing and printing of motion picture film.

PROCESS SHOT. A shot made by photographing foreground action against a translucent screen, upon which is projected from the rear another background. Also front projection.

PROJECTION. 1. Actors; speaking loud enough to be heard from a distance. 2. Film; throwing an enlarged image upon a screen.

RACK OVER. The device on a Mitchell camera that allows the film mechanism to be shifted to one side so as to permit viewing the scene directly through the lens.

RAW STOCK. Unexposed negative.

READING. Trying out for a part; part of a rehearsal.

REAR PROJECTION. See process.

REFLEX. A camera which allows the operator to view the scene being filmed through the lens.

REGISTER. 1. Acting; to indicate emotion by simulation. 2. Camera; to hold the moving film accurately in place as it receives its exposure.

ROUGH CUT. The first viewing of a picture after it has been put together.

RUSHES. Same as dailies.

SCENE. A unit of action. A succession of one or more shots within a sequence.

SCORE. The music for a motion picture.

SCREENPLAY. The script, which contains dialogue and action in a continuity form.

SCRIMS. Diffusion placed over lights to soften the effect.

SEQUENCE. A unit of action in which there is no lapse of time; sometimes contains several scenes.

SHORT FOCAL-LENGTH LENS. A lens that gives the feeling of depth to a set, from a 35 mm to 9 mm "bug-eye."

SHOT. A single piece of film within a scene, a take.

SHUTTER. The device inside the camera that rotates before the film, intermittently allowing it to receive exposure. It opens while the film is stationary, closes while the film is being moved to the next frame.

SLATE. The numbering board held before a take by the assistant cameraman; used to identify the film in the laboratory and cutting room.

SLOW MOTION. Obtained by speeding up the camera, or over cranking.

SOUND SPEED. 24 frames per second; 90 feet per minute.

SOUND TRACK. When recording, the magnetic tape. In projection, the optical area at one side of the picture on the positive print.

SPECIAL EFFECTS. A name given to almost any unusual effect to create an illusion in a film.

SPEED. 1. The state of things when the camera and recorder have reached their proper operation. The signal that the director can now say "action." 2. The sensitivity of film.

SPLICE. The place where two pieces of film are joined together.

SPLIT FOCUS. When two objects, one near to the camera and the other farther away, are both critically sharp.

SPLIT SCREEN. A procedure used to duplicate an actor in a scene. Used when creating the illusion of identical twins, or when one actor plays two parts.

STOCK SHOT. A scene taken from a previous picture and placed in the film library. Usually of scenic locales or hard to duplicate action.

STOP. The lens aperature in f. values.

STOP MOTION. The process of exposing a frame at a time as in animation.

SYNC. When the picture and sound track are properly lined up.

TAIL. The bottom of a picture, or the end of a film after it has been projected.

TAKE. An individual piece of film with no cuts. A shot.

TAKE UP. The mechanism that winds the film onto the spool in the magazine after it has received its exposure.

TAPE. The sound track.

TECHNICAL. In acting, playing a scene with limited emotion or genuine feeling on the actor's part, but not necessarily giving that impression to the audience.

TELEPLAY. A television screenplay.

THREAD. To place the film in the camera and make ready for shooting.

TILT. Moving the camera on its tripod in a vertical arc.

TITLES. The credit announcements that accompany a motion picture.

TONE DEAF. Said of an actor who cannot imitate another's reading of a line.

TREATMENT. A more detailed version of the story after the outline, but before the screenplay is started.

UNDERCRANK. To slow down the speed of the camera that gives the illusion of speeded up action. Fast motion.

UNDEREXPOSE. Allowing not enough light to reach the film.

UNIVERSAL FOCUS. When all objects, near and far, are in sharp focus.

UP SHOT. A shot made from a low position, camera angled upward.

WHIP. To quickly pan from one object to another.

WIDE-ANGLE LENS. Same as short focal-length lens.

WILD CAMERA. A silent camera, not in sync with sound recorder.

WILD TRACK A sound track made independently from the camera.

WILD WALL. A removable wall from a set.

WIPE. An optical effect that allows one scene to merge with another by moving a sharp line across the frame.

ZOOM LENS. A lens that can change its focal length from short to long, or long shot to close-up

BIBLIOGRAPHY

Clarke, Charles G. 1968. *Professional Cinematography*. Hollywood: American
  Society of Cinematographers.
Coleman, Hila. 1969. *Making Movies—Student Films to Features*. New York:
  World Publishing Company.
Gessner, Robert. 1968. *The Moving Image*. New York: E. P. Dutton & Co., Inc.
Jacobs, Lewis. 1970. *The Movies as Medium*. New York: Farrar, Straus &
  Giroux, Inc.
Kantor, Bernard R.; Blacker, Irwin R., and Kramer, Anne. 1970. *Directors
  at Work*. New York: Funk & Wagnalls.
Lewis, Colby. 1968. *The TV Director-Interpreter*. New York: Hastings House.
Lindgren, Ernest. 1968. *The Art of the Film*. New York: The Macmillan
  Company.
Mascelli, Joseph V. 1968. *The Five C's of Cinematography*. Hollywood:
  Cine-Grafic Publications.
Millerson, Gerald. 1969. *The Technique of Television Production*. New York:
  Hastings House.
Reiz, Karel, and Millar, Gavin. 1968. *Techniques of Film Editing*. New York:
  Hastings House.
Rilla, Wolf. 1970. *A–Z of Movie Making*. New York: The Viking Press.
Smallman, Kirk. 1969. *Creative Film-Making*. New York: The Macmillan
  Company.
Spottiswoode, Raymond. 1970. *Film and Its Techniques*. Berkeley: University
  of California Press.

Index

233